The Sublime Crime

Fascination, Failure, and Form in Literature of the Enlightenment

Stephanie Barbé Hammer

Southern Illinois University Press
Carbondale and Edwardsville

Library of Congress Cataloging-in-Publication Data

Hammer, Stephanie Barbé.
    The sublime crime : fascination, failure, and form in literature of
the Enlightenment / Stephanie Barbé Hammer.
        p.   cm.
    Includes bibliographical references and index.
    1. Literature, Modern—18th century—History and criticism.
    2. Crime in literature.   3. Enlightenment.   I. Title.
PN751.H26   1994
809'.93355—dc20   92-40551
    ISBN 0-8093-1831-8   CIP

The paper used in this publication meets the minimum requirements of
American National Standard for Information Sciences—Permanence of
Paper for Printed Library Materials, ANSI Z39.48-1984. ∞

For M. and D.

Contents

Acknowledgments

The idea of this book developed gradually from a 1982 conversation with some talented undergraduates at the University of California, Riverside. A campus lecture followed in 1983, as well as a paper at the 1984 MLA. A very early version of chapter 4 appeared in *The Comparatist* in 1986 and is reprinted here in a quite different form with the journal's kind permission. A version of part of chapter 2 was recently published in *Essays in Theatre*. The process of writing was supported by two pre-tenure awards from the Academic Senate and by two dedicated research assistants who patiently tolerated my chaotic instructions—Hal Swindall and Suzanne Mädler Marshall. At Southern Illinois University Press, Robert Phillips and Carol Burns served as my acquisitions and project editors respectively, and I am grateful to them for their assistance and enthusiasm.

This project has undergone several radical transformations, thanks primarily to the challenging encounters with my colleagues at UCR. Carole Fabricant encouraged me to consider two works that were to become central to this study—*The London Merchant* and *Caleb Williams*—while our fellow eighteenth-centuryist George Haggerty first called my attention to the homoerotic dynamics in Godwin's book and introduced me to the work of Eve Kosofsky Sedgwick. Other friends proved to be invaluable (and inexhaustible) storehouses of theoretical and critical information. John Ganim helped me to understand romance traditions, Zhang Longxi clarified my notions about Gadamer's hermeneutics, Reinhold Grimm reminded me of the important *Machtweib* tradition in classical German drama, while my readings of and conversations with Greg Bredbeck and Carole Anne Tyler greatly enhanced my understanding of gender theory. Kathleen McHugh's rare insights revised my appreciation for the masculinity problem in Schiller and Sade, while Theda Shapiro's observations were crucial for the discussion of Balzac in my conclusion. Finally, three smart graduate students taught me about Foucault, even as I thought I was teaching them, and my appreciation of that French theorist owes whatever sophistication it might have to Darnetta Bell, Kevin Bongiorni, and Christopher Wise. Non-UCR intellects also played a very important role. Katherine Ward guided me through the original version of *Gawain* and much of the Caleb Williams-Gawain connections came from our discussions. Larry Kritzman held my hand whenever the going got tough and gave me judicious advice as to how I might better articulate the deployment of Foucault in the introduction.

Two other people deserve special mention. They were the first readers of this book, which they tirelessly reread throughout its various permutations. The first of these was my outgoing chairman, Jean-Pierre Barricelli who made time in his busy schedule to mentor me, and I greatly appreciate the shrewd remarks and helpful suggestions of this great comparatist. My second reader was Robert Gross, who listened to countless incoherent verbalizations over the telephone and who quietly helped me to see what the book was really about. The influence of my fifteen-year-old running conversation with this brilliant scholar is everywhere in this study, and I could not have performed my reading of *Caleb Williams* without him, a reading that I dedicate to him, with love.

Family members were tremendously supportive. Judy Behrendt and Dave Baraff constantly asked about the book and listened to repeated rehearsals of its argument and contents. Charlotte Behrendt gave me sympathy whether I deserved it or not. Pamela Behrendt validated my feelings about college teaching. Peter Behrendt poured the scotch, and David Behrendt kept me smiling with his unforgettable impressions and impersonations. Emily Baraff and Lillian Behrendt soothed me through repeated viewings of *The Little Mermaid*, and the latter's entrance into my life halfway through the manuscript caused me to reread and rethink everything for the better. Larry Behrendt put up with much late-night hysteria and very little attention for three years. A truly patient soul, he listens to my tales of academic woe with unvarying generosity, gives sound advice, gets the computer running, sends out for pizza, turns on the hot tub, and in general solves all my problems in the most delightful way possible.

Looking over this study, I realize that this book is deeply connected to my parents, Leonard Hammer and Barbé Tirtov-Romanov Hammer, and to the ethical sensibility that has enabled them to lead lives of kooky dignity in a society that increasingly expects conformity and financial success from its citizens. They have consistently dared to be different, and I salute their difference, their courage, and their love, hoping they will not take it amiss that I heard their voices in the speech of fictional lawbreakers.

The Sublime Crime

1

Introduction

Hermeneutics, the Eighteenth Century, and the Challenge of Criminal Literature

Theoretical Overview

Readers of the present study might well ask why the artistic creations of the eighteenth century deserve the attention of a student of hermeneutics. To a certain extent, the answer to this question is already anticipated by the recent abundance of revisionist scholarship in the field of eighteenth- and early nineteenth-century literature and by the critical debates this scholarship has engendered—the sheer mass of which indicates both the importance that the eighteenth century holds for the late twentieth-century West and the difficulties which attend our attempts to grasp it (Crocker, "Enlightenment Studies" 376). Clearly, it is thanks primarily to the attention paid to the eighteenth century by Jacques Derrida and Michel Foucault that the past decade has seen a veritable outpouring of new approaches to the Enlightenment and its related movements. Equally clear is the fact that these new methods—ranging between and combining such critical perspectives as deconstruction, new historicism, feminism, and psychoanalysis—have contributed enormously to the field. Readings of the eighteenth century such as those by Josue Harari, Leonard Davis, Lincoln Faller, Hans-Jürgen Lüsebrink, and John Bender, as well as Felicity Nussbaum and Laura Brown (and the other authors of the essays in *The New 18th Century*) have achieved many important goals; in particular, they have refuted the well-known charge that Enlightenment literature as a whole represents an age of overt moral didacticism. Indeed, such readings have liberated particular works and authors from simplistic biographical analysis and opened up the canon to include heretofore forgotten and/or ignored writers.

Yet, strangely, many of these new readings—by their very insistence on the ideological grounding of artistic creation—risk losing sight of the peculiar aesthetic relevance that eighteenth-century art has for our own time, but as Nussbaum and Brown observe, this factor is still considered to be important by such prominent scholars as George S. Rousseau (13).[1] Given the considerable rift that now exists between "old" and "new" eighteenth-centuryists (Nussbaum and Brown 1–4), I contend that Hans-Georg Gadamer's hermeneutics offers a particularly helpful perspective from which scholars can approach texts in a field that is currently the subject of serious critical dispute.[2] Precisely because it is not a method, hermeneutics permits reading the literature of the eighteenth century in such ways as to include the valuable insights into the age brought about in particular by poststructuralism and feminism, without denying the aesthetic value that makes literature art and without disregarding the age's intellectual virtue and its profound concern with ethical matters. What follows is a summary of Gadamer's hermeneutics as it pertains to literature along with a brief explanation of the manner in which his work will be deployed in this present enterprise.

In his 1964 essay "Aesthetics and Understanding," Gadamer closes his analysis with the observation that the work of art confronts the observer with two dramatic exhortations: "The intimacy with which the work of art touches us is at the same time, in enigmatic fashion, a shattering and a demolition of the familiar. It is not only the 'This art thou!' disclosed in a joyous and frightening shock; it also says to us, 'Thou must alter thy life!'" (*Philosophical Hermeneutics* 104). In this manner, Gadamer stresses the directly personal nature of our understanding of what the work of art has to say; he also emphasizes the profoundly ethical content of that understanding. Art as a whole and literature in particular (for Gadamer privileges the literary work of art as the aesthetic site that testifies to "the sheer presence of the past" [*Truth and Method* 145]) engages the audience in an act of interpretation that consists in both a personal recognition and a kind of moral conversion, an urgent *prise de conscience* that one must change and that one has already been implicitly changed by the event of reading.

Gadamer's more recent essay, "On the Relevance of the Beautiful" (1977), develops this approach further, arguing that the process by which people understand both the art of the past and the present is essentially the same: "There is always some reflective and intellectual accomplishment involved, whether I am concerned with traditional forms of art handed down to us or whether I am challenged by modern forms of art. . . . For this reason, it seems a false antithesis to believe that there is an art of the past that can be enjoyed and an art of the present that supposedly forces us to participate in it by the subtle use of artistic technique" (*Relevance* 28). All art is by its nature contemporaneous—that is to say, art is art only when it makes an immediate claim upon its audience, when it "speaks" as though it had something to say right now. Therefore, art (and literature in particular) is not, nor can it be, historically determined, but rather of necessity it transcends the conditions that produced it (*Relevance* 12).

What then is the relationship between the work of art and history? To say, for example, that *Candide* does not comment upon life in eighteenth-century France would clearly be mistaken, yet it would also be a mistake to say that life in the eighteenth century constitutes and/or determines the meaning of Voltaire's satiric novel. If asked, Gadamer would probably conclude that Voltaire's work clearly comments on its society and time—and on ours insofar as we are the inheritors of them—but these contextual factors matter not at all in the determining of *Candide*'s meaning. Therefore, in order to come to an understanding of the claim staked by a particular artistic creation, it is neither necessary nor particularly useful to dwell upon the contexts that engendered it. Granted, literary productions are profoundly historical (that is, situated in history), and works from a particular period of time may share certain salient features, structures, and points of view.[3] However, Gadamer poses the issue another way; the profoundly historical nature of artistic creations enables audiences (subjects conscious of their own historicity [*Relevance* 11]) to understand them in the present and as present.

Gadamer's seemingly extreme view of art's autonomy from society has been echoed by critics who appear, on the face of things, to be ideologically opposed to him: the quintessential Marxist critic Theodor Adorno states in *Aesthetic Theory* that art can only be art when it is independent of and resistant to society (320–22) and poststructuralist feminist Hélène Cixous describes creative writing throughout *Newly Born Woman* in utopian, messianic terms—as getting out, as escape, as freedom, as a new world order. Thus, it is precisely because literature is autonomous that it can comment upon and resist society and undertake culture critique, as will be seen presently. And such a view of art is not a peculiarly "modern" (that is to say, post-nineteenth-century) one; one should remember that Plato too suspected that art was autonomous, which was why he suggested that all artists be banished from the Republic.

Furthermore, Gadamer's hermeneutics has particularly important consequences for the study of comparative literature. If all literature works in the same way (for it is not to be understood as an assemblage of cultural, political parts), then it becomes both possible and desirable to study the linguistic art of divergent cultures and periods, because all of these artistic creations have something intrinsically in common. Rather than casting about for exterior relations, the comparatist looks for internal ones—for symbols, metaphors, structures, and problems—that suggest that the ways in which the claims of different creations unfold might be mutually illuminating. This is the strategy that has informed the choice of texts in *The Sublime Crime*—a strategy that (despite its considerable perspectival differences) resembles the gesture of Eric Auerbach's *Mimesis*, a historical series of individual readings that address a central problematic. How do Gadamer's hermeneutics enhance a comparatist understanding of the eighteenth century specifically? In this regard, I have adjusted his approach somewhat. While Gadamer sees an enormous change during the early nineteenth century in the way art views itself, I will place this shift at an earlier date—namely, during, and especially at the end of, the eighteenth century. This placement is analogous to Michel Foucault's contention in *The Order of Things* that there is a crisis in *representation* (a word that designates but is not limited to artistic representation) at the end of the classical age (Foucault's term for the seventeenth and eighteenth centuries [236–42]). Thus, my assessment of the aesthetic importance of "Enlightenment" literature relies on Foucault's chronology as a helpful corrective to Gadamer's observation of the changeover in art's consciousness about itself—a consciousness that the German critic sees as the beginning of modern art. Gadamer defines this transition in the following manner:

> At the very start I pointed out how the so-called modern age, at least since the beginning of the nineteenth century, had emancipated itself from the shared self-understanding of the humanist-Christian tradition. I also pointed out that the subjects that previously appeared self-evident and binding can now no longer be captured in an artistic form within which new statements are made. The artist no longer speaks for the community, but forms his own community insofar as he expresses himself. (*Relevance* 39)

The three characteristics outlined by Gadamer as hallmarks of modernity—emancipation from humanism/Christianity, formal innovation, and the positioning of the artistic voice over and above (if not in direct opposition to) the community—are very clearly features that inform the works considered in *The Sublime Crime* in increasingly dramatic ways. Readers have only to compare the degrees to which criminal guilt is problematized in *Manon Lescaut* (wherein the seemingly religious Chevalier proposes an Augustinian confession that articulates not one ounce of regret) as opposed to *Caleb Williams* (wherein guilt conceals and reveals sexual deviance) to see that a progressive emancipa-

tion from Christian metaphysics is indeed taking place in literary art. Gadamer's second point—the problematization of form
—constitutes one of the mainstays of my argument. Accordingly, the latter half of this chapter will show the struggle of
Enlightenment writers to revise already existing forms so they
might tell the criminal's story in unprecedented ways. As for
Gadamer's third point, the artist's establishment of his or her
own community is observable on a variety of levels in the texts I
work with: in the actual presence of alternate societies in many
of the works (from *Jonathan Wild* to *Michael Kohlhaas*); in the use
of new styles and languages (sensibility, storm and stress, libertine, and disciplinary) to construct a new groundwork for communication; and in the fact that these works' prefatory/introduc-
tory remarks suggest (with increasing self-consciousness) that
both writer and reader belong to a special (and superior) social
group.

The Anglo-continental literature of the eighteenth and
early nineteenth centuries is of particular importance because it
represents the origins of modern art, as Gadamer defines it.
These origins have direct bearing on our understanding of
ourselves as late twentieth-centuryists and of our own contemporary aesthetic expressions. Moreover, this apparently esoteric
task constitutes part of what is perhaps the greatest challenge
facing the humanist at the end of this millennium—namely, the
recuperation of the connection with the Western tradition in a
manner that both affirms its importance and allows us to enter
into a dialogue with the tradition about new concerns. The art of
the eighteenth century, as the passage to modernity, represents
the ideal place to engage in this conversation.

Given the hermeneutic approach outlined above, readers
may be surprised by what might seem a strange reliance on the
work of Michel Foucault as a corrective to Gadamer's aesthetic
chronology. They may be further perturbed by my invocation of
the term *discipline*, as articulated in Foucault's *Discipline and
Punish*, in order to further my analysis of the later works
considered in this study. Nonetheless, I want to suggest that
Foucault's presence in this essentially hermeneutic enterprise is
in fact not so peculiar. Primarily, Foucault is important to this

study, not as a social historian but as a historian of representation, which has clear connections to the discussion of art. After
all, the model on which Foucault bases his notion of discipline is a
discursive one. Jeremy Bentham's plan for the penitentiary
called the Panopticon never actually came into existence; the
Panopticon is an imaginary, one might even say artistic, rendering of a possible penitential architecture. Further, Foucault's
own approach to his field(s) of study is not so different from
Gadamer's, as his 1984 interview with Paul Rabinow makes plain
(*Foucault Reader* 381–90):

> In the serious play of questions and answers, in the work of reciprocal
> elucidation, the rights of each person are in some sense immanent in
> the discussion. . . . Questions and answers depend on a game—a
> game that is at once pleasant and difficult—in which each of the two
> partners takes pains to use only the rights given him by the other and
> by the accepted form of the dialogue. The polemicist, on the other
> hand, proceeds encased in privileges that he possesses in advance
> and will never agree to question. (381–82)

The confidence in the possibility (necessity) of mutually
illuminating dialogue between free individuals, dialogue not
bounded by polemics, informs the work of Foucault as much as it
does that of more traditional hermeneutics.[4] This is not to say
that Foucault's relationship with the phenomenological tradition
as a whole is not an extremely complicated (and sometimes
openly hostile) one.[5] However, it is equally important to keep in
mind that the French philosopher's corpus is indeed connected
to hermeneutics—through the related problems of history, epis-
temology, and the identity of the subject.[6] Moreover, certain
aspects of Foucault's thought (especially in its later stages) actually share ecstatic features found in Gadamer's aesthetics.[7]

Furthermore, the work of Paul Ricoeur provides a defense
of what some readers may still persist in finding a perverse
marriage of theoretical perspectives. Ricoeur has argued
throughout his corpus for the simultaneous use of different
theories as counterbalances for each other, but nowhere does he
argue more eloquently than in the introduction to his immense
essay on Freud. In that study, he convincingly explains how the

deployment of opposing methods is actually crucial to enabling an interpretation to transcend its own perspectival mechanics (*De l'interprétation* 67–71). With this dialectic in mind, I have used Foucault's interest in the seventeenth and eighteenth centuries to counterbalance Gadamer's interest in the nineteenth century, and more importantly, I have enlisted Foucault's historical-sexual skepticism in order to modify Gadamer's faith in the value of the predominantly male (and officially heterosexual) Western literary canon. To further assist me in this latter task, I will add a third theoretical pin to this critical juggling act — namely, the feminist theory of Hélène Cixous, whose rereadings of such patriarchal texts as the *Iliad* (Cixous and Clément 73–76) point to the continuing importance of reading canonical literary texts by male authors with an eye to the ways in which they may actually subvert the values they appear to shore up.

Having laid my theoretical cards on the table, I want to remind readers that this analysis is not a "last word" which will silence all other voices and render further discussion unnecessary. Rather, it should inaugurate a critical dialogue about works which have been dismissed as failures, precisely because their aesthetic claims have not been understood or (as is the case of the Marquis de Sade, particularly) even recognized as being claims at all.[8] Therefore, the selection made here is intended to be provocative rather than exhaustive. This move may account for some unorthodox textual decisions, specifically the inclusion of Heinrich von Kleist, the exclusion of both John Gay and Daniel Defoe, and the periodic revision that such choices imply.

The works of Gay and Defoe have not been included here, not because they are unimportant, but because their considerations of criminality do not situate themselves within the modern arena as outlined by Gadamer and/or because these works do not exhibit the dialogue with criminality nor the revision of tragedy's connection with criminality — which will be discussed later in this chapter. These considerations caused me to leave out both *The Beggar's Opera* and *Moll Flanders*,[9] although a possible objection could still be made in defense of Defoe's *Roxana*, which is, arguably, a tragic novel (Starr 183), and whose heroine repeatedly speaks of herself as a criminal. Yet crime really signifies sin for Defoe's heroine. Maximillian Novak and others have already observed that Defoe's fiction unfolds within a Christian moralist sphere—a sphere that it critically investigates but never leaves— and that the narratives operate within the standard schema of the criminal biography (Novak, *Realism, Myth, and History* 99– 145; Backscheider 152–81) and the Protestant spiritual auto- biography (Starr).[10] In this context, Roxana's story proves to be a Protestant anatomy of guilt[11] (and a harrowing portrait of shame without repentance) far more than it is a discussion of criminality as a sociolegal category. Because of this perspective, the religious problematic articulated throughout *Roxana* allies it more closely with Ben Jonson's *Volpone*—and to the disturbing connections between sin and theatricality that Ben Jonson also raises—than to *The London Merchant*. While George Lillo's play superficially resembles Defoe's novel insofar as both tell the tale of the prostitute's criminal fall, the drama radically problema- tizes and covertly rejects any solution presented by Christian metaphysics.[12] Such factors as these do limit Defoe's usefulness for this particular study.

Conversely, Kleist—whose periodic affiliations are the sub- ject of some debate—has been included in what is otherwise a study of eighteenth-century literature because his work can be best understood within an eighteenth-century framework.[13] Kleist's *Michael Kohlhaas* simultaneously recapitulates eigh- teenth-century concerns surrounding the criminal and dramati- cally shifts the literary perception of the criminal's relationship to society—with lasting results. With Kleist, there is a move beyond a society that can be reformed by the presence of the outlaw within it. Instead, the unmistakable outlines of the edifice of the modern state as envisioned by Foucault in *Disci- pline and Punish* are present. In accordance with Foucault's penitentiary model, Kleist's Holy Roman Empire controls and shapes individual wills by the imposition of hierarchy, bureau- cracy, and norms of behavior. The disciplinary state thereby turns all citizens into cases—objects of scrutiny and figures in a documented history that will be used against them for purposes of subjection. The novella is itself a terrifying example of the power of such a history.

My insistence on including Kleist also derives from a desire to push the understanding of Enlightenment literature a bit further forward in time—a step that is legitimate, given the confusion surrounding this often-used, periodic term. While much contemporary scholarship still relies on the word without really tackling the ambiguity surrounding its actual characteristics and chronology, Peter Gay suggested twenty-five years ago that *Enlightenment* is at once a necessary and difficult concept because its rich meaning connotes so much that few companion terms are able to shed much light upon it (*Enlightenment* 9–10).[14] This problem of definition is compounded by critical arguments that propose the existence of many Enlightenments—which differ, not only in terms of national and linguistic boundaries (such as Scottish or Albanian), but also in terms of ideological ones (radical, dark and, even romantic), as well as the recent critical emphasis on the various minimovements (rococo, sensibility, storm and stress, and so on) that appear in different times in different places during the eighteenth and early nineteenth centuries.[15] Quite rightly, Lester Crocker asks with some exasperation (in his 1987 essay) that Enlightenment scholars think more critically about whom and what they are studying ("The Enlightenment: What and Who?").

Similarly, while the word *Enlightenment* is difficult to define, it is hard to say when the Enlightenment starts. While the term is often considered synonymous with the eighteenth century, Gay notes that the Enlightenment has been traditionally situated between two revolutions (English and French) and that it has its roots in the late seventeenth century (*Enlightenment* 17). This observation has been well substantiated by recent works such as Alan Kors and Paul Korshin's *Anticipations of the Enlightenment in England, France, and Germany* (1987). Moreover, it is even harder to say when the Enlightenment ends, as the recent array of works on that difficult transition from the eighteenth to the nineteenth century testifies.[16] Foucault well expresses the dual problem of defining and placing the era when (taking his cue from Ernst Cassirer) he observes that Enlightenment is really a very complex attitude—at once a mode of reflection "at the crossroads" between the critical and the historical and an ethos, which he sees as the germ of the "attitude of modernity." For him, this movement comes to the fore during the eighteenth century (although it does not necessarily begin there), and it finds its first philosophical articulation toward the end of the century with Kant's famous essay (although it is not bounded by the century):

> I have been seeking . . . to emphasize the extent to which a type of philosophical interrogation—one that simultaneously problematizes man's relation to the present, man's historical mode of being, and constitution of the self as an autonomous subject—is rooted in the Enlightenment. On the other hand, I have been seeking to stress that the thread that may connect us with the Enlightenment is not faithfulness to doctrinal elements, but rather the permanent reactivation of an attitude—that is, of a philosophical ethos that could be described as a permanent critique of our historical era. (*Foucault Reader* 42)

Although the strictures of Foucault's genealogy prevent him from characterizing the Enlightenment outright, it seems clear that he is describing a movement of thought possessing certain definite features: historical self-consciousness, an experimental ethos of self-critique in the present, and a will to remain on the frontiers of thought in order to move beyond them in the future. And it is worth noting that despite the vagaries of his language, Foucault's description is not very different from that of Lester Crocker who also sees the Enlightenment as a "diverse intellectual movement" rather than a period "whose general direction was to use free, critical reason, untrammeled . . . by authority and tradition, in order to understand the universe, man's place in it, human nature, and interaction" ("Enlightenment" 341).

This is very much the spirit in which the word *Enlightenment* is deployed in this study—namely, as a movement of historically self-conscious and self-critical thought that develops and culminates during the eighteenth and early nineteenth centuries. Further, I would like to suggest that such an admittedly broad understanding of the Enlightenment has three distinct advantages. First, it allows a look beyond (without overlooking) the apparent dissimilarities between diametrically opposed movements within the eighteenth century (such as German Sturm

und Drang and French libertinism), and it permits examination
of the extent to which such movements are concerned with the
same issues and go about exploring them in much the same way.
Second, an elastic view of the Enlightenment permits reex-
amination and repositioning of writers such as Kleist who have
had the misfortune to write at the turn of the century and who
have thereby been deprived of a periodic place. Third, the
stretching of Enlightenment literature toward the beginning of
the nineteenth century points in turn to the necessity of re-
evaluating the perennially fuzzy line that divides romanticism
(another problematic historical term) from the artistic innova-
tions which precede it.[17] Although such a reevaluation does not
lie within the scope of this book, the last two chapters strongly
imply that what is called romantic literature is not a rejection of
the Enlightenment so much as a continuation of (and not necessarily an improvement on) the modern attitude it heralds.

Crime and Formal Failure in
Literature of the Enlightenment

Within the context of hermeneutics and its insistence on the
ethical dynamics of literature, eighteenth-century works dealing with crime and the criminal present a special interpretive
challenge. For if art and ethics are bound up together, what is the
reader to make, not only of the frequency with which crime and
the criminal appear in the written texts of the period (ranging
from the legalistic tracts of Fielding and Beccaria to the sensa-
tionalist criminal biographies so popular in England), but of the
manner in which they appear? Denis Diderot's philosophical
dialogue *Rameau's Nephew* (*Le Neveu de Rameau*, early 1760s) is an
important literary case in point, for this novel-length conversation contains a surprising view of criminality: "If it is important
to be sublime in anything [en quelque genre], it is especially so in
evil. You spit on the petty thief, but you can't withhold a sort
respect from a great criminal. His courage bowls you over. His
brutality makes you shudder. What you value in everything is the
consistency of character [*l'unité de son caractère*]" (93). Rameau,
the nephew of the well-known composer also named Rameau,

expresses this opinion. A quintessential *artiste manqué*, he reveals that he also dreams in vain of being a criminal genius, and in so doing, he implicitly suggests that crime is itself a kind of art (462). Sublimity, he argues, is not only a possible but prominent feature in the commission of truly evil deeds, and the great criminal—a man of courage, atrocity, and psychological consistency—thereby achieves a level of pure excellence that others cannot deny.[18] The great criminal is, then, the exemplary male who forestalls our condemnation or indeed any judgment about him whatsoever; the criminal overwhelms with absolute greatness.

Equally important is the reverse of this implication; if crime can be sublime, then is not the artist (and his art) potentially criminal? Is art not in essence a transgression, a subversion of accepted values and rules?[19]

Moi, the virtuous philosopher and satiric spokesman of *Rameau's Nephew* is, needless to say, aghast at the nephew's panegyric of criminality which leaves him momentarily speechless but which he is unable to disavow. Soon after this bizarre exclamation, Rameau reveals that he is incapable of such grandscale criminal action, as he demonstrates with his tale of the *grison* (who proves to be none other than himself). Although he admires the statesman Bouret and the perfidious con man of Avignon, the nephew is incapable of the unscrupulous deception necessary to carry out a true crime. In the end, Rameau is only a charlatan dreaming of greatness, as much a failed criminal as he is a failed artist. Strangely, the dialogue ends at this point, without resolving any of the considerable array of aesthetic-moral questions it has raised—quite literally, a conversation that has gone nowhere.

Rameau's Nephew is in many respects a work about failure—of communication, of philosophy, of politics, and very possibly, of art—but the dialogue is particularly intriguing for two reasons. First, Rameau's passing remarks aptly summarize an odd dynamic of fascination and failure that pervades eighteenth-century literature of crime; second, the peculiar, self-collapsing form that frames those remarks tells (and shows) something important about the shape which literary considerations of the criminal can take.

The nephew's interest in committing crimes along with his interest in the person who commits them seems, to the late-twentieth-century mind, something of a representational commonplace. The aesthetic ramifications of this familiarity will be discussed in the conclusion of this study, but for the moment it is enough to remember that this interest acquired unprecedented proportions in the popular culture of the eighteenth century. Lincoln B. Faller has convincingly argued for the centrality of the criminal biography in the England of the late seventeenth and early eighteenth centuries (see *Turned to Account*), and this enthusiasm for the criminal mystique is manifest elsewhere, in England and abroad (Foucault, *Discipline and Punish* 300). However, it is also important to remember that, as I have tried to suggest in the foregoing theoretical overview, there is a difference between popular culture and literary art.[20] While the literary creations examined here certainly employ the formulas of popular writing,[21] they do so for considerably more complex (and critical) purposes—as will become evident.

Implicit in the first two works considered here—George Lillo's *London Merchant* (1731) and the Abbé de Prévost's *Manon Lescaut* (1731)—is the suggestion that crime exerts a powerful attraction over the potential malefactor, and since the attraction is irresistible, the criminal is not to blame. The criminal mystique is presented even more forcefully and problematically in Henry Fielding's *Jonathan Wild* (1754), where a professional thief repeatedly affirms the philosophical satisfaction of criminal behavior despite the fact that his profession leads to his downfall and demise. The same attraction asserts itself (with increasingly complicated ramifications) in the works of Friedrich Schiller, the Marquis de Sade, and William Godwin, where the lines of demarcation between the criminal and the law-abiding become more and more hazy. In fact, the allure of criminality in European literature moves beyond the chronological boundaries of the eighteenth century and grounds Heinrich von Kleist's startling *Michael Kohlhaas* (1810), a novella that both marks the culmination of the Enlightenment's investigation of criminality and profoundly influences Western literature's subsequent representation of the phenomenon.

Yet the criminal protagonists are all failures. The Chevalier des Grieux and Manon Lescaut, Barnwell and Millwood, Jonathan Wild, Karl and Franz Moor, Juliette and Justine, Caleb Williams and Falkland, and Michael Kohlhaas fail for one or more of the following reasons: they are inefficient transgressors who either cannot bring themselves to commit crimes and/or make fatal mistakes; they are guilt-ridden outlaws whose consciences catch up with them and bring about their destruction; they are innocents wrongly accused who take to illegal activities that they do not fully understand and whose scope transcends their control.

These characters' failure and subsequent downfall are of profound importance, for they link these texts to the artistic origins of criminal representation in Greek antiquity and at the same time indicate how these authors seek to restate the classical literary portrayal of criminality. Specifically, as different as these works are from each other, they all more or less overtly echo the fatal conflict between Prometheus and Zeus in *Prometheus Bound*, by pitting their obviously criminal characters against an apparently just society whose equitability proves dubious as the work unfolds.[22] Thus, despite their varied generic affiliations, these creations all possess a tragic resonance insofar as they attempt to rewrite that unequal struggle between the outlaw Titan and the Olympian tyrant. Certainly, these texts radically revise the Promethean formula—a fact already implicit in the substitutions that are made for Aeschylus' immortal outlaw, among them a prostitute, a professional thief, and an unemployed secretary. But the echo of the original is still discernible in the extreme seriousness with which these protagonists proclaim their criminality, the rhetorical energy that they expend, and the sacrifices that they make to justify their stances. In this sense, they all can be said to rely, to a greater or lesser degree, on what Eugene Falk has called "tragic renunciation"—a painful decision to renounce life itself, which is the result of the tension between the hero's will to live and his or her adherence to personal ethical values (4–5).

The influence of the *Prometheus Bound* conflict is, not surprisingly, most obvious in the only overtly tragic creation discussed here—namely in Lillo's bourgeois tragedy; certainly the

conflict between the rebellious Millwood and the authoritative
Thoroughgood, the patriarchal ruler of the miniature society in
The London Merchant, clearly resonates (while substantially alter-
ing) the Promethean juxtaposition of the unjust ruler and the
morally justified outlaw. At the other end of the spectrum lie the
other two works written during the first half of the eighteenth
century, *Manon Lescaut* and *Jonathan Wild*, in which the doomed
struggle between the criminal hero and his authoritarian nemesis is the least obvious because it is dispersed through a variety of
societal spokesmen.[23] The Chevalier des Grieux must defy, not
just one male authority, but indeed his best friend, his father,
and a veritable host of hypocritical male social powers in order
to affirm his love. Likewise, Jonathan Wild rails against a society
at large (of which the main proponents are Heartfree and oddly
enough, the book's own narrator) where all are thieves, and his
defiant performance at the block recalls Prometheus' refusal to
submit in the final moments of Aeschylus' tragedy.

The later works studied here undertake increasingly complicated and sophisticated combinations of these two early approaches. In them the confrontation between the rebel and the
tyrant is evident—as the contests between Justine and Juliette,
Karl and Franz Moor, Caleb Williams and Falkland, and Michael
Kohlhaas and the Junker von Tronka testify—but this core
antagonism is so radically problematized that it reveals both the
inadequacy of this power relation to define the actual struggle as
well as the very real difficulty that attends social rebellion or
indeed any form of individual resistance to the sociopolitical
status quo.

The problem of inadequacy leads to my second point about
the function of failure in the works selected here. These Enlightenment creations do not merely present criminal protagonists
who fail.[24] More importantly, like Diderot's dialogue, these texts
are *at once stories/dramas about and exercises in failure*, and in this
sense, their achievement is quite unlike that of their father-text
Prometheus Bound. By this I do not mean that they are artistic
failures. Indeed, I am arguing precisely the opposite, although
it is true that all texts considered here have been traditionally
received as flawed productions, precisely because their dynamic

has not been adequately understood. These texts "fail" insofar as the generic/formal modes chosen by the authors tend to self-destruct in much the same way that Diderot's philosophical dialogue dismantles itself as it proceeds, expressing ideas far different from those expressed by either Moi or the nephew (see Hammer, "The Dance of Dishonesty").

This self-destruction occurs because, as will be seen, the presence of the law-breaking figure causes the work that he or she inhabits to break its own generic and formal laws. Correspondingly, I shall argue that the rhetorical presence of Millwood in Lillo's bourgeois tragedy makes the drama covertly antibourgeois, while Manon Lescaut's silence transforms the Chevalier's confessional romance into a revelation of his destructive elitism. Likewise, the narrator's increasingly desperate efforts to marginalize Jonathan Wild propel Fielding's satire towards its generic opposite—a paean to the criminal's heroic mystique. The rivalry between the Moor brothers turns Schiller's republican Sturm und Drang drama of father-love, *The Robbers*, into a grisly performance of masculine violence, while the apparent juxtaposition between the fortunes of Juliette and Justine rewrites the libertine novel of license, *Justine*, into a narrative of imprisonment and repression. Most explosive of all are the self-annihilating dynamics of *Caleb Williams* and *Michael Kohlhaas*; fictions torn between opposing narrative modes (the defense and the romance), Godwin's novel and Kleist's novella rip themselves apart and in so doing, lay bare the deeply ambiguous character of their protagonists' criminal transgressions.

Seen from this perspective, the criminal protagonist's function in the works studied here looks something like that of Gilbert and Gubar's monster woman; one could argue that like that "vicious bitch outside," the criminal character repeatedly "gets away" from the male author who wants to imprison him or her in a textually ordained place (28–29). To a certain extent, there is indeed something feminine about the criminal, insofar as this person is profoundly "other," and like all "others" is endowed with many of the same enigmatic characteristics as the "second sex" (Beauvoir, *The Second Sex* 259); it is for this reason that the criminals in these selections are usually either sexually

ambiguous and/or express "suspect" sexual desires. These "per-
versions" are everywhere: the peculiarly obsessive quality of
Barnwell's and the Chevalier's platonic passions for Trueman
and Tiberge, Millwood's calculating coldness, Manon's thought-
less promiscuity, and Jonathan Wild's "lack of facility" with the
ladies, which stands in sharp contrast to Heartfree's fertility.
Even more striking is the incestuous and combustible combination of attraction and loathing that dominates the relations
between the Moor brothers, Justine and Juliette, and Caleb and
his father-husband Falkland. Eve Sedgwick's term, the *homosocial*, has particular relevance in the constitution of these criminal characters, as will be shown, and as the century progresses,
the literary representation of criminality becomes more and
more overtly connected to the representation of sexual deviance
and to a critique of gender roles in a masculinist society.

However, there is one important difference between the
Gilbert/Gubar monster woman and the criminal characters
considered here. The former evades her male author but is
unable, according to Gilbert and Gubar, to leave a meaningful
imprint on the text itself. In contrast, the criminal characters
under examination here invade the very center of the texts that
they inhabit, even as the work apparently tries to marginalize
(and silence) them within its boundaries. In other words, these
works all dramatize rather than submerge the criminal's struggle to assert him- or herself. Although, as I have already noted,
this struggle is effectively doomed on the level of plot, by
highlighting the problems involved in the struggle itself, these
authors allow their criminals to speak in a way that the Gil-
bert/Gubar monster woman never can.

Thus, the criminal effectively sabotages the official story
that the text wants to tell. This character deflects the plot, style,
and formal requirements of the work in question, subverting its
message—be it moral, sentimental, or libertine—through a kind
of structural sabotage, forcing the text beyond its own formal
boundaries. What might look at first like a relatively simple (and
ideologically safe) artistic dialectic—the subversive articulation
of the criminal mystique coupled with the neutralizing (and
nullifying) force of moral didacticism that ensures no criminal

protagonist ever actually "gets away with murder"[25] — is in fact a complex interplay of failure and innovation, subversion and affirmation, occurring at every level of the text. Through this interplay, the literary texts discussed here all inaugurate an ethical understanding that can neither be reduced to a rigid moralism nor to a deconstruction of the presented social values. Undoubtedly, this interplay articulates itself in different, increasingly complicated ways as the century progresses. The literature from earlier in the century promises itself as unproblematically moral (*The London Merchant, Manon Lescaut, Jonathan Wild*) but emerges as an occasion for highly critical reappraisals of the criminal's role in society and his or her reasons for coming into being. In contrast, the later literature utters a self-consciously problematic ethical challenge (usually in the form of an introduction or preamble), which it then apparently undercuts by presenting a pair of real and false criminals (*The Robbers* [1782], *Justine* [1792], *Caleb Williams* [1794], *Michael Kohlhaas* [1810]), but the result is still more complex. These works of the late eighteenth and early nineteenth centuries expose the inadequacy of our moral, political, and gender categories while they question (especially in Godwin and Kleist) the potential and the limitations of writing itself as a tool in the endeavor to think beyond imprisoning systems of thought.

The literary works discussed here employ the figure of the criminal and the concept of criminality as occasions for the reader's own ethical self-recognition and self-discovery; they demand with an increasing sense of urgency that the reader reevaluate his or her relation to the society in which he or she lives. As such, they function less as studies of the pathology of the criminal or as didactic (or antiestablishment) parables, than as aesthetic and philosophical explorations of what is right, and perhaps equally important, of the dangers involved in such explorations.[26] Thus, their very "failure" points paradoxically to their richness as works of art and to the complexity of the hermeneutic that informs them. Images, Gadamer notes in *Truth and Method*, are by nature inadequate, and it is their very deficiency that enables human beings to use them, by seeing beyond them, into that ineffability, which is the nature of real experience (316).

That such symbolic inquiries occasion primarily negative realizations while providing few or no answers, belongs, as Gadamer has noted, to the essential dynamic of experience, that is in and of itself negative, without being unproductive (*Truth and Method* 316).

Therefore, the criminal's subversive presence within these texts should be seen as both dangerous and potentially liberating; it inaugurates new insight while it exacts its price—removing certainty, without offering anything in its place.[27] In this sense, the creations of Lillo, Prévost, Fielding, Schiller, Sade, Godwin, and Kleist challenge the late-twentieth-century reader to continue the investigation that the works themselves have inaugurated, even as they outline the always imperiled nature of such an enterprise.

2

Economy and Extravagance
Criminal Origin in Lillo's *London Merchant* and Prévost's *Manon Lescaut*

An unexpected sort of criminal protagonist makes his appearance in George Lillo's bourgeois tragedy and in the Abbé de Prévost's preromantic novel, for the heroes of both works have little in common with earlier literary incarnations of the outlaw. George Barnwell and the Chevalier des Grieux resemble neither the brilliantly evil malefactors of Shakespeare nor the comic rogues of Grimmelshausen, Gay, Defoe, and Marivaux. In contrast to earlier characterizations of the criminal, the apprentice and the Chevalier are fashioned after a new and increasingly popular eighteenth-century character—namely, the man of sensibility (Bernbaum; Cory)—and consequently, both are presented to the reader/spectator as sensitive, virtuous, and noble (L. Brown 145). In fact, Lillo and Prévost exhibit the extreme selflessness of these innocent young men as a tragic flaw, for their loyalty to the unworthy objects of their attention drives them to commit similar illegal acts of increasingly serious nature—embezzlement, theft, and murder. But despite these transgressions, the other male citizens of Barnwell's and des Grieux's fictional worlds refuse to condemn them for the passion which has effected their criminal transformation; to the man, they recognize that the true cause of Barnwell's and des Grieux's malfeasance lies in their fateful encounters with Millwood and Manon Lescaut.

Both play and novel play a strange game with their outlaw
men of sensibility. While they offer these characters as alternative criminal types they also carefully insist that their criminal
status is but a seeming one. Instead, it is through the figure of
the prostitute that *The London Merchant* and *Manon Lescaut*
seemingly establish their female antagonists as the source of the
hero's criminality, and in so doing, both apparently reenact the
religious drama of Adam and Eve.[1] Like the first woman, Millwood and Manon harbor a facile carnality, which they use in turn
to tempt their lovers out of the exclusively male Edens that they
inhabit—the countinghouse and the monastery—in favor of a
life of crime. The image of woman as corrupt temptress is made
even more explicit by the fact that Millwood and Manon are
undiscriminating professional pleasure givers who cater to and
then capitalize upon men's basest carnal instincts.

On the surface, *The London Merchant* and *Manon Lescaut* not
only suggest a causal relationship between sexual desire and
malfeasance, but also specifically assign the role of instigator of
desire to woman.[2] It is the female's presence that produces desire
in the heretofore innocent male, and fittingly, the degree of
power that the female object exercises over the male desirer is in
direct proportion to the profundity of his moral fall. Seen from
this point of view, the drama and the novel both boast a straightforward, sexist didactic message: Passion is dangerous, because
one moment of sexual license suffices to transform a virtuous
man into a criminal.

But on closer inspection, this is not the case. Lillo's bourgeois tragedy and Prévost's novel of sensibility simultaneously
problematize their own explanation of criminal origin, even as
their moralistic demonstrations unfold. Gradually, another version of the presented events insinuates itself, subverts and eventually undermines the religiously based didactic parable that the
play and novel ostensibly tell. Intriguingly, this implied alternate
version offers a vision of criminality grounded, not in a metaphysics of female evil, but instead in a politics of male injustice.
Thus, while they stage apparent reenactments of the Judeo-
Christian connection between woman, original sin, and crime,
The London Merchant and *Manon Lescaut* also reveal this notion's

insufficiency and express a passionately felt intimation of social inequity—an intimation foregrounded by an "evil" female character who undermines unproblematic male "goodness."[3]

These opposing narrative versions manifest themselves through a war of words between sexually, morally, and financially opposed linguistic modes. While this discursive struggle is overt in Lillo's play (which establishes clear lines of rhetorical demarcation between Thoroughgood's realm of male goodness and that of Millwood's female evil), it is covert in Prévost's novel. Manon—who, like Millwood, incarnates female evil—does not speak here, rather it is her "fallen" victim's presentation of his seduction and descent into crime that unfolds against the contrasting backdrop of the Man of Quality's virtuously restrained narration. But the end result in both works is surprisingly similar: both drama and novel question the integrity of the dividing lines separating good from evil; they surreptitiously undermine the moral bases of male power; and they lay bare the inability of masculine metaphysics to account for the criminal's motivations and pleasures.

Economy in both its senses—as monetary system of exchanges and as thrift—forms the *modus operandi* of *The London Merchant*, and it consequently functions both as an econo-moral principle and as a rhetorical control. Like currency—which motivates the entire dramatic action—words themselves must be weighed carefully, invested wisely, and employed frugally (Foucault, *The Order of Things* 202). Thoroughgood himself announces economy's double role in the play's first scene, in which he demonstrates that he is not only a model businessman but a pattern of linguistic prudence as well. When Trueman praises his master, Thoroughgood accepts the homage but censures his apprentice's glibness: "You compliment young man. . . . Nay, I am not offended. . . . Only take heed not to purchase the character of complaisant at the expense of your sincerity" (act 1. sc. 1. line 30). With this remark, Thoroughgood clearly establishes the relationship between words and money; language possesses monetary value insofar as speech buys character, and thus, the way one speaks shapes the man and the manner in which others perceive him. Given this equivalence between speech and currency, it is vital that the businessman's language be economical in order to reflect the efficiency and integrity of his own trade.

In this way, the merchant's observation not only proclaims the frugality—rhetorical as well as commercial—of his own establishment, it also provides a work ethic of speech, which his employees should strive to emulate. Since the apprentices labor here rather than play, Trueman's language should eschew wasteful urbanity with its potentially costly risks of untruth. Rather, his speech should resemble that of Thoroughgood whose articulations throughout the play are succinct and usually didactic in flavor. His discourse consistently seeks to convey information in its most direct form, and the few metaphors occurring in it are either financial or religious—a revealing combination that assumes an inherent connection between commercial ventures and a virtuous Christian existence.[4]

Act 1, scene 1 already announces this implied affinity between business and righteousness, for Thoroughgood reveals that the individual's prudent linguistic investment not only indicates the virtue of the businessman, but indeed points to the moral power of commerce in general. He informs Trueman that he and his colleagues have employed their financial strength to support their queen and defend their country: "The merchants of this loyal city . . . all agreed to direct their several agents to influence, if possible, the Genoese to break their contract with the Spanish court" (1.1.36–39). In this manner, Thoroughgood demonstrates that he and others like him work, not for their own personal gain, but for the general good of their nation—an idea that he summarizes in suitably modest terms: "Thence you may learn how honest merchants, as such, may sometimes contribute to the safety of their country, as they do at all times to its happiness" (1.1.16–18). Thoroughgood's virtuous commercialism—grounded in his economical rhetoric—thus strives for financial success in order to more faithfully uphold society's political and ethical ideals.

In keeping with this vision, the apprentices employed by Thoroughgood resemble cloistered monks far more than ambitious worldly entrepreneurs; Barnwell and Trueman live modestly and chastely under Thoroughgood's roof, and their apprenticeship consists less in mastering the basics of a trade than in learning an ethical science, the application of which ultimately has global and messianic repercussions: "See how it [commerce] is founded in reason, and the nature of things; how it has promoted humanity, as it has opened and yet keeps up an intercourse between nations far remote from one another in situation, customs, and religions; promoting arts, industry, peace, and plenty; by mutual benefits diffusing mutual love from pole to pole" (3.1.5–9). Thoroughgood's commerce seeks the common good of all mankind and eventually unites even the most divergent races and cultures into one harmonious international business community. Thus, through the practice of virtuous commerce mankind may continually improve itself and might even create a kind of mercantile paradise; this commercial heaven on earth represents the ultimate goal of Thoroughgood's practices.

In this manner Thoroughgood's establishment presents itself as a mercantile monastery—a miniature theocracy where celibate, plain-speaking men enjoy a pure fellowship based on self-denial and unceasing commercial labor. We should note that the play repeatedly underlines the perfection of these platonic male relationships, while again stressing the importance of linguistic economy. For example, the friendship between Barnwell and Trueman is apparently such a close one that Trueman empathically shares Barnwell's as-yet-undisclosed troubles: "Before I saw your grief, I felt it. Since we parted last I have slept no more than you, but pensive in my chamber sat alone, and spent the tedious night in wishes for your safety and return. E'en now, though ignorant of the cause, your sorrow wounds me to the heart" (2.2.31–5). Such is the degree of intimacy in this relationship that no secrets can be successfully kept, even though they remain unspoken.

But while Trueman requires some verbal explanation from Barnwell, Thoroughgood is still less dependent on such clarifications, even when the latter mysteriously absents himself: "If my pardon or love be of moment to your peace, look up, secure of both. . . . Enough, enough, whate'er it be, this concern shows you're convinced and I am satisfied . . . I will not hear a syllable more on the subject. It were no mercy, but cruelty, to hear what must give you such torment to reveal" (2.4.6–36). The apprentice's expression of remorse provides all the information necessary. As his own reaction testifies, further explanation strikes the master as actually destructive to the perfect trust between the two men. Thus, in Thoroughgood's world, linguistic wastage is to be avoided at all costs, even though, as we shall see, such frugality exacts an unexpectedly heavy price.

The dangerous world outside the virtuous walls of the countinghouse neatly justifies the rigor of Thoroughgood's work ethic. His virtuous male directorship of the mercantile monastery—incarnating the virtues chastity, prosperity, self-denial and frugality—is dramatically inverted by Millwood's blatantly immoral female establishment (not a countinghouse but a house of entertainment), where promiscuity, poverty, self-indulgence, and wastefulness reign. Seen against the backdrop of the Christian mercantile monastery, Millwood looks like a satanic antibusinessman, whose management and methods ironically pervert those of Thoroughgood. She exercises her arbitrary power over her two depraved servants Lucy and Blunt and irresponsibly spends the money she has earned not for the benefit of humanity, England, or even her cohorts but merely for her own. Moreover, her dealings in no way resemble the honest commercial transactions of the London merchant, rather they are essentially dishonest manipulations of men—machinations that owe their success to Millwood's ability to recognize, and literally capitalize, upon male sexuality.

The absoluteness with which Millwood's philosophy opposes that of Thoroughgood is signaled immediately by her own distinctive manner of speech. In contrast to the merchant's terse rhetorical style that affirms the value of economy, Millwood's language celebrates extravagance. During her conversation with Lucy in act 1, scene 3, Millwood utters richly metaphorical speeches that dart from one image/idea to the next, and Lucy has trouble following her mistress' argument, so much does it express complexity, contradiction, and irony. Millwood should enjoy her beauty but does not, claiming that her very advantages have made her wretched; she says that she is a slave but speaks also like an enslaver, comparing her admirers to Latin American natives who toil under her conquistadorial whip, and she proudly concludes her rhetorical display of paradox by observing that artificiality is natural to womankind: "If I have any skill in physiognomy, he is amorous and, with a little assistance, will soon get the better of his modesty. I'll trust to nature, who does wonders in these matters. If to seem what one is not, in order to be the better liked for what one really is; if to speak one thing and mean the direct contrary, be art in a woman, I know nothing of nature" (1.4.7–13). According to Millwood, woman is naturally unnatural, and thus, the true character of the female is precisely that she has no true character; she is an infinite variety of masks.

Ergo, just as Thoroughgood's speech demonstrates plain language's virtue insofar as it represents the clear expression of truth, so does Millwood's speech display language's demonic potential to mystify and confuse, for everything and everyone that she describes appear under a double aegis of opposing characteristics. Men, according to Millwood, are both honorable and hypocritical, while she is both mistress of and slave to them. And just as Millwood proclaims herself to be both nature and artifice, so does Barnwell appear in a more complex light here: both modest and amorous, virtuous and sexually desirous, potential prey and potential predator.

Thus, in act 1 of his tragedy, Lillo establishes a dramatic tension between two clearly demarcated rhetorical spheres, which in turn represent opposing versions of human reality. If Thoroughgood's countinghouse and its language of economy represent the heights to which male culture can soar, then Millwood's house of entertainment and its language of extravagance portray the depths to which female sexual nature can plummet. Millwood looks even more sinister when compared to Thoroughgood's daughter, the virginal Maria. If the latter represents "the sweet heroine in the house," then Millwood just as clearly epitomizes the "monster-woman," an autonomous and therefore evil "vicious bitch outside" the boundaries of the male-dominated realm (Gilbert and Gubar 28–29).

The play's action unfolds in similarly absolute terms. As soon as the unsuspecting Barnwell literally steps beyond the physical bounds of his master's mercantile fortress, he is in danger, and the moment Millwood sets eyes on him, he is doomed. A brief conversation suffices to convince him that she loves him, and after one sexual encounter Barnwell realizes that he has irrevocably fallen from grace: "How strange are all things round me! Like some thief who treads forbidden ground, fearful I enter each apartment of this well-known house. . . . what must be my life? Ever to speak a language foreign to my heart, hourly to add to the number of my crimes to conceal 'em" (2.2.1–10). Although he has, as yet, committed no crime, Barnwell is already learning to speak the new (and consequently "foreign") language of criminality—as he himself is aware.[5]

Not surprisingly, this linguistic intuition proves to be a self-fulfilling prophecy. Although he understands exactly what is happening to him, Barnwell is unable to resist the criminal energies that passion has released in him; in spite of himself, he is speedily seduced into stealing money from his master and then murdering his uncle: "'What caused me to rob my gentle master, but love? What makes me now a fugitive from his service, loathed by myself and scorned by all the world, but love? What fills my eyes with tears, my soul with torture never felt on this side death before? Why, love, love, love! And why above all, do I resolve' (for tearing his hair, he cried, 'I do resolve') 'to kill my uncle?'" (3.3.97–110). In this manner Barnwell's brief moment of sexual license suffices to propel him into a short and fatal career in crime—reflected here by his own descent into the language of extravagance.

Moreover, in order to underline the danger of the eroticism it condemns, the play banishes the most crucial moment of Barnwell's fall to indirect report. The audience does not actually witness Millwood seduce Barnwell into murdering his uncle; we only hear of it from a discussion between Lucy and Blunt.[6] This omission clearly suggests that Millwood's power over Barnwell is so menacing that it can only be referred to but cannot be seen, like the Medusa's head. It is thus appropriate that it was Lucy and not Blunt who was present during this deadly conversation,

because as a woman she alone might be able to withstand
Millwood's seductive attractiveness. A male observer experiencing Millwood's powers of persuasion directly would be tempted
as Barnwell was, and in the polarized universe of the play, to be
tempted at all is almost necessarily to succumb, as Thoroughgood warns us: "Let his ruin learn us diffidence, humanity, and
circumspection, for we who wonder at his fate—perhaps had we
like him been tried like him we had fallen too" (5.1.48–51).

Millwood's destructive power is further corroborated by her
ability to overwhelm even Thoroughgood's good judgment when
he first meets her: "How should an inexperienced youth escape
her snares? The powerful magic of her wit and form might
betray the wisest to simple dotages and fire the blood that age
had froze long since. Even I" (4.16.79–82). With an uncharacteristic indirection that in turn marks his own brief weakening,
the merchant admits his own attraction to the prostitute who,
like the malevolent enchantress Circe, is able to suppress man's
intellectual forces and release the bestial (and therefore carnal)
tendencies in even the most virtuous, wise, and mature of men.

The fact that Thoroughgood himself is momentarily sus-
ceptible to Millwood's persuasive powers—notably her speech
("wit") as well as her appearance—seems to lay the ultimate
responsibility for Barnwell's malfeasance squarely on her, and we
should note that, at first glance at least, the utterances of
Millwood herself support this condemnation. She appears bru-
tally honest as regards her aims, which she claims are purely
mercenary: "Riches, no matter by what means obtained, I saw,
secured the worst of men from both [dependence and con-
tempt]: I found it therefore necessary to be rich, and, to that
end, I summoned all my arts. You call 'em wicked: be it so!"
(4.18.16–19). Further, Millwood feels no affection whatsoever for
the naive Barnwell, to whom she refers in the most scornful
manner possible, only once calling him by name (and that in her
conversation with Thoroughgood, where she is still trying to
disguise her guilt). Otherwise, she dismisses his youthful attractiveness with the indifferent observation, "Ay, the stripling is well
made" (1.3.48) and looks forward with anticipation to the time
when she will be "done with him." Likewise, Lucy reassures

Blunt that there is no chance whatsoever of their mistress falling in love with her victim: "There's no danger of that, for I am sure she has no view in this affair but interest" (1.7.27–28).

Correspondingly, when Barnwell fails to fulfill the function for which he was destined, Millwood coldly denounces and betrays him: "Whining, preposterous, canting villain, to murder your uncle, rob him of life, nature's first, last, dear prerogative, after which there's no injury, then fear to take what he no longer wanted; and bring to me your penury and your guilt. Do you think I'll hazard my reputation, nay, my life, to entertain you?" (4.10.39–44). In fact, Millwood's behavior toward Barnwell is so heartless that even her own servants grow horrified by her actions and turn her in to Thoroughgood and the authorities. Even after she has been caught, Millwood remains adamantly and arrogantly unremorseful as regards her evil actions: "I have done nothing that I am sorry for; I followed my inclination, and that the best of you does every day" (4.18.41–42).

Like Cain, Judas, and their ancestress Eve, Millwood is a depraved individual perversely drawn to evil, who in appropriate Christian terms, finds not joy in her transgressions, but despair. Millwood goes to the gallows, aware of her sinfulness but totally lacking belief in divine mercy, and her misery at the end of the play contrasts dramatically with Barnwell's pious willingness to redress the wrongs he has committed—appropriately, "paying" for these with his death.

However, while *The London Merchant* displays Millwood as evil incarnate, and thereby implies that she is the true malefactor—Barnwell being only the agent she uses to commit crimes—the play simultaneously suggests that her actions stem from motivations more complex than greed or even the perverse "female" desire to do evil for evil's sake. Although Millwood firmly declares that her malfeasance is the direct result of her poverty, her own speeches reveal that her criminal tendencies originate instead from a more sophisticated intuition of feminine deprivation: "Men, however generous or sincere to one another, are all selfish hypocrites in their affairs with us. We are no otherwise esteemed or regarded by them but as we contribute to their satisfaction. . . . We are but slaves to men. . . . Slaves

have not property—no, not even themselves. All is the victor's"
(1.3.21–22). Millwood observes that while male society has established a code of virtuous behavior that governs men's actions
with each other, all men unthinkingly violate this code in their
assessment and treatment of women. According to such a social
scheme, all women are enslaved prostitutes like Millwood herself; stripped of even their own self-possession, they are valued
only as unessential extensions of male desire.

This already-unjust conduct is rendered intolerable by another, more insidious injustice perpetrated by men on women:
"It is a general maxim among the knowing part of mankind, that
a woman without virtue, like a man without honor, or honesty, is
capable of any action, though never so vile: and yet what pains
will they not take, what arts not use, to seduce us from our
innocence and make us contemptible and wicked, even in their
own opinions?" (1.3.31–36). Having assigned women to a nar-
rowly defined and rigidly upheld social role, men consistently
strive to make them unfit for the only function society allows
them to fill; in this way, the male community perversely oblit-
erates the very quality in its female citizens that it claims to
admire and thereby all but sentences women to fall from their
already precarious social station.

Significantly, Millwood indicates that she has been the victim
of precisely such an action, and during her confrontation with
Thoroughgood, she recounts her painful history in terms that he
can immediately understand: "If such I had [perfections], well
may I curse your barbarous sex, who robbed me of 'em ere I knew
their worth; then left me, too late, to count their value by their loss.
Another and another spoiler came, and all my gain was poverty
and reproach" (4.18.11–14). At first glance, Millwood's analysis of
her victimization seems to ally itself with the mercantile system of
exchanges already affirmed by Thoroughgood (Flores 94). Virginity, she explains to the financially minded merchant, has a dollars-
and-cents value; it is the physical sign of virtue, just as money is the
physical token of wealth. Consequently, when virginity is stolen,
virtue and its accompanying perfections are taken along with it,
and the ethical as well as social value of the female individual is
thereby immediately diminished.

Yet it is important to note that Millwood's observation subtly criticizes Thoroughgood's linkage of virtue and commerce. As an innocent, Millwood naturally could not have known her virtue's "value," because such self-consciousness can belong only to someone who is no longer innocent—just as Adam and Eve realized their nakedness only after having eaten from the Tree of Knowledge. Thus, not only does Millwood suggest that true virtue exists without a price tag, for the obvious reason that it is priceless, but she also implies that the *very concept of value* is a postlapsarian one, belonging to a fallen society, that has made immanent standards of measure for transcendent, immeasurable qualities.[7] Equally important is the fact that Millwood's personal history revises the male/female roles played in the myth of original sin—for here, Millwood is the innocent and trusting Adam, while her male seducer becomes the morally weak and weakening Eve.

Millwood's picture of herself as innocent victim—a once-virtuous woman driven to and maintained in vice by the men who both ruin and condemn her—is useful because it sheds light on her plot against Barnwell—a project that at first seems highly inconsistent with what we know of her. Her apparently extreme materialism combined with her extraordinary intelligence and power to charm are clearly at odds with this foolish plan of action. First, given her exceptional attractiveness (a fact affirmed by everyone in the play), she surely could have attached herself to a man more powerful and more wealthy than Barnwell. Second, even if we grant her point that only the most innocent men can be fooled by women and therefore recognize the logic of her choice of victim, it seems clear that once she has procured the money from Barnwell, the best course of action would have been to simply abandon him, without involving herself in a highly risky murder by a man completely unversed in such matters, in which she is very likely to be ensnared as an accessory.[8]

However, when we consider Millwood's perception of herself as a victim of a spiritual robbery and her general evaluation of women's predicament in a male society, her plan takes on a psychological brilliance and an ironic appropriateness. If to deprive a woman of her honor (which equals her virginity) is to steal her most valued possession, that is to say her very self, then men's seduction/condemnation of women is nothing less than psychic and social murder. Given this suggestion, it seems likely that Millwood sees her affair with Barnwell as a rare opportunity to wreak vengeance on the male society that has rendered her worthless. By seducing Barnwell, she will demonstrate that even the most virtuous man is typical of his sex; her plan to make him rob and murder will corroborate what she believes men do to women every day.

Beyond this, through her dealings with Barnwell, Millwood can reverse their roles. In this context, it is no coincidence that she is consistently the aggressive party in this relationship; she pursues him, seduces him, follows him, seduces him again, and so on. Through this reversal, Millwood victimizes Barnwell in the same way that she herself has been victimized: she seduces an innocent, robs him of his virginity—and thereby his honor—destroys his reputation and turns him into a self-hating "wretch" like herself.

Millwood's project against Barnwell thus suggests itself to be both an act of revenge against a male-dominated society, which has collectively wronged her, and an attempt to procure personal justice from this unjust society: "What are your laws, of which you make your boast, but the fool's wisdom, and the coward's valor; the instrument and screen of all your villainies, by which you punish in others what you act yourselves, or would have acted, had you been in their circumstances?" (4.18.60–64). Again this point of view is sound, given Millwood's assessment of British society. If the male community is totally unjust, as she claims, then the only possible acts of justice meted out to the female individual must be of her own devising and will necessarily be considered criminal by the unjust authorities of an inequitable social system.

Despite the fact that Millwood is defeated and destroyed at the end of *The London Merchant*, the drama nonetheless corroborates her version of the events in act 4, scene 18, where the two spheres of opposing influences confront each other. No part of the play sends a more mixed message than this one, for if the

scene's action awards the triumph to the realm of Thoroughgood—since after all, Millwood is trapped, arrested by the
police, and unmasked as the real murderer, and thus the true
malefactor—rhetorically speaking, this scene tells another tale
altogether. Throughout, Millwood dominates, and all attempts
to accuse her backfire on the accuser, as Trueman quickly
discovers:

> TRUE.: Here thy power of doing mischief ends; deceitful, cruel
> bloody woman!
> MILL.: Fool, hypocrite, villain—man! Thou can'st not call me that.
> TRUE.: To call thee woman were to wrong the sex, thou devil!
> MILL.: That imaginary being is an emblem of thy cursed sex
> collected; a mirror wherein each particular man may see his
> own likeness, and that of all mankind. (4.18.1–7)

In the first exchange, Millwood repeats and improves on Trueman's syntax; she matches him epithet for epithet but strengthens her argument by making his three insulting adjectives into
three even more powerful nouns, that define rather than modify
his identity as "man." In the second, her mirror metaphor very
literally refracts Trueman's devil image back on himself and on
all men. We should also note that Millwood's refusal to allow
Trueman to name her succeeds to such an extent that the enraged
Trueman stops speaking altogether shortly thereafter and does not
speak again in this scene. Thoroughgood now takes over as inter-
locutor—a state of affairs that reinforces the already-strong suggestion that the younger man is unable to match the rhetorical skill
of the prostitute. But Millwood reverses the roles that Thoroughgood wants them to play; refusing to take the part of defendant,
she speaks as prosecutor of an unjust social order, which Thoroughgood must now attempt to justify.

The merchant's defense is a surprisingly feeble one. Having
attempted unsuccessfully in one speech to make Millwood's
guilt the issue of the conversation, Thoroughgood responds to
Millwood's invective in an increasingly weak manner.[9] In his last
two speeches, he no longer even addresses Millwood directly,
and his last response reveals an actual concession:

MILL.: Whatever religion is in itself—as practiced by mankind, it
has caused the evils you say it was designed to cure . . .

THOR.: Truth is truth, though from an enemy, and spoke in malice.
You bloody, blind, and superstitious bigots, how will you
answer this? (4.18.51–59)

In an uncharacteristic lapse, the highly intelligent Thoroughgood fails to understand the very core of Millwood's critique—
namely, that her indictment of religious institutions is directed
against men's use of religion and that therefore she includes *him
personally* in her attack. Moreover, this peculiar failure to com-
prehend Millwood's real target directly follows what appears to
be a clear recognition that she has made a valid observation.

These contradictory reactions point to Thoroughgood's
increasing discomfiture during his discussion with Millwood
and suggest that he might well have understood her meaning
after all but that he has used rhetorical question (conveniently
directed toward people who are not even present and who
therefore cannot possibly answer) to deflect the criticisms and to
conceal his own inability to respond to them in any meaningful
way. This impression is corroborated by the fact that after this
speech, he too is reduced to silence.[10] Finally, by giving her a
large closing speech, scene 18 clearly awards the rhetorical
triumph to Millwood; her scathing critique of the society Thoroughgood represents cannot be countered, because it is true.[11]

Thus, in the play's war of words, it is not Thoroughgood—
the virtuous masculine advocate of plain speech—but Millwood—the criminal feminine linguistic spendthrift—who
emerges triumphant. That this victory is itself an ironic one,
given Millwood's actual circumstances, corresponds perfectly
with her view of herself and of woman in society, and she
employs this paradoxical crisis point in the play (the moment
where victory and defeat merge) to make what seems at first to
be a grim prophecy. While Thoroughgood perceives the future
of man as a commercial striving toward a new Eden, Millwood
apparently sees the future of woman, not as progress, but stasis,
an infernal perpetuation of the vicious circle of injustice and
revenge, in that she herself is enmeshed:

O may from hence, each violated maid,
By flattering, faithless, barbarous man betrayed,
When robbed of innocence and virgin fame,
From your destruction raise a nobler name;
To right their sex's wrongs devote their mind,
And future Millwoods prove, to plague mankind!

                                                    (4.18.73–78)

This vision of violated maids punishing their seducers like the
mythical furies, reenacts Millwood's own fate, and in this way,
her dream of vengeance seemingly proposes a neverending
series of mirror images of herself.

And yet Millwood also uses her rhetorical pyrrhic victory to
affirm the value of woman over and against man's narrow
evaluation of her. Strikingly, she offers the female victims of the
future her own name with which they can replace their lost
virginal identity. This renaming is positive because it gives the
heretofore generically defined "maids" a common last name, an
appellation that marks an individual's relationship to a family
rather than her mere inclusion in a physiological category. With
this final grand linguistic gesture, Millwood re-creates woman
in her own image and thereby foresees much more than a
perpetuation of her own private rebellion. By sharing her proper name with faceless, nameless female victims, she both identifies and unites the violated maids to come and in so doing,
envisions a collective refusal of woman's male-determined status.
Seen from this point of view, these future Millwoods are not
mere carbon copies of the original; they are rather her daughters, who, like her, will affirm their own personal self-worth,
their "nobler name," until society does them justice.

In this manner, the play lends justification if not wholesale
condonation, to Millwood's actions, by making of her a heroic
character who displaces Barnwell as tragic focus of the piece.[12]
Her rhetorical triumph reveals the dark side of Thoroughgood's
enlightened realm, for the same virtuous commercialism that
has made him rich has made a commodity of her virtue (a
possession that can be purchased, sold, and stolen), condemning
the female victim rather than the male perpetrator of such a
robbery. Millwood bravely refuses to remain an object of mas-

culine exchange, but she purchases this refusal with her life. At first glance, the rhetorical dynamics of Prévost's novel have little in common with the clearly polarized histrionics of Lillo's play. *Manon Lescaut* reveals no apparent war of words at all, for the narrative control is firmly in the hands of two virtuous men—the Man of Quality and the Chevalier des Grieux—while rhetorical absence rather than presence characterizes the speech of their feminine opponent, the title character. Manon's silence is all the more surprising because it is she who ostensibly generates the Chevalier's entire story, as he himself indicates near the beginning of his narration: "Assuredly, constant and tender as I am by nature, I had been happy for life, had Manon been faithful. . . . O woeful alteration! That which is ground of my despair might equally have made my blessedness! That very constance that promised me the fairest of all fates and the most absolute rewards of love is that which has made me the most unfortunate of men" (20).

This Adamistic interpretation consistently guides the Chevalier's presentation of the facts. He maintains that his mistaken love for the unfaithful Manon Lescaut—a common and licentious girl—is the sole reason for his transformation from a potential Knight of Malta into a professional cheat, embezzler, and murderer. His rapid descent into criminal behavior proclaims itself rhetorically throughout his account, and in contrast to the Man of Quality's direct, self-consciously didactic introduction, des Grieux's use of language is quite reminiscent of Millwood's.[13] While Prévost's more aristocratic version of Thoroughgood weighs his words, carefully directing his reader toward an ethical analysis of the portrayed events, des Grieux wastes his, continually interrupting himself with superfluous exclamations, repetitious descriptions of his states of "transport," foreshadowings of the future, hindsight interpretations, and tortured philosophical speculation and discussion—all of which embellish a story that consists primarily of one episode, repeated and varied four times (Coulet 18).

This verbosity conveniently mirrors the monetary wastefulness of Manon Lescaut herself and the general extravagance of the Chevalier's life with her, while also signaling des Grieux's

fascination with his own progress into delinquency. This preoccupation is manifest, for in contrast to *The London Merchant*'s
summary account of Barnwell's fall and the acts undertaken, the
Chevalier dwells upon his descent into criminality with loving
detail and inflated style. For example, the protagonist describes
his entrance into the world of card sharks—his introduction to
criminal activity—as though he has been accepted by a holy
brotherhood (ironically appropriate given his former vocational
aspirations), and he even goes so far as to boast of his facility at
cheating at the illegal card game, faro:

> The principal theatre of my exploits was to be the Hotel Tran-
> sylvania, where there was a Faro table in one hall, and divers other
> games of cards and dice in the gallery. . . . I was not long in profiting
> by my master's instructions. I learned above all to be adroit in turning
> over, in playing the wrong card, and with the help of a pair of deep
> Ruffles at the wrist I had sufficient sleight of hand to deceive the eye
> of the cleverest, and to bring to ruin many an honest player. (71–72)

Although he prefaces his commentary with a moral disclaimer
(missing in the above translation is the key phrase in the original:
"Le dirai-je à mon honte?" [*L'Histoire du Chevalier Des Grieux et de
Manon Lescaut* 63]), the Chevalier subsequently reveals his pride
in his quickly mastered ability to ruin other players with a sleight
of hand. His stylistic emphasis is significant: des Grieux's tersely
stated feelings of shame are rapidly superseded here by an
extensive description of his prowess.

Even more important is the theater reference that situates
his depiction (Jones 48–59; Segal 28–32). With this implied
metaphor, the Chevalier elevates his cheating to both heroic
exploit and superlative performance in that he demonstrates his
talent and courage. Des Grieux is both hero and dissembler, his
gambling tricks are both chivalric exploit and theatrical performance, as he conceals his true identity (that of cheat) in order to
defend the honor of the lady he loves.

The Chevalier's suggestion that criminal activity is a kind of
drama and his implied attraction to theatricality crystallize in
his account of the proposed embezzlement of M. de G... M.... It
is no coincidence that this episode occurs at the novel's halfway

point, for it represents the novel's clearest dramatization of the Chevalier's fascination with his own criminal projects and the relationship between the erotic, the theatrical, and the criminal in his own mind.

Des Grieux ostensibly stages his deception, which consists primarily in playing the part of Manon's naïve brother from the provinces, for the benefit of the victim, the lecherous G... M.... However, the scene quickly becomes an ideal opportunity for des Grieux to demonstrate his powers of deception and rhetorical finesse to his mistress:

> The elderly lover seemed pleased to see me. He tapped me twice or thrice on the cheek, saying that I was a pretty lad, but that I must be on my guard in Paris, where young folk very easily fall into bad ways. Lescaut assured him that I was naturally so good that I talked of nothing but becoming a priest. . . . Our whole conversation at supper was much the same. Manon who was in a roguish mood was several times on the verge of spoiling all by her burst of laughter. I found the opportunity while at supper to tell him his own story and the ill fate that hung over him. Lescaut and Manon quailed as the tale went on, above all when I sketched his own portrait to the life: but his vanity kept him from recognizing himself, and I sketched it so adroitly that he was the first to find it highly comical. (91)

In this manner, the planned embezzlement assumes the nature of a diverting comedy with all the stock commedia dell'arte characters—the *senex amans*, the harlequinesque go-between Lescaut, and young lovers—all staged for an audience of one, Manon.

More importantly, the Chevalier's demonstration of his acting talent before the beloved serves as a kind of linguistic foreplay to two connected pleasures—first, that of procuring money, that leads logically to the second more important pleasure, namely, the sexual act, an even more private performance destined for the same audience of one. Seen from this point of view, the Chevalier's theft becomes double and therefore doubly pleasurable; he steals G... M...'s money *and* the object of the latter's desire, that G... M... has rightfully purchased.[14] But there is also an odd suggestion here. In this masquerade, des Grieux also momentarily supplants Manon as object of desire; as a "pretty lad," he not only steals G...

M...'s potential mistress, but actually fleetingly *becomes* that mistress himself. This is a somewhat jarring note in the sexual proceedings—to which we will return.[15]

But while des Grieux sensually outlines—and in outlining, relives—his lapse into criminality, he simultaneously blames this catastrophe on the object of his erotic passion, Manon Lescaut. Like Millwood, des Grieux's mistress seems to be a woman driven only by a lust for the material, although the Chevalier also insists with apparent generosity that she is not motivated by greed: "Never was a girl less attached to money than she: but she never knew a moment's peace of mind if there was any fear of lacking it. Pleasure and pastime she must have . . . to be constantly amused was so necessary to her that failing it one could count not at all on her humour or her inclinations" (69). To support this suggestion, des Grieux's story makes the same agonizing demonstration three times: whenever their finances falter, Manon offers to sell her sexual favors to a new, wealthy admirer. These episodes point, not only to Manon's total infidelity, but also to her actual inclination for prostitution, since this is always the means that she chooses to improve her lot. In contrast to Millwood, who repeatedly professes hatred for her "wretched" profession, Manon has no apparent moral objections to this employment, and the ease with which she sells herself suggests that, far from troubling her, this line of work may actually please her. Des Grieux also indicates that Manon is completely dishonest with him about her sexual business deals; with all three wealthy lovers—B..., the old G... M..., and the young G... M...—she deceives him, planning a betrayal which he always inevitably discovers.

Yet in the final episode, the Chevalier's narrative radically shifts gears from the temptation/fall story it seemed to tell to yet another kind of Christian parable—one of conversion and redemption. In America, Manon suddenly recognizes and confesses her moral and emotional inferiority to her lover. This confession reflects a profound moral transfiguration that enables her to stoically abandon all desire for material comfort and then offer her life to protect her lover from punishment by the Louisianian authorities. Manon's inner alteration in turn transforms the nature of the lovers' relationship and briefly, their place in society. This sudden metamorphosis is mirrored by the novel's dramatic geographical shift away from Paris (the seat of vice) to the American colonies, a place of poverty and simplicity:

> We lost no opportunity of doing a service or a kindness to our Neighbors; this obligingness and the gentleness of our bearing won us the trust and affection of the whole colony. In a short time we were so well thought of that next to the Governor, we ranked as the first people of the town. The innocence of our pursuits and the unbroken tranquillity in that we lived served to recall us, little by little, to a spirit of devotion and of religion. . . . Our conversations, which were always thoughtful, brought us insensibly to a desire for a virtuous love. (232)

Thus, while the first part of the novel stresses the fall of the Adam-like Chevalier, who has been fatally tempted by the weak and easily tempted Manon (Mylne 61), the last episode suggests a variation of the conversion of Magdalene, whereby the fallen courtesan is saved and transfigured by the pure devotion of her Christ-like lover, as she herself signals: "I feel too well that I have never deserved the amazing tenderness you have for me. . . . But you could not believe how I have changed. . . . I never cease blaming myself for my inconstancy, and my heart melts to see what love has made you do for a wretch who was not worthy of it, and who could not atone even with her blood" (231). In a romantic epiphany, Manon signals her gratitude to her savior for whom she is willing to spill her unworthy blood. In this context, her death represents, not the defeat, but the triumph of their love over the material circumstances that have controlled them throughout the narrative. Moreover, this is a triumph of spirit over body; through her sacrifice, Manon elevates herself morally to the level of the devoted Chevalier; in her death, she at last becomes worthy of him.

This new tale of redemption places the reader in an interpretational impasse. How can the same "criminal" love that impelled the Chevalier to malfeasance also instill a miraculous moral metamorphosis on the part of his temptress? How can the depraved Chevalier serve as an edifying example to his even

more depraved mistress? Only two responses seem possible and
neither are corroborated by the narrative as it has been presented to us: either the Chevalier has become a criminal because
his relationship with Manon is tainted and impure—she is an evil
woman and wholly responsible for his evil transformation—or
his love for Manon was not mistaken. In this case, she cannot be
evil, and therefore des Grieux's love for her cannot be the source
of his criminality.

In order to resolve this contradiction—on which depends
our understanding of the moral lesson promised by the Man of
Quality in his preface—the reader must further scrutinize and
evaluate the true character of the Chevalier's love for his mistress. But this proves an impossible task because, given the
paradoxical comments that the Chevalier makes about her, the
reader cannot determine who Manon Lescaut really is: she
appears under too-bewildering an array of diametrically opposed guises—temptress/martyr, virgin/whore, as well as faith-
ful/profligate, pure/perverse, honest/dishonest.[16] This uncertainty is exacerbated by the fact that des Grieux has actually
provided us with very little information about his mistress. He
never even so much as mentions any specifics as to her physical
appearance, mannerisms, or other traits, although he does
indicate that these features are enchanting:[17] "Her wit, her
heart, her sweetness and her beauty fashioned a chain so strong
and so enchanting that I should have counted myself happy
never to be free of it" (20). Even more importantly, we have no
clear rhetorical image of Manon. Curiously, in comparison to
Millwood's linguistic extravagance—which reflects her desire
for material wealth—Manon's extravagant life-style is in no way
indicated by her verbal self-expression, which is extremely mea-
ger as presented to us by the Chevalier (Fort 174).

Why does des Grieux so scrupulously silence the lover
whom he ostensibly mourns and whom his memoir seemingly
attempts to resurrect? The answer to this question is hinted at
whenever des Grieux's narrative does focus on Manon, for what
he says about her proves revealing in a most unexpected way. In
his account of their first meeting, for example, the Chevalier
implies strongly that it was Manon who seduced him, and he

emphasizes the fact that under her influence, he does not act like himself. As in the case of Millwood, the Circe image is helpful; like her British counterpart, Manon is also a sorceress of sorts, insofar as she magically releases the Chevalier's sexual yearnings (because until then he had never thought about women) and transforms him from a bashful schoolboy into a bold, decisive lover. Further, des Grieux describes Manon as totally self-possessed throughout this encounter. He tells us that she seemed unembarrassed by his attentions—which suggests that she is used to them—and her immediate comprehension of the purport of his declarations reveals to him that she is a sexually experienced woman with a history of wanton behavior: "She was far more experienced than I: it was against her will that she was being sent to the Convent, doubtless to check that bent toward pleasure that had already declared itself, and that was afterwards to be the cause of all her griefs and mine" (13).

Yet this scene also indicates that the Chevalier's interpretation of the events may well be an incorrect one. Manon tells des Grieux only that she has been sent to the convent by her parents in order to become a nun, but the actual motivations for this decision are open to conjecture, as des Grieux reveals with his lapse "doubtless" (*sans doute*). The above passage about Manon's history thus represents the Chevalier's assessment of the situation and not what she tells him. This clever employment of indirect discourse further confuses the issue as to what she actually says and what he interprets (Fort 174). Equally open to conjecture is whether Manon is unembarrassed by the Chevalier's declarations because she is licentious and experienced—as he thinks—or because she is a naive sixteen-year-old girl, swept away and herself transformed by the Chevalier's gallant attentions. The latter interpretation is implied by the Chevalier's report of his actions, which clearly reveal that he is the aggressor throughout the encounter; he accosts Manon in the street, subsequently convinces her to disobey her parents and follow him, and he takes charge of their flight, although she proves a skillful accomplice.

In this manner, des Grieux's account of his meeting with Manon contradicts his portrait of himself as the innocent victim in the hands of a sexually knowing manipulative female, for it is he who seduces Manon—not the other way around—the negative repercussions of which Manon already seems to foresee:[18] "She told me that she foresaw only too well that she would be unhappy" (13).

In similar fashion, the opening scenes of the novel establish the Chevalier's pattern of negative appraisal of his mistress— one that is borne out consistently, with the exception of the fourth episode. But this negative pattern repeatedly backfires on the Chevalier, revealing the darkness of his own character. Once again, the central G... M... affair provides the most dramatic example of this rhetorical ricochet action. When des Grieux learns of Manon's arrangement with the elderly man, he reacts with horror: "She is afraid of hunger: God of love! What grossness of feeling, and how ill a response to my delicacy! I feared it not at all, I who exposed myself there to so willingly for her, when I gave up my fortune and all the sweetness of my father's house" (79). Des Grieux's condemnation of Manon's materialism clearly bases itself on a Christian, chivalric ideal (Josephs 188). According to such a scheme, the virtuous lover seeks to emulate the perfect spiritual love exhibited by Christ; his passion is a totally selfless and disinterested emotion, which should inspire the lover to conquer fear of physical discomfort, pain, and even death.

Yet while it is understandable, given his religious training, that the Chevalier reacts to Manon's letter in precisely these terms, the wording of his condemnation betrays him, for it reveals that he is far more repulsed by Manon's base concern with her physical well-being than morally outraged by her planned sexual betrayal. We may be surprised to learn that it is not Manon's prostitution but her fear of hunger that offends the Chevalier's delicate sensibilities, as he himself indicates; he exclaims, not that Manon's sentiments are evil or depraved but merely that they are *grossier*, that is to say vulgar, common, and ordinary. Thus, the Chevalier condemns Manon, not on ethical grounds but according to a standard of discursive etiquette, that she has clumsily breached. How dare she, he asks, answer his noble declarations of love with such mundane and worldly concerns? Moreover his contemptuous repetition of the word *ingrate* in this soliloquy suggests that according to des Grieux, the base-born Manon has no right to express any emotion other than gratitude to him. How can she fear discomfort when he has grandly and voluntarily renounced his advantages and comforts for her?

In this manner the Chevalier's emotional response to Manon's letter suggests a very different source of distress than that of uncertainty as to the beloved's feelings and constancy. Here at least, these questions barely enter in and do not dismay the Chevalier as much as does Manon's worldview itself—based on physical well-being and material comfort—which he simply refuses to accept on the grounds that he finds it aesthetically displeasing. Most importantly, his reaction points to a conviction that his love is innately superior to hers for he insists that he and not she, is the absolute authority on the pangs of love: "It is I who can tell [*C'est à moi qu'il faut demander*] what cruel pains there are in being separated from what one adores" (80).

This scene and others like it force us to seriously reexamine the apparent generosity of des Grieux's philosophy of love.[19] His harsh assessments of his mistress suggest that, far from being the selfless ascete of love that he claims to be, he is instead an overly fastidious aristocrat who disdains any behavior that does not perfectly correspond to his ideas of the moment.[20] Seen from this point of view, des Grieux looks less like the romantic idealist that he says he is and more like a sentimental tyrant, a man so convinced of his own innate superiority that he is unable to recognize the value of any love other than his own, because he measures all emotions according to his own absolute and rigid standards. Moreover, his constant effort to render his beloved as unsubstantial as possible—by either silencing her outright or by editorially discrediting whatever she says or does—forces us to wonder if Manon Lescaut's function in des Grieux's narrative is not somehow very different than what he says it is.

These suggestions in turn point to the suspicious nature of des Grieux's insistences on his own sacrifices and sufferings, for what in fact has he forsaken? For all his rhetoric, the Chevalier's sacrifices prove to be rather trivial ones. Des Grieux never loses

the advantages of his social position; he always has economic
resources (his family and Tiberge), and he always has powerful
and/or aristocratic allies who intervene on his behalf at crucial
moments in the narrative. Thus, while the Chevalier claims to
have renounced his prestige, he conveniently has recourse to it
whenever his own personal welfare is seriously threatened. The
father of Saint-Lazare befriends and protects him even after
having been betrayed by him, Monsieur de T... is immediately
drawn to him despite his long standing friendship with the G...
M... family, and even his estranged father uses his influence to
bail him out of prison. The ship's captain and the colonial
governor befriend him, and surprisingly, even his rival, Synnelet, comes forward to protect him when he is accused of murdering his mistress. Des Grieux's school friend Tiberge constantly
lends him money and conveniently arrives at the end of the
novel, signaling des Grieux's physical return to the kind of life
for that he was destined—his *vie reglée et saine* in some kind of
religious institution. Most importantly of all, the Man of Quality
himself gives des Grieux financial assistance and is clearly so
won over by the Chevalier that he attempts his defense in his
preface to the story. Thus, in contrast to Barnwell, des Grieux is
never punished for his crimes; his privilege always protects him
(Donahoe 138). Instead, it is Manon who pays the debt to society
through imprisonment, public humiliation, deportation to the
colonies, and early death: it is she who loses everything.

Behind the metaphysical tale of an innocent young man
driven to destruction by a venal woman, who is in turn redeemed
by his love, a despotic narrative of male privilege and corruption
insinuates itself—that of a spoiled aristocrat's infatuation with a
common girl, of his indifference to the law, and of her payment
for their transgressions. This other story also suggests that the
source of des Grieux's criminal passion lies not in Manon,
whoever she may be, but in his own dangerous combination of
psychological traits—irresponsibility, egotism, lasciviousness,
dishonesty, and violence—all traits that Prévost's male society
covertly treasures and overtly admires in des Grieux himself.

In fact, the more that we think about the truth behind the
Chevalier's story, the more it becomes apparent that the role of

femme fatale that des Grieux foists upon Manon is in fact the role that he himself plays throughout the novel.[21] This becomes clear when we recognize that the Chevalier's adventures all contain the same component: the winning of favor from and the subsequent display of superiority to *another man*. As we have seen, the Chevalier is able to win (and usually manipulate if not outright betray) the devotion of a bewildering array of would-be masculine antagonists—men who should be and usually start out as des Grieux's opponents. Tiberge (the most positive moral authority of the piece and the representative of perfect Christian piety) seems to possess an admirable moral certitude, but in all his dealings with the Chevalier, he vacillates with surprising frequency between his love for his debauched friend and his sense of duty. This "love" is itself peculiar given Tiberge's strict principles, and it becomes more so when we realize that the Tiberge/Chevalier relationship mirrors the pure/impure dynamics of the one between the Chevalier and Manon; certainly Tiberge's behavioral pattern of alternating condemnation of and assistance to des Grieux repeats the Chevalier's own actions vis-à-vis his mistress.[22] And elsewhere, Prévost makes it clear that his hero is extremely talented at making other men love him—as the affections of such diverse personalities as the Man of Quality, Monsieur de T..., the prison chaplain, and the governor of Louisiana and his son repeatedly testify. The fact that, when they are not actually related to des Grieux, these men appear either as father/son pairs (the G... M...s, the governor and Synnelet) or as either father (B..., the prison father, the Man of Quality) or brother surrogates (Tiberge, Monsieur de T...) adds an ingredient of incest to these already perverse interactions—suggesting that the Chevalier is continually obsessed with besting the other members of his extended masculine "family."

The Chevalier therefore exudes precisely the fatal attraction over men that he claims is Manon's special property. Yet there is a big difference between them. While Manon manipulates only men who mean nothing to her and so remains true to her male family (brother and lover), the Chevalier is far more promiscuous; he uses everyone, including and especially the Man of

Quality, for what is the present narrative if not yet another attempt to seduce a powerful male into loving him?[23]

Seen from this point of view, Manon is not a love object or even an object of desire in a strictly heterosexual sense. Instead, she merely provides an opportunity for the Chevalier to affirm his male sexuality and at the same time, both his attractiveness to and his superiority over other men. Such an agenda is, as Eve Sedgwick has noted, typical of the homosocial man, for whom "desire and the structures for maintaining patriarchal power" are intimately connected (25); thus, the Chevalier uses Manon Lescaut primarily as a ploy to "cement his bonds with other males" (Sedgwick 26) as well as to display his power over them. This interpretation would explain why the Chevalier repeats the same episode over and over (the woman involved is always the same but the man is different), why des Grieux is consistently uninterested in proving his sensibility to his beloved, and why he experiences the ultimate heterosexual ecstasy, not with a living woman, but with a corpse: "I only laid her so after having kissed her a thousand times with all the passion of a perfect love [*du plus parfait amour*]. . . . Then I stretched myself upon the grave, my face turned to the sand" (247). With this chilling report (replete with necrophiliac overtones), des Grieux reveals that his love knows no exigency other than absolute possession and absolute mastery. It is not surprising therefore that the narrative does not revive the physical and rhetorical image of the beloved but rather triumphantly reenacts the process of erasure to which the Chevalier submitted her and that perforce proclaims his masculinity.

Does this narrative seduction succeed? Just as Millwood's rhetoric triumphs over her enemies in *The London Merchant*, so does the Chevalier's extravagant speech likewise reduce his auditor to silence; the narrative halts soon after the death of Manon, without a closing word from the apparently entranced Man of Quality. This lack of ending testifies to the power of the Chevalier's voice and returns us necessarily to the preface, that we now understand, is the real ending, insofar as it represents the Man of Quality's delayed response to the story he has heard.[24]

But insofar as the Man of Quality's preface celebrates the inner nobility of superior (masculine) souls and thereby prevalidates the Chevalier's self-defense, the older man proves no less blind than the younger one. The Man of Quality's complicity with this elitist of the heart thereby reveals his own profound emotional elitism, for the Chevalier's behavior has all too convincingly demonstrated the insidious nature of that spiritual noblesse oblige so touted in the novel's introduction:

> If, for instance, people of a certain order of intelligence and breeding will consider what is the most usual substance of their conversations or even of their solitary reveries, they will readily observe that these turn almost invariably on some consideration of morality. The sweetest moments in life for people of a certain habit of mind are those that they pass either alone, or with a friend, in conversing heart to heart on the charms of virtue, the sweetness of friendship, the means of achieving happiness, the weakness of nature that alienates us from it and the remedies that can heal them. . . . How then does it come that one falls so easily from these high speculations and so soon finds one's self on the level of common men? (lviii)

How, indeed. The Man of Quality's half-spoken suspicion that his moral code does not work is drastically confirmed by the very narrative he offers as a corrective: "Every adventure is a model on which one may form one's self: it has only to be adjusted to the circumstances in which one finds one's self" (lix).

In this manner, the very success of the Chevalier's narrative procedure with his auditor causes the entire narrative fabric to unravel. Just as Prévost uses the frame narrator to justify the protagonist in advance, so must the behavior of the protagonist now retroactively subvert the values put forth by the frame narrator. The preface does not explain the narrative, rather the Chevalier's story reveals that the narrator must have failed to grasp the significance of the story he transmits. Like his noble kinsman, the Man of Quality refuses to contemplate the flaws in his own moral-political system; he cannot understand the story he tells because he cannot "see" the problem, although he senses that it is there. But the novel's didactic circularity—whereby the moral conclusion that was deferred to our direct experience of the story is deferred once again to an ending that does not exist—warns us against that false security that derives from believing that we alone see clearly what others cannot. How much better readers are we than the Man of Quality? What hidden prejudices does our own judgment of the Chevalier contain? With this final ironic flourish, Prévost's novel invites our criticism and then reminds us to consider the flaws in our own moral systems.

Thus, the war of words between criminal and law-abiding, between feminine and masculine, and between evil and good yields surprising results in these two works of 1731. Millwood's sinful rhetorical "extravagance" subverts the integrity of Thoroughgood's mercantile monastery and its language of economy, and in so doing, it compromises the "purity" of the entire community. Seen from this point of view, the apprentices inhabit, not a pure male utopia, but a perverse and sterile dystopia, which not only thrives on exclusion, but which actually aggravates the very desires that it supposedly banishes. Certainly excessive emotions already seethe beneath the surface of Thoroughgood's self-controlled establishment, not only in the presumably debased form of Maria's passion for Barnwell, but also in the considerably more ambiguous passion between Barnwell and Trueman. Significantly, it is this relationship, and this one only, that is allowed to reach emotional heights directly presented on stage. And while the platonic "bedding" of Barnwell by Trueman on the former's prison floor (5.5) replaces the unseen and unseeable union between Barnwell and Millwood, the presence of these passions suggests that the commercial language of the mercantile monastery is by no means language of Christian goodness. Rather, it is the homosocial language of power—the rigid, hypocritical grammar of repression and oppression—that seeks to further the interests of men even as it announces and erases the possibility of men loving men (Sedgwick 3).

The language of homosocial economy is at once more universal and more invisible in *Manon Lescaut*, for it borrows the trappings of feminine extravagance only to more thoroughly assert its power and assure its place; ostensibly, the Chevalier speaks the way he does because he has been infected by his passion for his now-dead mistress. But there is something disingenuous about this rhetorical maneuver that allows des Grieux both to blame Manon Lescaut and at the same time to assume both her voice and her role as irresistible seductive force. Oddly, it is *because* he repeatedly excludes her that Manon escapes des Grieux's narrative grasp; because he will not describe her, she cannot be described, and she therefore evades the categorizations of woman that Millwood must deny and overcome. Thus, female absence rather than female presence undermines these paradoxical verbal proceedings—an imposed, false economy that in turn exposes the machinations of an extravagant speech that is indeed all too niggardly. Manon's shifting silhouette damns the Chevalier precisely because it does constantly shift; whenever he does include her—as he sometimes must—she immediately both pulls the story away from and brings us closer to the narrative's true concern—the Chevalier's power relations with other men.

Thus, rather than pitting the homosocial against the heterosexual, as does Lillo, Prévost points to the essential identity between them (Sedgwick 50), namely, by indicating that intermale transactions form an integral component of heterosexual passion. *Manon Lescaut* repeatedly emphasizes the importance of male bonding in sexual situations: the elder des Grieux smilingly procures his son a female replacement for the absent Manon; Lescaut proposes with jocularity that Manon support both himself and the Chevalier; the latter smugly reports being found in bed with Manon by a troop of archers, and he sympathizes all too ostentatiously with the rejected prince once his own primacy as preferred lover has been established. The novel's depiction of the Chevalier's passion certainly suggests that his love reflects all the flaws and perpetrates all the injustices of his male-dominated milieu, but it also does something else far more subversive. *Manon Lescaut* dismantles the mythology of romantic love—documenting that beneath man's passion for chivalric rhetoric lies his inability to truly love woman at all. Under the current system of exchanges and values, masculine love realizes itself physically only upon a dead woman's body (Sedgwick 76), while on the discursive level, it expresses itself most perfectly toward other men—therefore becoming at once murderous and at least potentially, covertly homosexual. This would explain why the Chevalier's tale has so little to say about Manon herself; the story is not really about her, after all. Through the rhetorical battle of economy and extravagance, both *The London Merchant* and *Manon Lescaut* problematize the source of criminality, although the revelation of criminal origin and the means to circumvent it have occasioned the works and provide the ethical ground upon which we are to base our reading. In both, the authors' apparent preoccupation with original sin gives way to a haunting dramatization of sociopolitical inequity—expressed in both works by the econo-sexual victimization of women. This shift is important in two ways. First, the immolation of these female characters—at the gallows and in the desert sands of Louisiana—displaces the sufferings of their "virtuous" male lovers, making the women rather than the men into tragic subjects. But equally important is the fact that the disruptive presence of these women in otherwise male universes also problematizes the relations depicted between men—calling our attention to the emotional anomalies lurking behind the walls of the mercantile monastery and the aristocratic brotherhood of sensibility. As Lillo's bourgeois drama rejects the values it seems to uphold, so does Prévost's novel of sensibility reveal the fallacy of the cult of sensitivity of which the Chevalier and the Man of Quality are both devotees. But the ramifications of the critique effected by both *The London Merchant* and *Manon Lescaut* are ultimately more radical still. The victimizations of Millwood and Manon point—at this stage of the Enlightenment, obliquely—to the bankruptcy of patriarchy and to the perversity of the emotions that it sanctions between the members of its male community, whose removed benevolence masks an anxious insulation that both desires and fears female penetration.

Hélène Cixous has argued that male writing has been run by a "libidinal, cultural—hence political, typically masculine— economy" ("The Laugh of the Medusa" 249). This masculine "economy" grossly exaggerates all signs of sexual opposition and ensures that woman never has her turn to speak. If this assessment is even partially correct, then *The London Merchant* and *Manon Lescaut* must be seen as particularly important works of the eighteenth century—intriguing exceptions to what Cixous sees as the rule of male writing. In this way, Lillo and Prévost transform the bourgeois tragedy and the novel of sensibility into a radical *mise en question* of the assumed correlation between criminality, evil, and femininity on one hand, and law-abidingness, good, and masculinity on the other. Through the problematic binarism of economy and extravagance, both authors expose and demand that we recognize the precariousness of the very literary-philosophical-political edifice that they seem to build up.

In closing, we should note that these works of the early eighteenth century already tentatively manifest the three features that characterize modern literature according to Gadamer. First, their covert rejection of the equivalence between original sin and crime marks their distance from humanist Christianity, and this distance will widen incrementally as we move from Fielding to Sade. Second, the play's and the novel's dismantling of the very generic frameworks within which they situate themselves implies that artistic form is itself a problem to be overcome, and this problem will become more visible, as the literary works considered here subject their own structures to greater and greater scrutiny. Third, *The London Merchant*'s and *Manon Lescaut*'s radical critiques of the societies that figure in their fictional worlds suggest that the present artistic statements are communities unto themselves that oppose rather than speak for the status quo.

Lillo's and Prévost's rethinking of the relations between masculine/feminine and crime adds yet another powerful dimension to their embryonic modern projects. Further, their reevaluations point in a critical direction, which becomes increasingly important to the works considered in this study, namely, the investigation of sexually nontraditional criminal protagonists—be they unmanly like Jonathan Wild, overtly effeminate as is Franz Moor, sadomasochistic as are Juliette and her mostly male cohorts, or homosexual, as is Caleb Williams. Only Michael Kohlhaas retains vestiges of traditional heterosexual manhood in the form of allegiance to wife and children, but he functions, oddly enough, in a world where sex has little importance. As these readings of *The London Merchant* and *Manon Lescaut* have suggested, we will see that linked to the eighteenth century's literary consideration of crime-form-failure is an increasingly problematized discourse on the nature of masculinity itself and its relation to the unjust society of which it seems to be an integral part but for which it also proposes itself as a potential, subversive cure.

3

Greatness, Criminality, and Masculinity

Subversive Celebration and the Failure of Satire in Fielding's *Jonathan Wild*

As we have seen, an overt didacticism operates—albeit super-ficially—in both *The London Merchant* and *Manon Lescaut*. In comparison with these seemingly conservative dynamics, *Jon-athan Wild* strikes us at first as an even more reactionary step backward in the literary portrayal of the criminal and of the power of criminality.[1] First written in 1741 and considerably revised for its second, definitive publication in 1754, *Jonathan Wild* operates on a transparent satiric premise—that of ironic inversion—and this method is deployed consistently through-out.[2] Henry Fielding's satirist designates his blatantly unrealistic fiction as scrupulous, factual biography (Wright 15–19; William R. Irwin 85) in order to drive home a clear satiric message.[3] The ironic refusal of historical accuracy in the "biography" will reveal a higher truth as to the nature of such criminal types than any "true" account ever could. This fiction will demythify the nefar-ious lawbreaker and will show him up for what he really is—not a hero, but a villain, a figure worthy, not of admiration but of contempt. Consequently, Fielding's satirist attacks not only his obvious scapegoat, Wild, but also all those who mistakenly see any shade of greatness in him; such a critique, therefore, neces-sarily includes the hack writers of criminal biography and all

potential readers of his history. Ultimately, it is the condemnation of Jonathan Wild and with it the revision of our notions of
greatness that constitute the strict moral corrective urged by
Fielding's satire.[4]

Fielding's two hundred-odd pages repeatedly demonstrate
that criminality is not just morally wrong but also practically
speaking, self-defeating. Banished to America for seven years,
Wild returns to England no better off than he was before, and he
thenceforth meets with failure on all fronts; unable to win Miss
Tishy's sexual favors, he is equally incapable of ruining the hated
Heartfree. Like Millwood, he is eventually betrayed by his own
people (the arrested Blueskin stabs him, whereby it is discovered
that Wild has been stealing through other people [168]) and like
her, is summarily hanged. In corroboration with the already
overwhelming experiential evidence against criminal behavior,
Wild's accomplices find themselves at Newgate at the end of the
novel; even his wife is facing criminal charges by the conclusion.
In this manner, Fielding's satirist shifts the grounds for his
condemnation of criminality toward empirical rather than
metaphysical considerations. While Providence is still appealed
to, as it was in both *The London Merchant* and *Manon Lescaut*, the
appeal is considerably qualified by an ethical pragmatism that is
reminiscent of John Locke.[5] Criminality is evil, because real life
(which the "true history," for all its distortions, *does* reflect)
proves that criminality does not and cannot succeed.

As though this demonstration were not clear enough, Fielding's satirist joins to the proof of Jonathan Wild's criminal
failure a most disparaging evaluation of his male sexuality. It is
noteworthy that in contrast to both Barnwell and the Chevalier
des Grieux who are repeatedly shown as active, effective sexual
desirers (who are also sexually attractive to others), Jonathan
Wild's sexuality is consistently and dramatically thwarted in its
expression. He does not seem to be at all attractive to women,
and although his physical desire is insistently heterosexual, it
always proves inadequate to the obstacles blocking it. In Wild's
three ill-fated sexual encounters, the narrator suggests that his
protagonist does not procure satisfaction because he is physically unable to overpower the women in question. Wild's inability

to have his way with the lady of his choice is made abundantly clear in his courtship of Miss Tishy—a would-be rape that is easily averted by the physical force of the latter. The affair with Molly Straddle echoes this implication; Wild must pay for services that Molly (as her last name implies) often gives away. We are told pointedly that he cannot "make" her do otherwise, and moreover he himself is robbed during the process. Even the delicate Mrs. Heartfree is able to summon up the strength to physically resist him, at least until the ship's captain arrives on the scene.

Thus, integrally connected to the satiric demonstration that Wild is not a "great" man is the equally damning implication that he is not exactly a "man" period. Fielding's narrator suggests that Wild is a kind of eunuch—a creature who possesses the desires of a male but lacks the virility to carry out such desires. The sterility of his marriage to Miss Tishy bears out this suggestion, especially in contrast to the Heartfree marriage, which is both passionate and biologically fruitful. Real men, the narrator seems to suggest, are law-abiding citizens, as the fertile, well-loved Heartfree would seem to exemplify.

And yet, for all its clarity, the satiric demonstration in Fielding's novel does not work, for the narrative proves, not Jonathan Wild's failure, but rather the failure of his satiric attacker. Correspondingly, the struggle over the suppression of the criminal's voice—and the subversive point of view that this voice articulates—as enacted in *The London Merchant* and *Manon Lescaut* inaugurates even more dramatic formal problems in this seemingly "simple" satiric work. Through the telling of the tale, the narrator of *Jonathan Wild* discovers what the Chevalier has already suspected and tried to forestall in his own story: by allowing the criminal other to speak, one gives him or her a subversive power that, if unchecked, could wreck the entire narrative enterprise. But rendering Wild a demasculinized object of ridicule proves insufficient to invalidate his articulated point of view. The very fact of him, his very existence in the story seems so disruptive to the present satiric project that Fielding's narrator finds it necessary to displace him altogether from the narrative center. He summons an entirely different protago-

nist—Heartfree—and in so doing, he eventually splits his story
in two, offering two distinct narratives that have less and less to
do with each other. But this strategy fails as well. The satire in
Jonathan Wild ruptures; while the satirist ostensibly directs his
attack against Wild and the criminal glamour he exemplifies,
this narrative retreat from the satiric target reverses the entire
argument—reinforcing rather than demystifying the ineffability of both Jonathan Wild's criminal mystique and his uncertain
masculinity.

Chapter 1, book 1 announces this paradox by displaying a
critical strategy that compromises itself even as it is pronounced.
Having informed us that his present history will be modeled on
those of classical antiquity (and hints at his satiric intent with the
mention of the cynical Suetonious), the satirist informs us that
greatness and goodness are completely incompatible, for he
ironically defines *greatness* as the ability to practice evil (ironically understated as "mischief") on a particularly grand scale:[6]

> But before we enter on this great work we must endeavor to remove
> some errors of opinion which mankind have, by the disingenuity of
> writers, contracted: for these . . . have endeavored as much as possi-
> ble, to confound the ideas of greatness and goodness; whereas no two
> things can possibly be more distinct from each other, for greatness
> consists in bringing all manner of mischief on mankind, and good-
> ness in removing it from them. (40)

In keeping with his announced allegiance to the methods of
Roman historians, the satirist proves this contention by offering
two famous classical models whom he describes with a peculiar
twist:

> In the histories of Alexander and Caesar, we are frequently, and
> indeed impertinently reminded of their benevolence and generosity,
> of their clemency and kindness. When the former had with fire and
> sword overrun a vast empire, had destroyed the lives of an immense
> number of innocent wretches, had scattered ruin and desolation like
> a whirlwind, we are told . . . that he did not cut the throat of an old
> woman and ravish her daughter, but was content with only undoing
> them. And when the mighty Caesar, with wonderful greatness of
> mind, had destroyed the liberties of his country, and with all the

means of fraud and force had placed himself at the head of his equals
. . . we are reminded . . . of the largess to his followers and tools, by
whose means he had accomplished his purpose, and by whose
assistance he was to establish it.

    Now who does not see that such sneaking qualities as these are
rather to be bewailed as imperfections than admired as ornaments in
these great men? (40–41)

These two ancient heroes—usually thought of as the quintessence of intelligent rule, military leadership, and manly courage—thus reveal themselves under the satirist's incisive gaze to
be tyrannical monsters. The "virtues" of Alexander and Caesar
are stripped down to meaningless gestures that have been
highlighted by those incompetent historians foolish enough to
call these villains heroes in the first place.

    With these introductory remarks, the narrator signals how
his satiric message should be decoded, for he gives the key
equivalence here. From now on, the term *greatness* refers not to
any grandeur of spirit or mind but to the very opposite: to
despotism, violence, lust, in short, to all the characteristics that
are normally considered vile in human behavior. Correspondingly, he will designate goodness with such derogatory terms as
meanness, baseness, and so on (Hatfield 107). Thus, precisely
because the protagonist of the narrative is a notorious thief, and
therefore a destructive and marginal member of society, the
satirist will present him as a "Great man," superior in every way
to the average law-abiding citizen: "As our hero had as little as
perhaps is to be found of that meanness [i.e., goodness], indeed
only enough to make him partaker of the imperfection of
humanity, instead of the perfection of diabolism, we have ven-
tured to call him *The Great*" (41).

    But if Wild's hesitations in malfeasance are indeed flaws
that make him contemptible—as the narrator's ironic remark
suggests—then his lack of greatness lies, not in his deficiency of
good qualities, but strangely enough in his inconsistent practice
of evil. The narrator has already paved the way for such an
interpretation earlier in the chapter when he notes that Wild's
character is, like most men's, a mixture of good and bad:
"Though nature had given the greatest and most shining endow-

ments, she had not given them absolutely pure and without alloy" (40). Such a suggestion implies in turn that had Wild possessed such persistence in villainy, he might be able to command the terrible respect that diabolical greatness inspires. Moreover, if it is impossible for human beings to be perfectly evil—as the narrator has just implied with his reference to the general "imperfection of humanity"—then this new standard of greatness appraisal must also apply to Caesar's and Alexander's paltry exercises in virtue; apparently even they are not perfectly evil either (McKeon 384). In this peculiar manner, the narrator's criticism of Wild's imperfection in evil implies that Wild is not great, not because he is not vicious, but because, like these falsely great tyrants of the past, he is an imperfect perpetrator of vice.

In this manner, the narrator's satiric introduction argues that the loathsome Wild has no claim to greatness whatsoever because he imperfectly emulates famous men of the past who are in fact no better than he. He also suggests that our conceptions of greatness are false, for how can there be such a quality, if such ancient heroes as Caesar and Alexander—our standard of measure—do not qualify? This judgment suggests in turn that greatness, as we construe it, is a dangerous myth and that consequently the individual's quest for such an elusive quality must of itself lead to ignominy (Golden 9). Implied in this condemnation is a call to rethink the criteria for masculine heroism, for if these patriarchs of Western culture are villains, then representatives of exemplary virile behavior must be found elsewhere.

Where are these positive masculine models to be located? On one hand, the narrator's ironic introduction suggests that, in reality, no man can be considered great because mankind in general seems to be capable only of relative virtue and viciousness. Yet according to such a theory, Jonathan Wild may not be great, but then neither is any other male, including the ancients to whom he has been compared. In this circuitous fashion, the narrator's remark about male imperfection points away from the thrust of his argument—the baseness of Wild—and toward the uselessness of the term on which he has based his satiric attack upon Wild. Greatness, he suggests, is not a gauge that we can employ to any meaningful purpose when we assess a man, because without valid anterior models, we no longer can say with any certainty what greatness is, and, more importantly, if it is even possible. Moreover, seen under this lens, "masculinity" itself becomes a potential problem, for if it is no longer to be tied to the classical tradition of the warrior-hero, then *what is it?*

To make matters more confusing, the narrator briefly mentions that male greatness—both the evil and good kind—is possible, if rare: "Though we sometimes meet with an Aristides or a Brutus, a Lysander or a Nero, yet far the greater number are of the mixt kind, neither totally good nor bad" (39). This suggestion in turn raises another question. If greatness can be evil—if a Nero can be as impressively wicked as a Brutus is impressively good—then do not Caesar and Alexander have some just claim to this elevated status, precisely because they were ruthless conquerors with surprisingly few virtuous flaws? And if these heroes are great because they were extraordinary malefactors, does not the villainy of Jonathan Wild have some access to this grandeur also, insofar as he seems to hesitate no more than they themselves do, and insofar as he aspires to their level of achievement?

In this way, the apparently unproblematic satiric attack on Jonathan Wild's greatness inaugurates far more serious and complex queries: What is the nature of greatness, good, or evil? Is male greatness possible, and if so must it be absolute? The narrator seems to want it both ways: good greatness is possible but evil greatness is not, and yet the very comparisons he uses to convince us further confuse the issue.

Book 1, chapter 1's ambivalence as to the nature of a masculine quality whose moral content seems ambiguous and whose very attainability is questionable undermines the narrator's critical project from the outset, making a seemingly simple task an arduous one. As was the case in *Manon Lescaut*, whenever the narrator does discuss Jonathan Wild's personality at any length—especially when he pays attention to his thoughts, feelings, and opinions—the passages meant to ridicule him point instead to an interpretation of his character that, not only subverts the satiric analysis proposed by the narrator, but indeed *proposes a "satire" of its own.*

The second chapter of book 1 for example, traces Wild's genealogy and reveals that he is descended from a long line of thieves, traitors, and scoundrels. Wild's family history functions as a bathetic device that demonstrates how indeed ignoble Wild's background may be. However, it also suggests that he cannot be entirely blamed for his character, for it seems that he is, after all, precisely what his own family has made him. This impression is reinforced by chapter 3's account of Wild's childhood instruction, which proves to be one of total noneducation. The young boy is quickly abandoned to his own devices at school by an indifferent master, and therefore he learns virtually nothing. The possibility that Wild possesses some native intelligence and interest in knowledge that might have been better guided is indicated in his extreme albeit warped enthusiasm for the classics, which he excitedly misreads (or does he?) as models—and therefore justifications—for his own emerging delinquency.

This not-so-benign neglect of Wild's formation culminates in his father's decision to have him live in London. The fact that the elder Wild believes that the younger Wild's exposure to the Snap family will further the latter's education suggests, not only that the father is indifferent to his son's development, but that indeed the profession which the younger Wild chooses is not very different from the profession which the elder Wild has envisioned for him. Accordingly, Jonathan's entrance into the world reminds us of the Chevalier's criminal apprenticeship, and it functions in a similar manner; just as des Grieux's association with Lescaut makes him look good in comparison, so is Wild introduced to an assembly of characters so immoral and downright crooked (the unscrupulous Mr. Snap, his promiscuous and greedy daughters, and the Count La Ruse, a professional cheat and embezzler) that it is hard not to see him in a positive light—at least in comparison to his base companions.

Given the kind of formal education and adult company to which he is exposed, we must ask if Jonathan Wild ever had a chance to be anything other than what he is. His prehistory—which the narrator has offered us as evidence of Wild's ignominy—actually serves to mitigate his baseness by suggesting that Wild's professional inclinations have been formed by circumstances beyond his control. In this manner, the narrator's attempt to establish the vileness of Wild's nature by lampooning his family and childhood environment threatens instead to make the thief more, rather than less, sympathetic, insofar as Wild, the victimizer of society himself, appears to be a victim of his own father and the debased social world within which he has been placed.

However, this is not at all Wild's view of the matter; he sees himself, not as victimized, but as privileged, for he regards his profession in a completely positive, even ideal light, as his conversation with the count and his soliloquy concerning Bagshot make plain. Wild's discussion with La Ruse represents our first direct exposure to the former's discourse, and we should note that Wild's opinions contain an unexpected logic that contrasts dramatically with the emotionalism of both Barnwell and des Grieux. Unlike them, Wild makes no claim to an original, now-lost innocence; he does not blame his criminality on an outside (female) force, for he sees his criminal identity as a social advantage rather than a metaphysical curse. Significantly, his mode of speech sounds much more like that of Millwood than like either of his male predecessors, and like her, he appears to view his role in society with a cool, objective detachment. When the count criticizes the young man's contentment with petty thievery and urges him to rise socially by means of his powers, the latter gives an astonishing and eloquent answer:

> I am far from agreeing with you, that great parts are often lost in a low situation; on the contrary, I am convinced it is impossible they should be lost. . . . In civil life, doubtless, the same genius, the same endowments, have often composed the statesman and the prig. . . . The same parts, the same actions, often promote men to the head of superior societies, which raise them to the head of lower; and where is the essential difference if the one ends on Tower Hill and the other at Tyburn? Hath the block any preference to the gallows? . . . A guinea is as valuable in a leathern as in an embroidered purse; and a cod's head is a cod's head still, whether in a pewter or a silver dish. (52)

Again, the satiric irony breaks down. The satirist uses this dialogue to display the perverse immorality (and laziness) that guides the already-evil seventeen-year-old boy. And yet the argument itself exudes sound reasoning. Wild claims that, in a world where most men are thieves, social elevation is inconsequential. Since men from the bottom and from the top of society's hierarchy—prigs and statesmen—hunger for the same material things—food and money—and since both run the same risk of being apprehended and punished for stealing them, perceived differences of social status lie in the most superficial, unimportant distinctions: embroidered purses versus leather ones, silver versus pewter dishes, and death at the block versus the gallows.

Further, when the count bewails Wild's lack of ambition, the latter replies in a similarly philosophical vein:

> If, therefore, you had only contended that every prig might be a statesman if he pleased, I had readily agreed to it; but when you conclude that it is his interest to be so, that ambition would bind him to take that alternative, in a word, that a statesman is greater or happier than a prig, I must deny my assent. . . . The same degree of heat which is common in this constitution may be a fever in that; in the same manner, that which may be riches or honour to me may be poverty or disgrace to another for all these things are to be estimated by relation to the person who possesses them. (54)

Having staked his claim as a man of sense, Wild now displays his sensibility. He explains that the rationale for men's choice of profession lies, not in their differing abilities, but rather in the different cultivations of their taste. Thus, in a world where all social distinctions are indifferent, the appeal of a criminal career over a legitimate, political one is in fact a matter of personal inclination. But Wild goes further; he grounds his taste in a peculiar sort of morality, for he implies that there is something implicitly more honest about stealing than in so-called legitimate business. Professional priggery is consequently more appealing morally than the infinitely more dishonest and ruinous prigdom of the powerful: "How easy is the reflection of having taken a few shillings or pounds from a stranger, without any breach of confidence, or perhaps any great harm to the person who loses it, compared to that of having betrayed a public trust, and ruined the fortunes of thousands, perhaps of a great nation!" (55).

And Wild's profession provides the individual with more satisfaction than does the illusory recognition gained by a leader of men: "What are the flattery, the false compliments of his gang to the statesman, when he himself must condemn his own blunders, and is obliged against his will to give fortune the whole honor of his success? What is the pride resulting from such sham applause, compared to the secret satisfaction which a prig enjoys in his mind in reflecting on a well-contrived and well-executed scheme?" (54). In a speech that would do credit to Calderon's Segismundo, Wild skillfully deploys the *Vanitas* theme to imply that the power of the powerful is itself a sham. Because he deceives himself as to the real nature of his profession, the politician is necessarily deluded by his visions of his own grandeur; he fails to recognize that he is in actuality as much a victim of fortune as everyone else, and because of his apparently legitimate, though reprehensible, actions, he will necessarily be condemned and hated both during and after his tenure of office.

In this manner, the narrator's account of Wild's discussion with La Ruse neatly turns the tables upon his satiric project, for the intended attack on Wild transforms itself into a defense of him. This transformation occurs because the ostensible satiric target himself articulately indicts society in general and the government in particular—suggesting that these institutions, and not he, are the true guilty party.

Wild's implication that his particular brand of thievery conforms to some unwritten but valid law of social behavior crystallizes in his reveries about his accomplice Bagshot. Contemplating what is to become his usual practice of capturing the entire booty, which his underling has stolen for him, Wild justifies himself with the reasoning that he is only improving upon the normal practices of commerce:

> Mankind are first properly to be considered under two grand divisions, those that use their own hands, and those who employ the hands of others. The former are the base and rabble; the latter, the genteel part of creation. The mercantile part of the world, therefore, wisely use the term employing hands, and justly prefer each other as

they employ more or fewer; for thus one merchant says he is greater
than another because he employs more hands. (78)

Since, Wild continues, conquerors and absolute rulers use the
labor of others only to further their own interests, he is taking
actions that are perfectly appropriate, given his desires for
greatness:

> Now suppose a prig had as many tools as any prime minister ever
> had, would he not be as great as any prime minister whatsoever?
> Undoubtedly he would. What then have I to do in the pursuit of
> greatness but to procure a gang, and to make the use of this gang
> centre in myself? . . . and thus (which I take to be the highest
> excellence in a prig) convert those laws which are made for the
> benefit and protection of society to my single use. (80)

Thus, Wild's innermost thoughts reveal that he is ambitious
after all; he dreams of becoming an absolutely great thief, a
criminal Alexander, who rules completely over an army of
robbers whom he may reward or put to death as he pleases. This
is a perfectly logical pursuit, he believes, since this practice has
been traditionally validated by and admired in great leaders of
the past and is encouraged in the present by the regular abuses
of current statesmen. In this way, Wild's vision of himself and his
profession suggests, not that he is a perverse social outcast trying
to attack society's foundations, but that he wishes to excel to the
utmost of his abilities in accordance with the social practices of
the great from the past and present.

Wild's two speeches in book 1 outline a surprisingly effective
defense of priggery on both personal and social grounds. Taking his cue from Millwood, he argues that thievery is practical
and popular—many men of all stations use its principles. Moreover, it provides pleasure and satisfaction to the perpetrator,
first, in the exercise of one's natural talents and predispositions,
and second, in the contentment that one feels when these talents
have been successfully carried out. His particular mode of
robbery is politically efficacious and socially correct in that it
actually improves on the financial principles of mercantilism; it
conforms to the practice of respectable merchants and imitates

the usage of all great leaders who use the labor of others for their own personal profit.

Like that of Millwood, Wild's criminal philosophy claims an exemplary moral honesty as to how the world really works and what society really expects of the individual, although he chooses to subvert rather than rebel against those social principles. Unlike his female counterpart, Wild determines to attain the uppermost reaches of the hierarchy of mercantile exchanges—a reasonable decision on his part, since as a man he has no reason to wish to absent himself from the exchange altogether, despite the fact that he does not seem to profit much sexually speaking. Nonetheless, in contrast to the respectable members of his society who hypocritically deny their priggish intentions, Wild, like Millwood before him, appears to be completely forthright, at least with himself and his associates, as to his true priggish character. Consequently, his affirmation of the superiority of criminality over legitimacy points to his own superior integrity. Unimpressed by the masks with which crime disguises itself as legitimate behavior in order to gain power, undistracted by love, Wild determines to achieve greatness in a purely and truly criminal realm. Seen from this point of view, the great criminal is in fact greater than the great statesman, insofar as his thoughts and actions boast a greater consistency.

The empirical force of Wild's defense is sustained by the fact that, in book 1 at least, the protagonist is surrounded by characters who are indeed thieves of one sort of another—a state of affairs that bears out Wild's picture of an essentially dishonest society that unofficially sanctions thievery: the count and Wild steal from each other; Bagshot steals from the count; Wild steals from Bagshot; even Smirk and Bagshot steal Miss Tishy's favors away from their "rightful owner," Wild. Viewed in this social context, Wild's defense of priggery appears irrefutable—an impression that will render the introduction of Heartfree absolutely essential to rescuing the narrator's faltering satiric critique.

In this manner, book 1's attack on Wild effects a subversive transformation of him from satiric target into satiric spokesman and philosopher of crime. During his speeches, he usurps the narrator's power of invective and himself sheds a damning light

on a hypocritical society that condemns, yet tolerates and practices, thievery. Moreover, among such as his companions, Wild
does indeed lay claim to greatness, for he clearly surpasses the
others in talent and ambition, in the sophistication of his machinations, and in his philosophical commitment to stealing. Book
1 shows that though Wild may have been influenced by his
nefarious family background, he also strives to surpass it. Not
content with his forefathers' tradition of petty larcenies and
betrayals, he aims at a higher goal of complete criminality.

We should note that the ascendance of Wild's criminal point
of view spills over into the transitional book 2. During his
soliloquy in chapter 4, Wild contemplates the vanity of acquisitions and possessions, the vulnerability of the thief to his own
accomplices, and he justifies his choice of life in the following
way: "Why then should any man wish to be a prig, or where is his
greatness? I answer, in his mind: 'tis the inward glory, the secret
consciousness of doing great and wonderful actions. . . . These
must bear him up against the private curse and public impreca-
tion, and while he is hated and detested by all mankind, must
make him inwardly satisfied with himself" (96–97). This speech
is important because it represents a counterargument to the
discussion of greatness inaugurated in book 1, chapter 1. Again,
Wild affirms the deeply personal satisfaction of crime, but he
now pointedly connects this notion with the concept of greatness,
which is likewise measured on a subjective basis. Wild believes that
greatness lies in the individual's personal intimations of that
quality in himself, and he strives to actualize this potential in
whatever field of activity is most congenial to him. Thus, against
the narrator's problematic claim for an objective criterion of
greatness that can be assessed historically—and that may or may
not exist—Wild puts forward a radically subjective yardstick; as
greatness lies in the self, it is the self alone that decides and judges
how far it meets its own standard of excellence.[7]

But if this soliloquy reinforces Wild's defense of priggery by
lending a subversive dignity to his feelings about himself, book 2
as a whole marks a new direction in the narrative. In response to
the surprising intimations in book 1 that there might be some
logical foundation for Wild's criminal actions and that crimes

might possess a certain subjective value for the perpetrator, the narrative now begins to shift away from Jonathan Wild as main character and allows Heartfree, the real hero of the piece, to take his place. The jeweler's tribulations at the hands of Wild and his stoic forbearance throughout are clearly meant to place Wild's restless villainy in grotesque relief; the narrator signals his intention ironically at the beginning of the new book: "It [Heartfree's character] will serve as a kind of foil to the noble and great disposition of our hero, and as the one seems sent into this world as a proper object on which the talents of the other were to be displayed with a proper and just success" (84). Of course, the exact opposite is true; Wild is the foil for Heartfree, whose sterling qualities should shine out all the more brilliantly. The portrait that follows makes this intent even more explicit:

> He was possessed of several great weaknesses of mind, being good-natured, friendly, and generous to great excess. He had, indeed, too little regard for common justice, for he had forgiven some debts to his acquaintance only because they could not pay him. . . . He was withal so silly a fellow that he never took the least advantage of the ignorance of his customers, and contented himself with very moderate gains on his goods; which he was the better enabled to do notwithstanding his generosity, because his life was extremely temperate. (84)

Through his inversive irony, the narrator gives a portrait of the quintessential Christian gentleman. A Barnwell before the Fall, Heartfree is a scrupulously honest businessman for whom great achievements mean nothing and who is happy to operate within the small spheres of his personal business and his domestic life. At the same time, much is made of the fact that Heartfree is a virile, sexually potent man, as his wife's utter devotion to him and their two children suggests.

In support of this new character, the narrator gradually alters his tonal register when he describes Heartfree and his family.[8] This deviation is particularly apparent in his account of the couple's reaction to Mr. Heartfree's arrest:

> Mrs. Heartfree was no sooner informed of what had happened to her husband than she raved like one distracted; but after she had vented

> the first agonies of her passion in tears and lamentations she applied
> herself to all possible means to procure her husband's liberty. . . .
> After many fruitless efforts of this kind she repaired to her husband,
> to comfort him at least with her presence. . . . The moment he saw
> her a sudden joy sparkled in his eyes, which however, had a very short
> duration; for despair soon closed them again; nor could he help
> bursting into some passionate expressions of concern for her and his
> little family, which she, on her part, did her utmost to lessen . . . she
> conjured him, by all the value and esteem he professed for her, not to
> endanger his health, on which alone depended her happiness, by too
> great an indulgence of grief; assuring him that no state of life could
> appear unhappy to her with him, unless his own sorrow or discontent
> made it so. (105)

The narrator's style shifts from the language of satire into the
language of sensibility (Dircks 73). The mock-heroic tone and
the ironic linguistic reversals that have characterized the story of
Wild thus far all but disappear; when they occur, they bracket
the passage in question, which is otherwise devoid of such
details. In what is arguably the sexiest scene in *Jonathan Wild*, the
narrator places the Heartfrees in a des Grieux-esque kind of
transport where suffering and ecstasy merge in an orgasmic
outpouring of feeling. Here the narrator repeatedly emphasizes
the intensity of emotions experienced by the couple: horror, joy,
despair, selfless concern for the other, along with boundless love
that husband and wife feel for their children, and these passions
are further dramatized by such violent, sexually suggestive
verbs as *rave*, *vented*, and *bursting*. It is only at the end of this
passage, that the narrator returns formulaically to his irony—a
strategy which strengthens rather than lessens the pathos of the
foregoing scene: "In this manner did this weak poor-spirited
woman attempt to relieve her husband's pains. . . . Heartfree
returned this goodness (as it is called) of his wife with the
warmest gratitude" (105).

   This portrait of Heartfree echoes the narrator's implication—voiced in his introduction—that greatness does not exist
in human terms and that consequently our conception of the
hero must be revised accordingly. Not Alexander or Caesar, but
rather humble, plain Heartfree embodies an exemplary character which we can in reality strive for he—the good, truly mas-

culine, if naive protagonist—is the new ideal (Wendt 312).

On closer inspection, though, it becomes obvious that the establishment of Heartfree as hero owes itself to a number of narrative machinations that distort the story to an enormous degree. In fact, the dice are so obviously loaded against Wild, narratively speaking, that it becomes virtually impossible to regard the narrator's point of view as a reliable one. While book 1 presents an ambiguous view of Wild, the subsequent books are careful to depict the prig's inexorable decline; from here on, he makes nothing but errors and undergoes only increasing misfortune. In book 2, Wild is outsmarted by the count, robbed by Molly Straddle, and outmanned by the ship's captain when he tries to rape Mrs. Heartfree. In book 3, he betrays his true nature by urging Heartfree to commit murder to escape from prison. Then his planned stagecoach robbery miscarries, his right-hand man Fireblood sleeps with his intended, and members of his gang, led by Blueskin, rebel against their leader, albeit in vain.

But the narrative *coup de grâce* occurs when book 3 reveals that Wild's manner of speech is not truly his own; the narrator informs us that he has been refurbishing his "hero"'s discourse in order to render it more impressive. This narrative reversal specifically demolishes Wild's defense of priggery in book 1 and generally invalidates all that Wild has said and can ever say in the future. But with what result? We now understand only that we cannot ascertain with any certainty *what* Wild's real opinions are, because his own voice has been, and will continue to be, disguised and distorted—the only evidence of his "real" speech being the one orthographically absurd, brief letter to Miss Tishy.

Fielding's satirist uses—much more clumsily—a variation on the same technique of suppression that the Chevalier employed with Manon Lescaut. But as was the case in Prévost's novel, the narrator's retroactive denial of any direct access to his title character tells us little about Wild but instead reveals a great deal about himself. The narrator's tardy censoring of Wild's speech after the fact uncovers his own fear of the danger that Jonathan Wild poses, should he ever be allowed to speak directly to us again (which he never does), and of the danger that even his "refurbished" speech already presents, should it go unnoticed. Beyond that, the satirist's curious insistence on making his own language unambiguous in retrospect points to his suspicion that the fictional speech assigned to Wild for mock-heroic purposes has been accomplishing the opposite of what he intended it to. The announcement itself betrays the fact that Wild's fabricated voice has escaped the narrator's control and is making suggestions about Wild that the narrator does not wish us to consider in our evaluation of him. The satirist's declared suppression of Wild's manner of speaking thus testifies to his increasing anxiety as to the equivocal nature of his message.

The growing intensity of this struggle is reflected in the increasingly blatant acts of narrative omission in book 4. While Jonathan Wild's adventures in America have been eliminated from book 1 on the claim that they were not varied enough, the reader receives an exhaustive account of Mrs. Heartfree's equally repetitive adventures in Africa—a report that requires the length of four chapters. More importantly, although the chapters in book 4 alternate roughly between Heartfree and Wild, the information concerning the latter becomes increasingly fragmented, and his character functions more and more as an interloper in a story that is no longer about him. For example, Wild's discovery of Miss Tishy's infidelity in chapter 10 briefly interrupts but cannot halt Mrs. Heartfree's inexorable account of her admirers and helpers on her journey. Moreover, the account of Wild's final days in Newgate achieves continuity in narration only at the end of the book as an afterthought, now that the misfortunes of the Heartfrees have been reversed. But even these adventures are maddeningly fragmentary, as the partial record of the conversation between Wild and the ordinary makes plain (205–10).

In this manner, the novel increasingly reserves its satiric tone for Wild alone; in the Heartfree sections, the narrative veers away from satire into a combination of sentimentalism and picaresque romp (M. Irwin 48–49), where the good, sensitive, but foolish hero and heroine find their happiness in the end. Correspondingly, Wild ceases to be the center of his own story and becomes marginalized and silenced. At the same time, the fact that Jonathan Wild's adventures are usually replaced, not by those of Heartfree himself (for he is in jail), but by Mrs. Heartfree suggests that he is being silenced in a most unusual way. We have already seen how Wild is demoted to the level of buffoonery, appearing as a frustrated, cuckolded villain who cannot even rape "well." This emphasis on his sexual failures clearly demasculinizes him. But the degree to which he is made a visual rather than audible presence in books 2 through 5 also indirectly *feminizes* him. This process of feminization—which would explain the similarities between Wild and both Manon Lescaut and Millwood (rather than with Barnwell and des Grieux)—occurs through two related narrative strategies. First, Wild's feminization is covertly indicated structurally by the very juxtaposition of his defeat with Mrs. Heartfree's series of triumphs. As the novel progresses, it is not Heartfree but rather Heartfree's wife against whom we are to measure the success of Fielding's criminal; this implicit connection is strengthened by Mrs. Heartfree's demonstration, during her adventures, of many of Wild's most cherished qualities—among them self-interest, self-reliance, and adaptive mastery (McKeon 390–91). Secondly, as we will see in a moment, Jonathan Wild resorts to a peculiarly "feminine" mode of self-expression—namely, the grotesque rebellious "dance." This silent art has particular gender ramifications. Rituals of tortured dancing exemplify, according to Catherine Clément (Cixous and Clément 13) and Sandra Gilbert and Susan Gubar (43), the patriarchal pattern whereby visual expression takes the place of verbal as a means to allow the "feminine" to vent its frustrations and to restrict this overflow within a safe, social context. Indeed, Jonathan Wild's death scene is a kind of ironic tarantella, although it proves to be anything but "safe."

Although the narrator scrupulously avoids giving us any direct information about Wild's reaction to dying, the snippets of dialogue that are given reveal a man determined to play out his role in life to the best of his abilities, while clearly articulating the image of the danse macabre: "Instead of shewing any marks of dejection or contrition, he rather infused more confidence and assurance into his looks. . . . Being asked whether he was afraid to die, he answered: "D——n me, it is only a dance without music" (211). Having failed in a suicide attempt, Wild goes to the gallows undaunted, with a glass of wine in his hand and a thievish prank in his heart:

> Then shaking hands with his friends (to wit, those who were conducting him to the tree), and drinking their healths in a bumper of brandy, he ascended the cart. . . . in the midst of a shower of stones, etc. which played upon him, [he] applied his hands to the parson's pocket, and emptied it of his bottle-screw, which he carried out of the world in his hand. . . . Wild had just the opportunity to cast his eyes around the crowd, and to give them a hearty curse, when immediately the horses moved on, and with universal applause our hero swung out of this world. (213–14)

We should note that, while we do not hear anything that Wild says before he dies, this narrative reportage only seemingly removes us from the immediacy of the action; by distancing us verbally from Wild, the satirist perforce places us in a visually privileged position. The result of this strategy is that we are able to observe Wild's interaction with the public all the more closely, as though we were watching a series of close-ups in a silent documentary; these mute images prove powerful indeed.[9] Wild nonchalantly confronts the hostile crowd with a series of gestures, each of which articulates a key aspect of the thief's self-understanding and his vision of his relationship to his society. With his simultaneously convivial and ironic toast to his executioners, Jonathan Wild silently proclaims his gentility and his superiority to the law enforcers who have condemned him. He then demonstrates his priggish talents for the last time. This action provides visual testimony of Wild's earlier words—namely, his affirmation that thievery provides personal satisfaction. Such a claim is manifest here; the pleasure of Wild's final theft clearly transcends the practical, for he can gain nothing from this gratuitous robbery of a ridiculous object. Under these dire circumstances, Wild's last criminal statement is very literally the quintessence of gallows humor. His act takes on the quality of a supreme joke, a final dig at the authorities (religious as well as social) that condemn him. Lastly, Wild's inaudible curse on the crowd who stones him (again, a feminine role, insofar as this situation ironically recasts the plight of Mary Magdalene) dramatizes his conviction that those who condemn him are indeed no better than he, and he repudiates them, as much as they reject him.[10]

Wild's theatrical refusal to die a repentant criminal signals his conviction that there is nothing that the criminal should be sorry for, and with this refusal, Wild again—briefly—supersedes the narrator as social critic. His "dance without music" unfolds as a silent, satiric performance, a pantomimed critique of those who survive him, and who mistakenly believe that they are any different from him. But even more important is the fact that this refusal either to repent or to be an object of others' derision allows Wild to transform his execution—a scene, among other things, of public humiliation—into an ironic celebration of his own criminal savoir-faire. By the subversive alchemy of irony, Fielding's villain transforms sociopolitical defeat into personal triumph.

In this way, Wild's final claim to greatness echoes and improves upon Millwood's claim to nobility.[11] For both, the moment of defeat becomes the most perfect moment of victory. But while Lillo's criminal villainess, Millwood, declaims extravagant rhetoric at her unmasking only to falter at the gallows, Fielding's feminized villain uses extravagant gesture, and he uses it, not at his arrest, but at the very moment of his execution—demonstrating a firmness of purpose not seen before.

Wild's final performance reveals without a shadow of a doubt that he possesses an unimpeachable commitment to his philosophy of crime, and Fielding's satirist unwillingly recognizes this. In corroboration with Wild's refusal to die a "mere" thief, in the final lines of the novel, the narrator grudgingly concedes that Wild is indeed exemplary in his practice of villainy: "Not one in a thousand is capable of being a complete rogue; and few indeed there are who, if they were inspired with the vanity of imitating our hero, would not after much fruitless pains be obliged to own themselves inferior to Mr. JONATHAN WILD THE GREAT" (220). Although he continues to deny Wild the possibility of being perfectly evil, the narrator admits that Wild has gone as far as any man can go in the direction of complete malfeasance, and his criticism of those who would imitate the prig also signals his awareness that Wild's example is—unavoidably—inspiring to others.

The absolute insufficiency of Wild's defeat in Fielding's novel reflects back in turn on the triumph of Heartfree, which we now realize is equally inadequate. Although the new hero profits at the end of the novel, in the social landscape presented, he certainly represents the exception rather than the rule of human behavior (M. Irwin 47), especially when one considers how his clients, neighbors, and friends (with the exception of Friendly) react to his imprisonment. Further, although Providence (in the form of the good magistrate) does reward Heartfree, it seems equally likely that Fielding's hero will be tried again by the brutal world in which these characters operate. And if this is so, then it is clearly not easier, as the narrator argues, to be an honest man rather than a rogue.

For these reasons, the narrator's intended lampoon of Jonathan Wild falls far short of the mark, and the incomplete picture of the criminal that his twisted narrative outlines points instead to the dubious nature of his own talents and of the classical genre in which he works. Point by point, Fielding demonstrates the degree to which his own satiric spokesman is incapable of hitting the target that his irony aims at, and at the same time, he hints at the impossibility of satirizing a creature whose very lowness proves his highness, and whose sexual incapacity oddly reinforces his criminal potency. Ironically, it is within the virile confines of that quintessentially male genre, satire, that demasculinized, feminized Jonathan Wild finds the perfect, grotesque, skewed place to present and defend his values. Proclaiming that his deviance from the norm is in fact not deviance at all, he cannot be brought down by the norms of satire (Frye 223), for those norms now mean nothing; in its confrontation with a half-man, manly satire cancels itself out and becomes the sexually ambiguous locus for a subversive celebration of all that traditional satire abhors: greed, hypocrisy, confusion.

Yet if the narrator's satiric attack on Jonathan Wild unravels even as it unfolds, the satire itself makes suggestions about the criminal that far outstrip the limited view the narrator has insisted on showing. We have seen that Wild is not "simply" evil; he is not after all a foolish and base personality who can be easily categorized, condemned, and dismissed. Instead Fielding displays an individual who interacts with his society in a complex manner; Wild is at once social victimizer, victim, and paragon of hidden and unspoken social values—both a product of, and a rebel against his milieu. Moreover, he represents a point of view that cannot erased. If the narrator incrementally demasculinizes, marginalizes, and feminizes Jonathan Wild by making of him a silent object of scrutiny rather than a speaking subject, the satire itself suggests the futility of such gestures, for the exemplary criminal possesses his own subversive power, which resists suppression and elimination and which doggedly insists on expression and recognition of itself on its own terms.

Seen from this point of view, Jonathan Wild's character presents a far more complex problem for the reader than does the thief/highwayman of the standard criminal biography of which Fielding's novel is at once a parody and an elegiac revision. While the thief of eighteenth-century popular culture is only a "convenient enemy" whose critique of society is in no way threatening (Faller 188), Fielding's satiric recasting of just such a biographical figure suggests the exact opposite. Jonathan Wild cannot be silenced and therefore can never be killed definitively; he will always find another way to "speak" and thus he lives on in the very work that wants to execute him. As we have seen, the narrator's attempt to ridicule Wild and (thus make him forgettable) instead, ironically, memorializes him and guarantees his immortality. By marginalizing his antihero, the narrator does not demystify the criminal, but rather renders him all the more mysterious. Moreover, because we cannot know in the end for certain who Jonathan Wild really is, we cannot judge him, and therefore the question of his greatness must remain open. Like Manon, he eludes our interpretative grasp, and his enigmatic character gives him power.

Correspondingly, the openness of Fielding's novel shows how far literary representation of the criminal has come since *The London Merchant* and *Manon Lescaut*. Lillo's and Prévost's clearly demarcated zones of gender, moral, and political opposition are at the end of both works superficially reconciled with a master morality—be it Thoroughgood's or the Man of Quality's. While it is clearly artificial (and therefore deeply problematic, as discussed in chap. 1), this formulaic reconciliation provides the *The London Merchant* and *Manon Lescaut* with the outward trappings of traditional closure mandated by their generic structures. On the surface at least, the dual punishment of both the virtuous man and the vile woman (the executions of Barnwell and Millwood on one hand, and the death of Manon and the reformation of the Chevalier on the other) makes the play and the novel "look like" the genres that they are in fact defamiliarizing; cosmetically speaking, they still resemble a bourgeois tragedy and a novel of sensibility, even though their very unfolding surreptitiously devours their own generic innards.

Yet the formal "failure" that occurs in Fielding's satire is much more dramatic. The narrative center upon which Fielding's satirist focuses cannot hold, and he gradually abandons his central character because he proves too dangerous. Through this regression, Fielding's satire dramatizes both the subversive critical possibilities of the criminal's story as well as the problem of containing it within the boundaries of literary form. The novel's double narrative articulates both an anxiety about the criminal's disruptive power and a sneaking delight in his stubborn refusal of what we call "goodness" even as it explodes traditional invective into an interplay of critical perspectives inimical to its own enterprise.

Far from being a conservative defense of moral values, *Jonathan Wild*, like *The London Merchant* and *Manon Lescaut*, proves to be a sophisticated attack launched at society. But Fielding's refusal to "speak for the community" (Gadamer, *Relevance* 39) in his satiric novel is far more radical than that of Lillo and Prévost. While they are content to critique the hypocrisy of Anglo-European masculinist society, Fielding calls into question a cluster of ideas crucial to that society's very being: heroism, greatness, and masculinity itself. While they reveal the homosocial power struggle that conceals itself behind the metaphysical ploy of making woman the origin of crime, he takes that critique one crucial step further. Fielding's novel observes that it is not woman's but man's shifty identity and his contradictory constructions of himself that lie at the root of both the fascination with the criminal and his curious status as both social insider and outcast. Because he is and is not a hero, a lawbreaker, and a man, because he hovers at once within and without the accepted social order, Jonathan Wild becomes, to paraphrase Emily Brontë, "more ourselves than we are."

In this sense, the narrator's fictionalized biography does indeed point to a higher truth, although it is a truth that he cannot personally apprehend. For all its apparent self-conscious didacticism, *Jonathan Wild* expands the satiric critique of criminal "greatness" into a simultaneous revelation and questioning of our historical and therefore traditional attraction to (and unwilling validation of) masculine behaviors that overstep the norms of civilized behavior and that have, it seems, little to do with virile heterosexuality. It is Wild's criminality—his violations of the law and his insistence on the sociopolitical validity of "evil"—which impresses us (William R. Irwin 77), and it is in his weirdly courageous adherence to his principles that his claim to greatness lies. Seen from this perspective, Jonathan Wild is perhaps the "real" man here, after all. His problematic claim to greatness and to maleness—at once so vigorously denied and so vigorously proclaimed in a satire that self-destructs as it constructs its argument—is not resolved in Fielding's novel. It lingers on, an exhilarating, frightening alternative that rocks our understanding of heroism and which points to the construction of a society founded on an altogether different political ethos and on a very different notion of manhood. With his unrepentant, philosophically confident, and only nominally heterosexual antihero, Fielding outlines new representational possibilities for the criminal in Western literature—possibilities that Friedrich Schiller and the Marquis de Sade will explore thirty years later in greater, and more disturbing, detail.

4

Criminal Kin

Gendered Tragedy, Subversion of Inversion, and the Fear of the Feminine in Schiller's *Robbers* and Sade's *Justine*

Jonathan Wild's conviction that the prig and the statesman resemble each other is grounded in his refusal to distinguish between the criminal and the law-abiding; this refusal of difference becomes the focus of attention for Friedrich Schiller's prerevolutionary *The Robbers* (*Die Räuber*, 1782) and Alphonse de Sade's postrevolutionary *Justine* (1791).[1] Despite their obvious tonal differences and the nine tumultuous political years separating them, both the play and the novel undertake similarly complex critiques of the dichotomy criminality/compliance by means of a pair of false doubles—in both cases represented by same-sex adversarial siblings. As we have seen, a law-abiding double is used frequently in conjunction with the criminal protagonist in eighteenth-century literature. Barnwell/Trueman, Millwood/Thoroughgood, des Grieux/Tiberge, Jonathan Wild/Heartfree are all variations on the criminal-compliant dichotomy examined here, but the doubles in *The Robbers* and *Justine* strike us immediately as being very different from their predecessors. This difference derives from the fact that Schiller and Sade reverse the traditional linkage of good-compliant and evil-criminal from the outset, while the oppositional couples

80

from earlier in the century are only gradually problematized as the works in question unfold.[2] This overt subversiveness marks a new moment in eighteenth-century literature's evolution, and it is useful to refer once again to Gadamer's definition of modernity (see chap. 1). In both *The Robbers* and *Justine*, we can easily perceive the three elements to which Gadamer refers, even before undertaking any in-depth analysis: the radical degree to which Christianity becomes an object of derision here (separation from Christian humanism), the new literary forms that Schiller and Sade deploy (formal problematization), and the self-consciousness of their appeals to their readers (the author who is a community unto himself over and against his audience).

Let us now consider these points of modernity in greater detail. Schiller's and Sade's separation from Christian humanism is manifest in their outright foregrounding of the criminal protagonist's heroism—an effect achieved by the inversion of the roles which we might expect the criminal and law-abiding characters to play. In both the drama and the novel, the "good" sibling (Karl, Justine) is unfairly recognized by society as a dangerous outlaw, while the "evil" sibling (Franz, Juliette) prospers through the same injustice; in both cases, the latter is, not only an accepted member of society, but actually gains thereby through surreptitious criminal activity. Through this inversive maneuver, Schiller and Sade accomplish two important goals early on: first, they establish that the practices of Christian morality and effective personal action are totally inimical to each other within their fictional societies; second and more importantly, their repeated insistence on the practical efficacy of criminal versus compliant deeds reverses the connection between metaphysics and politics made explicitly by Lillo and implied by Prévost and Fielding. While politics must be made subservient to and indeed derives from metaphysics in *The London Merchant, Manon Lescaut* and even (although somewhat tenuously) in *Jonathan Wild*, in the worlds of *The Robbers* and *Justine*, it is metaphysics that must not only cede to politics, but must also admit its essentially political grounding.

Likewise, Schiller and Sade encase their inversive aesthetic explorations in equally new, subversive, "revolutionary" forms. The Sturm und Drang drama radically develops the bourgeois tragedy (Geyer-Ryan 218) away from threatened domestic bliss (Jonnes 143–44) and toward the expression of violent emotionalism, while the libertine novel represents an outrageous amalgam of the bildungsroman and the novel of sensibility (Reichler, "On the Notion of Intertextuality" 207) in which sensibility is transformed into sexuality and moral education reformulates itself as an exposé of increasingly refined, unauthorized sexual practices.[3]

Moreover, rather than insisting on the self-evidently didactic character of their artistic enterprises, both Schiller's and Sade's prefatory remarks pointedly refuse to present themselves as authoritative guides (Prévost, Fielding) that will shape the interpretation of an already sympathetic reader. Instead the *Vorrede* and the "Lettre à Constance" *problematize communication* with their audiences by two related strategies. First, they issue a paradoxical challenge to a potentially hostile reader, charging him or her to undertake a moral reading of what seems to be an immoral, dangerous text. Secondly, they explicitly appeal to a gendered audience (masculine in Schiller, feminine in Sade), and at the same time, they signal that reading according to the gender ideals that they outline may prove impossible. In this manner, Schiller and Sade overtly connect the understanding of criminality with the issue of gender identity—which is signaled at the offset to pose a serious problem.

Rather surprisingly, Schiller's *Vorrede* proposes that his drama not be put on stage at all, lest it be misunderstood by the crowd; instead, the author covertly appeals to a virtuous male reader much like himself who will come to the play with an open mind and who sincerely desires to fully understand it as well as the honorable intentions of its author (xii). But this appreciation will be no mean feat because, Schiller warns, the present work will stress not the beauty and power of virtue but the overpowering strength of vice:

> Whoever proposes to discourage [*rächen*] vice and to vindicate religion, morality and social order against their enemies, must unveil

crime in all its deformity and place it before the eyes of men in its colossal magnitude; he must diligently explore its dark mazes [*nächt-lichen Labyrinthe durchwandern*], and make himself familiar [*sich hineinzuzwingen wissen*] with sentiments at the wickedness of which his soul revolts. (viii)

Two significant gender images are introduced here: on one hand, a statue of "colossal magnitude," which coyly suggests that the undisclosed but terrifying shape of crime may be phallic, and on the other hand, the feminine womblike labyrinth, which is already impregnated with (and already partially masculinized by) a symbolic Minotaur—here incarnated by "wicked senti-ments." Thus, Schiller likens his play's confrontation with evil to both a David and Goliath battle and Theseus' pursuit of Minos' monster stepson in one of Western myth's most frightening spaces. We should retain this peculiar image of seeking a mon-strous masculinity inside of femininity, and note further that it connotes both overt and covert dangers—a life-and-death strug-gle with one who is both more and less than a man *and* losing one's way on the treacherous testing ground. In this manner, Schiller implies that both writing and reading *The Robbers* (for the above description applies equally well to both author and reader) is a test meant only for the most stouthearted male who must prove himself as exemplary as a classical hero; only he can disarm the dangers of this work and master its moral meaning.

Sade appeals in even more radical terms to his destined female reader—his friend Constance who is not only a model of virtue, but also of good judgment, and enlightenment:

But throughout to present Vice triumphant and Virtue a victim of its sacrifices, to exhibit a wretched creature wandering from one misery to the next; the toy of villainy; the target of every debauch; exposed to the most barbarous, the most monstrous caprices; driven witless by the most brazen, the most specious sophistries; prey to the most cunning seductions, the most irresistible subornations . . . to employ the boldest scenes, the most extraordinary situations, the most dreadful maxims, the most energetic brush strokes, with the sole object of obtaining from all this one of the sublimest parables ever penned for human edification. (455–56)

Like Schiller, Sade seems to rely on an exemplary reader to do precisely what most others cannot. Constance must also resist and master the meaning of a narrative whose graphic depiction of evil is so irresistible that any other reader would easily succumb to it. Yet there is a suspicious shiftiness in the language of this argument. Sade's letter not only predicts, but actually seems to seductively look forward to the multiple sexual degradations performed on yet another moral woman in the novel to come. This eager anticipation—signaled stylistically by the overwhelming rush of superlative constructions, which all derive from *le Vice triomphant* and *la Vertu victime*—raises several questions. Why has Sade selected a woman to assess the merits of a narrative that completely opposes the logic informing that selection and what can his book have to say to Constance (and by extension, to us, since we should read as she does)? Is Sade in fact submitting his book to the authority of a superior female judge, or is the letter itself an exercise in libertine seduction that will probe the limits of her (our) virtuosity by continually outraging it?[4] Thus, we cannot help but wonder if reading Sade's proposed narrative will "do" to Constance and to us what his characters will do to Justine. Dare we continue?

In this manner, both Schiller and Sade present *The Robbers* and *Justine*, as litmus tests of our own moral, intellectual, and sexual capabilities. This is clearly a perilous appeal, for the way in which Schiller and Sade frame the interpretive challenge of their work suggests two dangers: first, that the failure to discover the moral of the tale reveals one's own moral, intellectual, and generic failings, and second, that failure to meet the standard is very likely, if not almost certain. Thus, even as their potential readers are constituted as gendered, interpreting subjects, Schiller's and Sade's prefaces set them up to fail as those subjects, and in this manner, the authors self-consciously expand the problem of formal failure (explored in Lillo, Prévost, and Fielding) *to include the reader*, and by implication, the very process of textual interpretation itself. There is in the prefaces of Schiller and Sade a sinister warning of an imminent hermeneutic breakdown that will not leave us unscathed. And as we shall see, *The Robbers* and *Justine* break themselves down and threaten to disassemble the reader as well in a particularly troubling way. The masculine universe of *The Robbers* contains fewer women than any other work discussed in this study,[5] and its story unfolds as a homosocial nightmare, where manliness must for the most part define itself without the benefit of its necessary biological counterpoint—with tragic results. And yet according to Karl Moor, Schiller's Rousseauian robber captain, it is precisely femininity that is to blame for the current sorry state of societal affairs in Germany. Even before his conversion to a life of crime in the forests of Bohemia, the elder Moor brother scornfully refers to his emasculated era as a *Kastratenjahrhundert*, which needs a powerful injection of masculinity in order to restore it: "I am supposed to lace my body in a corset and straitjacket my will with laws. . . . The law has never yet made a great man, but freedom will breed a giant, a colossus. . . . Give me an army of fellows like me to command, and I'll turn Germany into a republic that will make Rome and Sparta look like nunneries" (pp. 36–37; act 1. sc. 2). Karl explicitly connects lawbreaking with a salutary masculine virtuosity (positively reiterating Schiller's opening image of the Colossus), even as he compares the effect of law to a feminizing corsetry. Like Prometheus, the mythic father/criminal/hero, the great man oversteps the law to do higher good and to establish a new and better society. Lawbreaking, according to this view, fulfills a revolutionary and restorative function—it undermines the letter of the law in order to more fully express the spirit of the law, namely the enforcement of justice and the protection of freedom.[6]

This sense that the criminal is indeed a masculine social paragon is further reinforced by the manner in which the robber band is formed: "Swear loyalty and obedience till death! Swear by this man's right hand of mine! . . . I swear to you to remain your captain in loyalty and constancy till death" (49–50; 1.2). Through this ecstatic ritual of male bonding, Karl's founding of the robber band recalls, not the crass formation of a conspiracy of thieves, but rather the establishment of a regiment complete with oath of allegiance to its commander.[7] This is indeed an alternative society—a military oligarchy devoted to a charismatic leader, which enables the men to do great things.

Just as the Spartans were able to hold Thermopylae against
insuperable odds, so does Moor's detachment win the day
against society's troops in act 2. The men's loyalty to each other
and to their captain emphasizes the strength of the pledge as
well as the power of Karl Moor's personality.
In this manner, Schiller's Sturm und Drang drama reverses
the geographical demarcations of gendered good and evil in the
The London Merchant. Karl Moor's robber band seemingly provides an equally idealized, though now criminalized, variation
on Thoroughgood's mercantile monastery, precisely because it
lies outside of compliant society. Here too, as in Lillo's countinghouse, plain-speaking, celibate men love each other and labor to
create a better world. And like Prévost's des Grieux, Karl is a
genius at homosocial negotiation. In fact, he improves on the
record of *Manon Lescaut*'s hero by almost immediately assuming
his position at the very summit of the male hierarchy—all
without an actual woman in tow—although this very genius will
prove his undoing.

There is, of course, a woman in Karl's life, but she exists in a
more obviously marginal relation to him than do either Millwood or Manon with their men. Like Lillo's Maria, Amalia is a
paragon of virtue ensconced as the one woman in an otherwise
all-male household. As such, she, like her British predecessor,
simultaneously shores up the probity of the drama's hero and
sexually sanitizes the male community in the play. Her unshak-
able belief in Karl's inner nobility (reminiscent of des Grieux's)
imbues him with an heroic aura, while her physical desire for
him—so strong that she feels its power even when she does not
recognize her fiancé (act 4)—authenticates (and authorizes) his
irresistible manliness. Thus, despite the fact that she spends
little of the play's duration actually with him, Karl's fiancée
fulfills a key function in *The Robbers*; her devoted, admiring,
descriptions of him repeatedly confirm his exceptional masculinity: "Why then, the world is turned upside-down, beggars
are kings and kings are beggars . . . the look with which he begs
for alms must be a noble and kingly look—a look to wither the
pomp and splendor, the triumphs of the great and rich!" (55;
1.3). In an inverted moral universe, Karl becomes a heroic

beggar king in Amalia's eyes. In a later speech, Karl is a Christ-like angel who will wash away the tears of his guilt-ridden father (69), and in this same scene, Amalia compares Karl indirectly with Hector, whose farewell to Andromache she is so fond of singing and actually performs twice in the play.

Hector is clearly an important metaphoric choice, for Homer's character is at once a warrior, an heir apparent to the realm, and a husband whose devotion to his wife and family dramatically contrasts the sexually ambiguous, quasi-pederas-tic, and bloodthirsty ambitions of his archenemy, Achilles. And accordingly, when measured against this ideal of virile hetero-sexuality, Franz Moor looks weirdly effete—an effect reinforced most strongly by Amalia, who is, not surprisingly, the most articulate defender of the difference between the two brothers. Significantly, Amalia's evaluation of Franz resembles that of Fielding's narrator vis-à-vis Jonathan Wild, for she too implies that the younger Moor brother may not be a "man" at all. Appropriately, she alone of everyone in the play recognizes Franz's true, hidden emotions toward Karl; because she is a woman, she is best suited to understand his real "feminine" identity, as her first scene in the play with him already signals: "Oh I beg you—do you pity your brother? No, inhuman creature [*Unmensch*], you hate him!" (51; 1.3). Amalia's epithet for Franz is apt; *Unmensch* literally designates an "un-man" in addition to the word's figurative denotation, "monster."

Her later reactions to Franz are even more telling. Amalia despises Karl's younger brother so thoroughly, as she herself tells him ("*Ich verachte dich!*") that although she is briefly taken in by the story that Karl died in battle, she never fears the threats of the new master, including and especially the sexual ones. The inadequacy of Franz's sexual energy is eventually demonstrated in the same way as that of Fielding's satiric protagonist—namely, through an unsuccessful rape. But here the critique goes even further. Franz's sexual menaces are met with a series of increas-ingly aggressive moves on the part of Amalia: she strikes him in the face, adroitly takes his dagger (the same kind of phallic instrument that Karl will use to kill her), and then uses his weapon to chase *him* offstage (95–96). Interestingly Franz never again attempts to overpower her; this scene marks the end of their sexual interaction. Unlike Wild, who, despite repeated failure, remains an avid pursuer in the heterosexual hunt, Franz is permanently unmanned by the object of his desire, forcing us to wonder if Amalia is indeed what he desires after all. In further support of this view, Schiller contrasts Karl's charismatic leadership (Leidner 65–66) and ease in male bonding with Franz's extreme isolation and alienation from the other men of the play. The fact that he is neither feared nor respected by any of them, from his father on down to the crotchety manservant Daniel, suggests that no man should ever take him very seriously.

Thus, in an even more radical rewriting of the odd gender dynamics that occur between Jonathan Wild and Mrs. Heartfree, Schiller suggests that the only woman in his play proves more of a "man" than his villain does. In this way, while Schiller employs Lillo's dichotomy of masculine good/feminine evil, he dramatically alters the nature of their spatial and generic separation. Just as Lillo's mercantile monastery moves outside society in Schiller's *Robbers*, so does feminine evil now lurk within society rather than without and even more importantly, no longer resides within a biologically female body. Instead, feminine evil hides *within masculinity itself* rather than in its ostensible sexual other. This is a crucial change, to which we will return at the end of this chapter.

Admittedly, this view of Franz as feminine agent of evil seemingly contrasts with his rhetoric, which is vociferously violent and which presents, early on, an unmistakably phallic vision of total tyranny: "Now you shall see Franz naked as he is, and cringe in terror! . . . My brows shall beetle over you like stormclouds, my imperious name hover like a threatening comet over these mountain-tops, and my forehead shall be your barometer! . . . I will set my pointed spurs into your flesh, and see what a keen whip will do" (71; 2.2). Interestingly, Franz's fantasy also invokes the preface's image of the (here emphatically naked) Colossus, and he envisions himself as a quasi-deified master, who will repeatedly penetrate the flesh of his subjects with sharp objects.

But it is precisely because his references to the violent domination of others contrast so dramatically with his actual achievements (we need only remember the discrepancy between Millwood's powerful rhetoric and her real powerlessness) that Franz looks and is treated so much like a woman. Certainly, as a villain, he has more in common with Medea and Phaedra than with *King Lear*'s Edmund, to whom he has been often compared (Kraft 501). These languishing, overly emotional, disenfranchised malefactresses of classical and neoclassical drama resemble Franz far more than does the promiscuous, aggressive, and highly attractive bastard son of Shakespeare's play.

Through these generic juxtapositions, the play suggests that Karl's transgressions are both implicitly more noble and more masculine than those of his brother and that whatever misdeeds he is guilty of must be excused within the context of Franz's own criminal project. After all, were it not for Franz's forged letter and Karl's subsequent belief that he had been disowned, he would never have joined the robber band in the first place, as he himself exclaims: "*A villain's trickery [spitzbübische Künste]*! ... I could have been happy—oh villainy, villainy [*Büberei*]! my life's happiness vilely, vilely betrayed" (120; 4.3). Even as he recognizes the efficacy of Franz's machinations, Karl denies their power by comparing them to boyish pranks, which stand in sharp contrast to his manly, if misguided, crimes.

The drama's resolution seemingly corroborates such an interpretation of the two brothers. Fittingly, Karl again asserts his allegiance to the politico-ethical values that he has only seemingly violated; in a grand gesture, he gives himself up to the authorities—himself exacting society's punishment of him. In contrast to this display of *virtu*, Franz dies hysterically at his own hand, cornered by the robber captain's men; once again, the death scene reminds us more of mad Dido's suicide than that of reasoned Socrates. In this way, *The Robbers'* conclusion supports the suggestion that the robber Moor is both the real innocent and the real man, while Franz, the ostensible law-abiding citizen, is the real criminal and the false man; as such, he represents the hidden, corrosive, effeminate evil within a society that should be and must be an exclusively masculine place.

However, as the play proceeds, the inversive validation of real manhood through lawbreaking in *The Robbers* subverts itself and collapses. Two strategies undermine it. First, Schiller makes it clear that the two brothers are not in fact as different as they (and others) say they are (Donnes 148). Second, any judgment of Karl and Franz is problematized by the fact that their false opposition plays itself out ad infinitum between each one of them and the other male characters in the play—situating the reader/audience in a dizzying hall of Franz/Karl mirror images.

We should remember that while Karl and Franz certainly speak very differently—the one swearing and repeatedly emphasizing the importance of manly behavior, the other resorting to complex imagery and French cognates—they both agree on the dismal nature of German society.[8] Within this context, Franz's criminal activity also acquires revolutionary overtones, insofar as his plans represent an explicit (personal rather than collective) rebellion against the injustices of his father: "I should like to know *why* he made me? Not out of love for me, surely, since there was no *me* to love? Did he know me before he made me? Or did he think of me while he was making me? Or did he wish for me as he was making me? . . . Can I acknowledge any love that does not rest on respect for my person?" (34). In this critique of what Adrienne Rich calls "the kingdom of the fathers," Franz exposes the emotional emptiness of father-love under patriarchy—a critique that extends his earlier remark that "not flesh and blood, the heart makes father and son" (30). Masculine relationships based, not on regard for a particular individual, but on mere blood ties cannot be recognized as love. Such ties are the result of the father's own *mise en preuve* of virility, the product of which he deploys to perpetuate both his power and his biological self.

Thus, just as Franz takes the place of Millwood in Schiller's rewriting of the bourgeois tragedy, so does his soliloquy in scene 1 suggest that his will to power through illegal acts stems from motivations very much like hers. Although he too invokes the materialist ethics of pure self-interest seen in Lillo's play ("Swim who can, and let sink who is too clumsy"), it is clear that he does not act out of the desire to do evil per se but rather from an intimation of personal injustice, a gnawing sense of inferiority and the despair of winning any affection from others—as he himself admits: "And master I must be, to force my way to goals that I shall never gain through kindness [*Liebenswürdigkeit*]" (35). In this manner, Franz hints that he does not in fact want to be a "master," but that he sees no other alternative.

Like Millwood's solitary revolt against the mercantile monastery, Franz's equally lonely rebellion against his father represents an attempt to reject and circumvent patriarchy and the contradictory values that it incarnates. This revolt and the price it exacts culminate in his death scene. Shaken by an apocalyptic nightmare in which he alone is damned for all eternity, Franz fears divine judgment, but he refuses to beg for God's mercy. Convinced that he is going to hell, Franz still resists the ultimate male authority, even as he plunges into madness: "No, nor will I pray—Heaven shall not have this victory, hell will not make this mock of me" (121; 5.2). With this enraged rejection of gendered Christian metaphysics—represented here by masculine heaven (*der Himmel*) and feminine hell (*die Hölle*)—Franz sacrifices his own religious belief on the altar of a criminal project which is a complete failure. Unable to compel any of those he holds thrall to do his bidding (his underlings all either openly defy or secretly disobey his orders[9]), the fratricide and patricide Franz envisions, lead inexorably to his one successful murder—his own.

In this manner, Franz's own speech and actions undermine his claim to villainy, while the rebelliousness of his plans links him with Karl. But the two brothers share other characteristics as well. Despite what Amalia says, Karl Moor is no Hector; in fact, he too has much more in common with Achilles. Addicted to the glories of battle, Karl is, for the duration of the play, even less interested in Amalia than Franz is. Having mentioned her cursorily in act 1 (41), Karl forgets her utterly in his devotion to his robber band, which is consistently his emotional priority. He does not think about her again until act 3, when the sufferings of a young recruit (who has had his fiancée, also named Amalia, stolen from him) remind him to check up on his own property. Tellingly, Karl always links his discussion of Amalia with his father, and his soliloquy which opens act 4 (in which Karl contemplates his home from afar), has more to say about father, fatherland, and becoming a father than it ever has to say about Amalia: "Soil of my fatherland. . . . Sky of my fatherland! Sun of my fatherland! . . . Here you were one day to wander, a great man . . . here to live your boyhood once more in Amalia's blossoming children. . . . No, I must see her—and him—and let me be annihilated! (106–7; 4.1).

In fulfillment of his bloodlust, Karl even goes so far as to kill Amalia at the end of the play when he is asked to give her up by his fellow bandits. Thus, Karl consummates his love for Amalia by running her through—an apt symbol for the degree to which violence has replaced and becomes identical with desire in the masculinity-obsessed world of Schiller's play. But ironically, it is through this very sacrifice that Karl Moor makes a fatal mistake; his prioritization of the robber band's fellowship over the love of Amalia goes too far, as the robbers' uncharacteristic condemnation of their captain makes explicit:

ROBBERS: Captain, captain! What have you done? . . .
MOOR: I have slaughtered an angel [einen Engel] for you. . . . Are you satisfied now?
GRIMM: You have paid your debts with interest. You have done more than any man [kein Mann] would do for his honor. (158; 4.2)

The closing exchanges between the captain and his troop (which effect the final rift between Karl and his band) are replete with trenchant metaphoric gender shifts that testify to an increasing uncertainty as to who represents what, sexually speaking. Significantly, Karl transforms the now-dead Amalia into a masculine angel—a fitting reaffirmation of both his manliness and his devotion to his homosocial bonds. But Karl's cohorts are shocked by this sacrificial slaughter—an act that they emphatically claim no "man" would make.

This is, on the face of things a surprising reaction, given the violently sexual nature of the robbers' own exploits.[10] Furthermore, the closing dialogue makes it clear that the robbers do not object to Amalia's death on moral grounds but are rather for the first time both frightened and repelled by their adored leader.

What is happening here? There is, according to the chop logic of the homosocial, a good reason for the robbers' curious condemnation of Karl's murder. Through his grand gesture of actually killing Amalia in order to remain faithful to the robber band, Karl has interrupted and bypassed the compulsory homosocial circuit of man-woman-other men so scrupulously maintained (though consistently problematized) in *The London Merchant*, *Manon Lescaut*, and *Jonathan Wild*. It is consequently no wonder that the robbers immediately recognize this act as a serious transgression, while Karl, in his turn, realizes that the oneness that he hoped to achieve with this male community is impossible:[11]

> ROBBERS: Ha! have you lost your courage? Where are your high-flying plans? Were they but soap-bubbles, that burst at a woman's breath?
> MOOR: Oh, what a fool that I was, to suppose that I could make the world a fairer place through terror . . . what is ruined is ruined—what I have overthrown will never rise again. (159)

With this horrifying twist, Karl's makes the ultimate sacrifice to masculinity only to see his faithful explicitly reject the masculinity of his act and place him in that same cowardly feminized context as the play situates his brother.

In this manner, Karl's machismo and his homosocial genius lead him to make a sacrifice as futile as that of Franz. Moreover, this consummation proffers a disturbing variation on Franz's sexual inadequacy, for if Franz's impotence is tied to his inability to commit acts of violence, that of Karl derives from his lust for force. The difference between real men and false men, the play ironically observes, is that real men kill—especially those whom they love. But the end result is the same, because love, pleasure, or even a modicum of contentment are possible for neither the false man nor the real one—a state of affairs which suggests that there *is* no "real" man.[12] Karl's virility and Franz's effeminacy thus prove to be two sides of the same coin—two necessarily false views of sexual identity as projected by patriarchy.

Which of them, then, is the true criminal? Schiller makes this already-impossible question even more difficult to answer through the peculiar distribution of minor characters in the play. Disturbingly, in the alternate criminal regimes of Franz and Karl, both father-figures and subordinates mirror those falsely gendered roles that the two brothers play within the Moor family.[13]

This gender trouble is most evident in the father himself. It is noteworthy that the head of the family, the Count von Moor — who is the cause of so much that happens in the play (Koc 95)—is an oddly effeminate parent. He is a sentimental, ineffectual, and weak father who—like Amalia—is so in love with his elder son that he is completely blind to his very real flaws—an interpretation that sheds light on the reasons behind the count's indifference toward his younger, equally "feminine" son.[14] If the elder Moor's love for his firstborn son is more "maternal" than "paternal," then as a "feminine" parent, he would understandably be more attracted to his "masculine" child.

In ironic contrast to the elder Moor, the two father-surrogates of the drama are highly aggressive, power-mad disciplinarians who delight in asserting authority over the recalcitrant sons. Assigning one to each brother, Schiller shows these macho religious authorities—the Catholic father (Karl) and the Protestant pastor Moser (Franz)—to be no better fathers than the count is, although they are his diametric opposites.[15] Through these falsely opposed paternal authorities of order, Schiller sketches out a strange patriarchal society, which is governed both by rigid discipline and by lax indulgence, a society that either blindly punishes or blindly condones but that never judges and never reforms—at once emotionally uncontrolled and emotionally bankrupt.

The other minor characters repeatedly play out the Karl-Franz conflict surrounding the problematic father to a degree that suggests that, while the roles can be differently distributed, the story must always remain the same. Hermann plays "Franz" to Franz's "Karl," for Hermann is also a disenfranchised son who longs to have and fails to obtain what Franz wants (Amalia) and who also eventually betrays his older brother-master. Kosinsky plays the part of a younger, more naive Karl, complete with his own Amalia; by attempting to dissuade Kosinsky from joining the robber band, Karl briefly becomes a father figure to this earlier version of himself—as he himself is aware. Finally, Spiegelberg plays Franz's role as Karl's jealous sibling in the robber band; like Franz, Spiegelberg resents Karl's popularity with the others, and like Franz, he both plans to steal his enviable position as captain away from him and takes only indirect action against him.

In this manner, neither brother escapes the complex of masculine family relations that has precipitated their rivalry, and that family drama repeats itself over and over again throughout *The Robbers*. Franz is undone in part by his disloyal surrogate brother (Hermann) just as Karl is partly undone by his (Spiegelberg). Karl's banishment from his father leads him to play father, not only to Kosinsky, but to the entire band (whom he not infrequently calls "children"), and leads him to a confrontation with the angry father-figure of the priest. Franz rejects one father only to have to deal with two others—the pastor and his servant Daniel who cared for the two boys (in this play, even the nursemaid is a man)[16] and whose senile sentimentality clearly echoes the Count von Moor.

Through these dramatic mirrors, the same male power-relationships recur constantly in Schiller's play, and in this manner, the structures of masculine intercourse in the robber band and within the disrupted Moor household prove virtually identical. Consequently, Karl and Franz find themselves trapped in a pernicious system of masculinist behavior from which there is no escape, and which they both seem doomed to repeat, in the same way that their energetic battles against their own intimations of personal injustice lead them to reincorporate that same injustice in their own usurpations. The play's very insistence on the geographical space between Karl and Franz (who never meet on stage) reinforces the fact that they inhabit the same inescapable psychic, political, and sexual architecture.

Seen from this perspective, Karl's criminality strangely resembles that of his brother. Both are unauthorized usurpers of male authority—from without and within the domain of law-abiding society—and both are unable to fulfill what they set out to accomplish. Just as Franz fails as a tyrant, so does Karl fail as a revolutionary and paradoxically proves a more effective despot than his own brother (Steinhagen 142). And both fail the test of masculinity, one by effeminacy a breath away from homosexuality, the other through a more profound irony. Karl's masculinity oversteps the conventions of homosociability to such a degree that it *becomes feminine*—landing him beyond the pale of acceptable behavior among men.[17]

Given this state of affairs, the "preservation of patriarchy" (Koc 102; Geyer-Ryan 222; Donnes 158) that the plot achieves must be seen in completely negative terms. Through the dual fates of the Moor brothers, Schiller exposes the insidious power of a male authoritarian regime that perpetuates its injustices through its own male progeny. This society unthinkingly sacrifices its offspring in order to preserve itself, despite the fact that this preservation is a horrible reversal of natural order—one, which carried to its furthest extreme, guarantees obliteration. In this sense, Schiller radically extends Lillo's exposure of both the sanctity and the viability of the masculine community. If the mercantile monastery's future is in doubt in *The London Merchant*, the masculine society of *The Robbers* is locked on a course of self-destruction, from which it cannot/will not avert itself. Thus, homosocial patriarchy is both the phallic colossus and the monstrous evil of the preface, waiting in a womblike nightmare labyrinth of false passages and false exits—an image that well describes the process of the play itself. Here every man (and every reader who would read like a man) must lose himself and must contemplate, kill, or be killed by his false other—the monstrous, imprisoned half-man Minotaur—without ever understanding that the nature of the beast is in fact his own.

We should note that, despite the greater number of actual women in *Justine* in comparison to *The Robbers*, Sade's fictional landscape still very obviously constitutes a man's world (Carter 38).[18] But it is precisely against this backdrop of masculine domination that the criminal achievement of Juliette looks so remarkable. It is no coincidence that the novel begins with her portrait rather than that of her sister—the ostensible heroine—because Juliette's history not only represents a model criminal history, but also offers an inspiring example of femininity triumphant under patriarchy at its most physically threatening to women. In fact, the contrast between the successful career of Juliette and the disastrous fate of her sister (and that of so many innocent women in the narrative) strongly suggests that it is only through criminality that woman may hope to achieve parity with and economic independence from man.

Like Millwood, Juliette is a professional malefactor who singlemindedly commits whatever crimes necessary to procure the wealth and power which she apparently desires. But unlike Lillo's villainess, she is never exposed as a malefactor and punished for her repeated transgressions; instead, with each act, she progressively gains more money and more social stature. Thus, as a treacherous and murderous courtesan, Juliette fulfills Millwood's criminal dream of transcending the masculine exchange by overtly trafficking herself within it and at the same time, covertly violating the exchange to her own advantage. As her English predecessor hoped, Juliette successfully wreaks her revenge on the male sex, even as she moves up the social ladder:

> Until she reached the age of twenty-six, Madame de Lorsange made further brilliant conquests: she wrought the financial downfall of three foreign ambassadors, four Farmers-general, two bishops, a cardinal, and three knights of the King's Order; but as it is rarely one stops after the first offense, especially when it has turned out very happily, the unhappy Juliette blackened herself with two additional crimes similar to the first: one in order to plunder a lover who had entrusted a considerable sum to her, of which the man's family had no intelligence; the other in order to capture a legacy of one hundred thousand crowns another one of her lovers granted her in the name of a third, who was charged to pay her that amount after his death. (466)

Thus, it is precisely because Juliette suffers the added social disadvantage of being a woman that her history sets the standard of behavior against which the novel will measure that of its other characters; her ability to rise contains an inspiring message of hope to all societal underlings, as the book's only other female criminal porte-parole, the adventuress Dubois makes explicit:

O Thérèse! the callousness of the Rich legitimates the bad conduct of
the Poor; let them open their purse to our needs, let humaneness
reign in their hearts and virtues will take root in ours; but as long as
our misfortunes, our patient endurance of it, our good faith, our
abjection only serves to double the weight of our chains, our crimes
will be their doing, and we will be fools indeed to abstain from them
when they can lessen the yoke wherewith their cruelty bears us down.
(481)

Crime is the great equalizer, and as such, it must be practiced on
ethical as well as political grounds. Thus, Dubois implies that,
not only does crime make a woman as good as man, but through
this aggressive practice of self-assertion, she virtually becomes a
man as well[19] — as her own relaxed "fraternity" with Coeur de
Fer's otherwise all-male robber band would seem to signify.[20]

Juliette's (and Dubois') successful criminal entrance into the
realm of the masculine contrasts markedly with the much longer
tale that follows. Justine's narrative unwittingly demonstrates
that what might be dismissed as one individual's freak good luck
with crime is not the exception but the rule of human experience, for in the various episodes of the novel, all who imitate
Juliette's deeds are rewarded in like manner.

A brief list bespeaks the overwhelming character of Sade's
"demonstration." The usurer M. du Harpin obtains great wealth;
Dubois goes on to make her fortune by serving the libertine desires
of France's most illustrious citizens; the pederast Count Bressac
murders his aunt and enjoys her fortune; the surgeon Rodin
vivisects his daughter and wins honors and a post with the empress
of Russia; one of the evil fathers of the libertine monastery is made
general of the benedictine order; Roland the counterfeiter makes
his fortune and leaves for Italy; and the judge Cardoville sexually
abuses the prisoners whom he then convicts, and he subsequently
becomes governor of a province.

Just as their successful criminal actions mirror those of
Juliette, so do these antagonists' arguments elaborate her philosophy, so succinctly put at the beginning of the novel: "She
[Juliette] rebuked Justine for her sensitiveness; she told her, with
a philosophic acuity far beyond her years, that in this world one
must not be afflicted save by what affects one personally; that is

possible to find in oneself physical sensations of a sufficiently voluptuous piquancy to extinguish all the moral affections whose shock can be painful" (460). The other criminal antagonists echo and amplify Juliette's argument that while crime is practical, it is necessary to find pleasure (*volupté*) in crime in order to successfully combat the negative and disagreeable influence of the moral code one has learned.

The necessity of establishing a morally counteractive connection between crime and pleasure culminates in Roland's argument for the interdependency and interchangeability of crime with sexual satisfaction:

> I have discovered myself, while thinking of crime, while surrendering to it, or just after having executed it, in precisely the same state in which one is when confronted by a beautiful naked woman . . . now, if pleasure-taking [*jouissance*] is seasoned by a criminal flavoring, crime, dissociated from this pleasure, may become a joy in itself; there will be a certain delight in naked crime. . . . Thus, let me imagine, the abduction of a girl on one's own account will give a very lively pleasure, but abduction in the interests of someone else will give all that pleasure with which the enjoyment of this girl is improved by rape; the theft of a watch, the rape of a purse will also give the same pleasure. . . . from this moment on, one tastes the greatest pleasure in everything criminal, and, by every imaginable device, one renders simple enjoyments as criminal as they can possibly be rendered. (680–81)

Taking its cue from Jonathan Wild's emphasis on criminal self-fulfillment (and shedding retroactive light on the character of his satisfaction), Roland's theory of pleasure synthesizes Juliette's principles and explains how criminal activity automatically masculinizes the perpetrator. As far as he is concerned, not only does pleasure make crime without guilt possible, crime has now become indispensable to him for pleasure; in fact, crime *is* pleasure, as his rhetoric demonstrates. Roland understands the word *rape* as both sexual coercion and robbery; stealing a watch and violating a woman procure him the same kind of enjoyment. Thus, Juliette's recommendation to her sister that she purposely find a pleasure in the commission of a crime has succeeded to the degree in Roland that such a process has become second nature for him; it is no longer a conscious exercise of the will and the imagination, but it has become instinctive and automatic. At the same time, though, Roland's metaphor implies that a woman can be *potentially as effective a rapist as a man* when she undertakes a robbery (Paglia 239). In this way, Roland's theory unites law-breaking and voluptuousness into one seamless gratification, which seems pointedly masculine regardless of one's actual gender.

In like manner, Sade's characters collectively construct a seemingly impenetrable edifice of arguments that defend crime as practical, potentially pleasurable, and therefore irresistible, since it serves all individuals' primary interests. The power of these arguments stems, not only from their sheer mass, but also emerges from the confident urbanity of the criminals themselves. Like Dubois, Roland, and Juliette herself, Sade's other criminal portes-paroles resemble equally well-educated, rational eighteenth-century philosophes, who cheerfully put forth their arguments in order to enlighten Justine and to thereby free her from the prejudices that blind her to her felicity (Klossowski 3–22). With the rhetorical ease and firmness of purpose displayed by Jonathan Wild, Sade's criminals appear unwavering in their principles, speak with equally impressive rhetorical skill, and represent a wide range of professions and classes.[21]

Seen from this point of view, the malefactors of the novel seem to actually inhabit the criminal society envisioned by Rodin, who concludes that "everyone in a criminal society [would be] . . . either very happy indeed, or else in a paradise of unconcern " (547). Taken together, Sade's criminals appear to constitute this odd utopia, an inverted El Dorado where women as well as men freely practice criminality regardless of class distinctions.[22]

Conversely, within the inverted framework of a criminal society, a virtuous person would emerge as an outlaw, and such is the case for Justine who consistently violates the criminal code that Sade's citizens live by. The novel carries out this inversive agenda to the letter by systematically punishing Justine whenever she commits a virtuous and/or lawful deed, in the same way that her sister is rewarded for her vicious, illegal behavior.

Justine herself announces her deviance at the beginning of the
novel when she affirms her adherence to an orthodox Christian
vision of goodness to which she consistently remains true:

> I am aware of all the dangers I risk in trusting myself to the honest
> sentiments which will always remain in my heart; but whatever be the
> thorns of virtue, Madame, I prefer them unhesitatingly and always to
> the perilous favors which are crime's accompaniment. There are
> religious principles within me which, may it please Heaven, will never
> desert me; if Providence renders difficult my career in life, 'tis in
> order to compensate me in a better world. (480–81)

Justine tirelessly (and tiresomely) reiterates this position, despite
the fact that all her virtuous deeds are met with betrayal and/or
precipitate her downfall. Again a list will suffice: St. Florent, the
man whom she rescues from the robber band, rapes her and later
delivers her into the hands of M. de Cardoville; Roland rewards
her aid with imprisonment in the counterfeiters' fortress; and a
beggar woman to whom she gives money robs her. Justine's
charitable acts almost invariably prove either useless or outright
detrimental, hastening on the deed that she hoped to avoid, as
her attempts to prevent the murders of Mme. de Bressac,
Rosalie, and Guernande's wife show. The futility of her benefi-
cence culminates near the end of her narrative in the failed
attempt to save an infant, whom the child's mother left behind
during her panicked escape from a fire—an accident that lands
her in jail as an arsonist.

In response to Justine's behavior, the episodes of the novel
gradually impose increasingly cruel and complex forms of sexual coercion upon her. The first and last sexual episodes make this
progression clear: the beating Justine receives from the robber
band because she refuses sexual intercourse culminates in the
baroque orgy at Cardoville's home complete with complicated
instruments of sexual torture. This intensification and compli-
cation of sexual coercion suggests that the degree of Justine's
punishment increases incrementally, the more intractably law-
abiding Justine proves to be.[23] Correspondingly, Justine is incarcerated with increasing frequency and longer duration in prisons and in communities like the libertine monastery, which are

so extremely regimented that they resemble a penitentiary en-
forcing discipline on prisoners far more than they do any harem.
In like manner, the connection between sexual coercion and
incarceration becomes increasingly strong in the second half of
the novel—culminating in Antonin's sodomizing Justine in her
prison cell.[24] The heroine's recalcitrance is reinforced by the
"last chance" opportunities provided her by M. de Guernande
(whose desire to kill his wife recalls the murder of Bressac and
whose bloodletting propensities are reminiscent of Rodin) and
Dubois who urges Justine to murder and rob M. Dubreuil. In
both cases, Justine would have been rewarded if she had agreed
to help them.

Thus, Justine's narrative unfolds at once as a vindication of
her sister's conduct and a condemnation of her own, for each
episode demonstrates the falsity of the Christian virtue to which
she claims allegiance and the consequent futility of her law-
abiding behavior. The novel's demolition of Christian morality
reaches its climax in the monastery where that very religious
authority that Justine so respects is exposed as a violation of the
principles it allegedly defends. Dom Severino proudly declares:
"To whom then will you have recourse? to what? Will it be to that
God you have just implored with such earnestness and who, by
the way of reward for your fervor, only precipitates you into
further snares, each more fatal than the last? to that illusory God
we ourselves outrage all day long by insulting his vain command-
ments?" (568). And just as the speech and fates of the novel's
secondary criminal antagonists mirror the principles of Juliette,
the characters who falter in these principles or who refuse on
some level to live by them are also punished or destroyed.
Bressac's disapproving aunt is summarily done in; Rodin's recently Christianized daughter Rosalie is killed; Omphale is put
to death after her unwilling service to the monastery is done;
Roland's successor, the kind counterfeiter, is the one who is
arrested and thrown in prison; Dubreuil offers to marry Justine
and is poisoned.[25]

According to this inverted point of view, if Justine is a
criminal because she refuses to obey the laws governing the
world in which she lives, then she is also perverse in her deter-

mination to act in ways that contradict her own experience: "However much I ought to have forbidden myself the self-indulgence of sympathy, however perilous it was for me to surrender to the impulse, I could not vanquish my extreme desire to approach the man and to lavish upon him what care I could offer" (665). As she fleetingly recognizes, Justine too finds pleasure (*volupté*) in actions that can only bring misfortune.[26] Elsewhere, Sade obliquely suggests that Justine is in some way attached to her own suffering (Didier 89; Gallop 62). Revealingly, the one man in the novel for whom she feels both physical and emotional attachment is also the one man who has no interest in women. Furthermore, Justine's peculiar reaction to her new-found happiness near the end of the novel ("I was not born for such felicity" [741]) suggests, not only that she dreads some unforeseen calamity, but also that her suffering defines her destiny and her identity. This may be why Justine's life as Justine is very short; it is her existence under her alias Thérèse—the ecstatic martyr—that is long, and for her at least, meaningful.[27]

The novel's indictment of Justine's behavior culminates in her death—a freak accident that grimly parodies the work of divine retribution, for death by lightning bolt is the traditional punishment for liars and sinners. This absurd demise under-lines the misguidedness of Justine's religious devotion, a mere superstition to which she is more perversely devoted than are the criminals attached to their socially unacceptable gratifications.

And yet, as in *The Robbers*, Sade's inversion of criminali-ty/compliance and his vision of a universally masculinizing criminality give way and break down. At the end of the novel, we make the surprising discovery that the entire argument has been in the process of disintegrating even as the narrative proceeds, because Justine's story has been accomplishing her sister's undo-ing even as it unfolds. Consequently it threatens—potentially at least—to undo Sade's other criminal antagonists as well. Cer-tainly, Justine's danger has already been indirectly alluded to by the very time and effort that the libertines devote to arguing with their victim. Why are they not content to just victimize her but deem it necessary to try repeatedly to convert her to a point of view that she will clearly never espouse?[28] This state of affairs

suggests that, in spite of all their statements to the contrary, the
criminal antagonists of the novel take Justine's moral arguments
seriously enough to perceive her steadfastness as a threat and to
regard her presence as somehow hazardous to them.

This danger becomes manifest when we consider the fate of
Juliette, who eventually disobeys the criminal code by which she
has vowed to live. Even at the beginning of the novel, Sade
signals Juliette's vulnerability by inserting an important passing
remark in his introductory portrait: Juliette is "a trifle wicked,
unfurnished with any principle, allowing evil to exist in nothing
[*ne croyant de mal à rien*], lacking however that amount of de-
pravation in the heart to have extinguished its sensibility" (458).
Despite the fact that she seems peculiarly gifted for a life of
crime, Sade reveals that Juliette is still emotionally sensitive, and
this will prove to be a fatal flaw. This weakness begins to display
itself right away, for Juliette contradicts her principles by taking
an interest in the criminal stranger she sees at the inn. What
seems at first like a mere device to set the narrative in motion
proves vital to Juliette's subsequent actions after she has heard
Justine's story.

The peculiarity of her reaction to the tale is especially
striking considering how Juliette should react to it. It is important to remember that during her narration, Justine reveals that
she has already related the story of her accruing misfortunes
many times, and that each time, this narrative recital provokes
indifference to her suffering and eagerness to victimize her in
turn.[29] In fact, Justine's story seems to possess a distinctively
seductive quality, insofar as it seems to actually encourage its
hearer to commit violent deeds (Gallop 4). Ironically, the telling
of the tale provokes the continuation of that which its teller
hopes to avoid; wishing to evoke pity and generosity in her
auditors, Justine usually awakens the exact opposite emotions.

Given this pattern, we would expect Mme. de Lorsange to
react according to the criminal principles to which she has
painstakingly adhered, and which Sade has so painstakingly
spelled out again and again. But this is not what happens:
"'Mademoiselle,' said she to Justine, 'it is difficult to listen to you
without taking the keenest interest in you; but I must avow it! an

inexplicable sentiment, one far more tender than this I describe, draws me invincibly toward you and does make of your ills my very own'" (738). Juliette's own words reveal that during the telling of the tale, she has not only recognized her sister, but feels sympathy for her, identifies with her, and is driven to recognize not only their long-denied kinship of blood, but a kinship wrought by affection, which welds them into one person experiencing identical woes. In an unusual articulation of female homosocial desire, Sade has his heroine who loves no man, fall into virtue by the seductive narrative of another woman.

This recognition of a kinship that is both biological and emotional effects a dramatic transformation. Juliette immediately acquires aspects of her sister's virtuous character, for she leaps to Justine's assistance, has her lover Corville protect her sister from the authorities, takes her into their home, and sets about establishing her innocence and restoring her good name—all of which goes completely counter to her consistently wicked behavior heretofore. In this surprising way, Juliette reacts to Justine's story, not as she should, but as Justine herself and Constance would, Sade's perfectly moral reader addressed in his prefatory letter.

Yet while Juliette's recognition of her sister implies her own moral self-recognition, the novel's conclusion suggests more sinister reasons for Juliette's transformation. Mme. de Lorsange's identification with her sister culminates in her peculiar interpretation of the significance of the latter's death:

O thou my friend! The prosperity of Crime is but an ordeal to which Providence would expose Virtue, it is like unto the lightning, whose traitorous brilliancies but for an instant embellish the atmosphere, in order to hurl into death's very deeps the luckless ones they have dazzled. And there, before our eyes, is the example of it; that charming girl's incredible calamities, her terrifying reversals and uninterrupted disasters are a warning issued me by the Eternal, Who would that I heed the voice of mine guilt and cast myself into His arms. Ah, what must be the punishment I have got to fear from Him, I, whose libertinage, irreligion, and abandon of every principle have stamped every instant of my life! What must I not expect if 'tis thus He has treated her who in all her days had not a single sin whereof to repent! (742)

Believing that there is a connection between her sister's fate and
her own, Juliette reads Justine's death as proof of divine retribution, despite the fact that as far as she can tell, her sister was a
paragon of virtue. If God has chosen to punish some mysterious, imperceptible, secret sin in Justine which Juliette cannot
see, this act must represent a warning of her own fate—an
indication of an even greater punishment to come.

Thus, Juliette's recognition of her sister has led not only to
identification with her, but also to substitution for her; Juliette
now takes Justine's place in the convent that the latter grieved to
leave at the beginning of the novel. With this sudden, drastic,
and uncharacteristic reversal, Sade suggests that his criminal
paragon espouses principles that she scorned, because she cannot transcend the moral education which she received despite
her own reasoning powers and the overwhelming proof of her
own experience. Seen from this point of view, Juliette's "moral"
transformation is neither positive nor moral; her rejection of her
life of crime is the product, not of reason and of intelligent
choice, but of irrational fear and the influence of her childhood
convent education, which she has, in spite of everything, been
unable to overcome.

At the end of the novel, Juliette violates the standards of
which she herself is supposed to be the most perfect representative—a state of affairs that implies, in turn, that the other
criminal antagonists may not be as firmly entrenched in their
principles as it seems and that they too might succumb; this
would explain the virulence of their reactions against Justine's
narrative and would account for their persistence in the obviously impossible task of converting her to the libertine world
view.[30]

How should *we* interpret Justine's history? Sade challenges
us to perform a moral reading of his novel but employs Juliette's
own misinterpretation of its meaning to lay bare the "morality"
of precisely this kind of reading. If to interpret Justine's tale
morally is to read it as Juliette does, then to read morally is to
misread, and to understand the moral lesson is to misunder-
stand drastically and self-destructively. In this manner, Sade
subverts the inversive authority of his ideal, female moral reader,

suggesting, that we should not, in the last analysis, want to read the story as Constance does, although like Juliette, we may not be able to do otherwise.[31] Seen from this perspective, the name of Sade's destined reader is both darkly ironic and frighteningly appropriate, for *constant* not only describes a person who is faithful, dependable, and stalwart, but also designates things which are uniform, unchanging, and fixed.

Thus, Sade's female reader Constance refers also to a *constantly feminine* act of reading, which cannot embrace change, deviation, or randomness. Therein lies the significance of the female gender in the "Lettre à Constance" and elsewhere in *Justine*. Sade uses "femininity" in much the same way that Schiller uses his self-collapsing "masculinity"—namely, as the contradictory marker for the degree to which our society acts upon our morals even while we think that we act upon it. If we are all false men in Schiller so are we all potentially, inescapably "feminine" in Sade[32]—hence the persistent emphasis throughout the novel on pederasty in general and on sodomy in particular. Through the common possession of the anus, men and women become the same feminine body (Sartre 457), which is dangerously penetrable, malleable, and docile as both Justine and her false double Juliette prove to be.[33]

Through the problematics of "feminine" interpretation, Sade's novel expresses a new criminal awareness: society is riddled with lawbreakers, but their criminal behavior is menaced by influences more insidious still, coercions that cannot be seen and felt but which control human destiny even more powerfully than do Rodin's surgical instruments and Roland's noose. Yet if we can no longer blindly trust our morality then on what basis are we to undertake a moral reading of Justine's tale? The novel itself implies that we cannot fulfill the challenge it has issued us, unless or until we recognize, construe, and transcend the limitations of our moral training, for as Juliette demonstrates, it is not enough to simply rebel against it.[34] The insufficiency of the libertine revolt is hinted at even before the novel's surprising conclusion; the apparent freedom of the criminal libertines is undercut by the extreme regimentation of the environments they inhabit (Barthes, *Sade, Fourier, Loyola* 129). In fact, the more we see of Sade's hidden pleasure palaces, the more they resemble penitentiaries rather than brothels. These are not lush spaces of spontaneous orgiastic abandon but rather barracklike, stripped down, confining areas where strict rituals are enacted.[35] The elaborate sex crimes perpetrated by the libertines prove to be, not active (masculine) rebellions against, but rather passive (feminine) products of a society that controls them more than they know.

With the subversion of inversion—by inverting the relationship between good/evil and criminality/compliance and then sabotaging the dichotomy altogether—Schiller's drama and Sade's novel double back on themselves; even as they definitively redraw and redefine the distinctions between the criminal and law-abiding, they blur the boundary lines between those distinctions more dramatically than any of the literature considered thus far. Through this double hermeneutic twist, both works undertake two important demonstrations: first, criminality's identity as an antisocial force is already contaminated by a compliance that is not its social opposite but merely its social extension (its twin, its false other); second, the figure of the criminal is inextricably bound to the powerful distorting lens of gender under patriarchy. In fact, Schiller and Sade explicitly suggest that the lens of gender may predetermine and consequently invalidate any proposed reading of the criminal text (including this one).

Through these complicated maneuvers, Schiller and Sade both skillfully yank the interpretive ground from under us, forcing us to wonder if we can ever break out of our own falsifying dichotomies, even enough to fully understand the works that we have before us. At the same time, the unrelenting grimness of their fictional worlds implicitly demands that we reinvent ourselves ethically, politically, and generically, despite the fact that such a reinvention proves possible for none of the characters in either *The Robbers* or *Justine*.

Schiller transforms the Sturm und Drang revolutionary drama into a work so subversive that it exposes the "phallacy" of the genre's own revolutionary concepts as well as the bankruptcy of the patriarchal social-familial values that ground them, while Sade's libertine novel unpacks the very real limitations of the libertine revolt and suggests ironically that the libertine is no more free than anyone else. The obvious failure of these revolutionary forms (together with their corollary—that the authors suspect the reader may fail to understand them) announces an incremental intensification of the formal problematics at work in this study since Lillo. Through texts that dismantle themselves, not once but twice, Schiller and Sade make the important suggestion that any genre (and the formal elements that it predicates) may be itself doomed on some level to fail both the artist, who would tell the criminal's story anew, and the reader, who would understand it differently.

Thus, both the play and the novel expand the query "Who is the real criminal?" into a *mise en question* of the very intellectual/gender/genre frameworks within which the question is raised. For how can we ask "Who is the criminal?" when our conceptual models for such behavior no longer suffice to explain the criminal and the nature of his or her crime or indeed even the gender identity of him or her? And where is the form that can successfully contain this difficult story? If *soi-disant* revolutionary genres cannot, then what can?

Through the clustered problematics of moral reading, gender, and genre, Schiller and Sade point the way to the cusp of Enlightenment portrayals of criminality. Godwin and Kleist will raise the issues of interpretation and formal failure to crisis proportions and they will further solidify two major directions of modern criminal representation, which Schiller and Sade so forcefully herald. The problematization of the homosocial, which begins with Lillo and culminates in Schiller's depiction of a masculinist society obsessed with its hidden effeminacy, will spill over into an explicitly homosexual domain in William Godwin's *Caleb Williams*. Correspondingly, Sade's interest in a perverse sexuality already determined and directed by the invisible controls that institutions (rather than persons) exert over citizens looks forward to the bureaucratic nightmare world of *Michael Kohlhaas*. In his tableaux of constricted libertine spaces Sade traces the silhouette of Foucault's disciplinary architecture—an edifice that will emerge with all its terrible clarity in *Michael Kohlhaas*.[36]

But before examining these works, I want to briefly explore the ramifications of these two crucial directions, both for the literature of criminality thence forward and for the orientation of this present study. From now on, the dichotomy between criminality and compliance will be always already false, and this falseness will usually manifest itself in three related *disciplinary* ways. First, the outlaw's double ceases to be a law-abiding citizen and will become either another outlaw or a member of a "surveillance" team from a detective/police force or a legal institution; this will be the case in both *Caleb Williams* and *Michael Kohlhaas*. Second, the criminal's actual criminality may have little if anything to do with actual law breaking and even less to do with "good" versus "evil" (Foucault, *Discipline and Punish* 251–52) but rather with vague suspicions and complex allegations. Third, the scenery against which the criminal protagonist acts will look more and more like a Foucaultian network of interlocking punitive systems that shape the criminal's story from without by meticulously measuring degrees of deviance from a "norm" which grows increasingly difficult to precisely articulate (Foucault, *Discipline and Punish* 182–83).

More importantly, *The Robbers* and *Justine* dramatize a crucial shift in the gender dynamics of literary criminality, and this shift will force one of the prevalent theoretical perspectives in my argument to take a back seat for the remainder of this study. In the interstices of this analysis of predominantly male criminal characters (in male-produced literary works), I have been attempting to outline some of the possibilities for female representation in the criminal text. These possibilities are forcefully voiced by Lillo, Prévost, and Sade, for all of whom the criminal heroine displaces the criminal hero of the piece (in Sade, significantly, there is no designated male hero) and becomes a potential model of an alternate behavior and an alternate truth. Still, while Sade represents in many ways the culmination of this interest in the criminal feminine during the Enlightenment,[37] his work also, along with Schiller's, marks the end of significant female presence in the literary text of crime for a long time to come.

This is, to be sure, quite a paradox, but if we compare the relationships between masculine/feminine in *The Robbers* and

Justine, the problem emerges with disturbing lucidity. Despite the obviously different sexual emphases in the drama (male doubles) and the novel (female doubles), both works stress the importance of an aspiration toward a criminalized masculine ideal, which is seen in terms of political and sexual supremacy. This objective is explicitly demonstrated in Karl Moor's military will to power which allows him to at once reign supreme over his outlaw community and be an object of adoration to them. And as we noted earlier, this masculine ideal of political/sexual force is also implicit in the aggressive *arrivisme* of Juliette's libertine philosophy which empowers her at once to live as well as a man (and a rich, aristocratic man, at that) and be an irresistible object of desire in a man's world.[38] Conversely, the great fear expressed by the characters in both works (overtly in Schiller, covertly in Sade) is of becoming feminine—of being a passive, powerless, and disregarded instrument rather than a subject of power/ pleasure, as are both Franz and Justine.

And it is here that a strange literary event occurs. Curiously, Sade's criminal femininity, which aspires toward virtual masculinity meets with the same fate as Schiller's physiologically based outlaw virility. The fact that both the macho Karl and the seductress Juliette ultimately find themselves in the same "place" as their feminine counterparts suggests that both men and women striving for the masculine find themselves forcibly propelled into the feared feminine—a no-man's-land of passivity, contradiction, misunderstanding, and self-obliteration. Thus, in both *The Robbers* and *Justine*, the feminine domain represents at once the hateful but inevitable destination for members of both gender affiliations, *be they criminal or compliant, be they physically male or female.*

Seen from this perspective, the critique of criminality undertaken by Schiller and Sade points far beyond itself indeed— to a precocious vision of a phallocentrism so vast (and a phallic ideal so unattainable) that it tragically undermines any and all courses of action (by men and women) and possibly preconditions (and thereby prevents) any means of understanding those actions. In contrast to the critiques of Lillo and Prévost, which expose a patriarchal edifice that is to be contemplated (and dismantled) from without, Schiller and Sade uncover a phallo-centrism that is the imprisoning condition of contemplation itself and that shapes understanding and interpretation from within. But how are we to think our way out of gendered thinking? In this urgent, late-twentieth-century question lies the impossible yet unavoidable challenge issued to us by *The Robbers* and *Justine*—failed works about failure that nonetheless dare us not to fail, even as they suggest that we must.

Having made this digression, I would like to stress that the interpretational precipice toward which Schiller's and Sade's explorations of gender lead have far-reaching representational consequences. These self-erasing geographics, which draw everything over to the feminine side of the gender dichotomy, indicate the radical degree to which the role of masculine/feminine in relation to crime has altered in Enlightenment literature. Again, it is productive to contrast this view of gender with that of Lillo and Prévost, who specifically employ woman as the first cause for man's criminal behavior. In startling contrast to Millwood and Manon Lescaut, and in a further refinement of the direction taken by Fielding, Schiller's and Sade's criminal feminine no longer resides necessarily within a female anatomy. The female now is the "feminine," and *it* (rather than *she*) becomes a kind of floating signifier (Cixous and Clément 64)—displaced into men specifically (Schiller) or indifferently into men and women both (Sade).

It is essential to recognize that this move away from woman as site of the feminine inaugurates a new danger—at once making possible a great gain and incurring a great loss for the literary exploration of criminality in the West henceforth. On one hand, with the feminine set loose in masculinity, the story of crime is potentially freed up to address both homosexual desire and homosexual panic (Sedgwick 89). Consequently, literature of criminality is empowered to focus—when it dares—on the erotic vagaries and contradictions within masculinity in general and within the homosocial circuit in particular. In the next chapter, we will see that *Caleb Williams* marks an important example of that critique. However, as I will make apparent in my conclusion, the critique of masculinity and the homosocial/

homosexual connection is not, for the most part, carried forward
in literary criminal representation of the nineteenth and twentieth centuries. Indeed, quite the opposite will prove to be the
case. After Godwin and Kleist, literature of crime in the West
will turn away from the contested masculine territory that the
Enlightenment discovers and maps out.

Further, if every character is now potentially feminine, then
there is little need for an actual woman in the literary text. This
reasoning explains why, after Sade, female criminals all but
disappear from the story of crime, while women as a whole play
increasingly marginal roles in it.[39] Henceforward, the trouble-
some, exciting space that Lillo, Prévost, and Sade open up for
the criminal actress is usually camouflaged by a patriarchal
writing that by and large refuses—even at its most radically self-
critical—to recognize woman as problematic, dangerous, and
therefore important in her own right. We will see that in Hugo
and other nineteenth-century explorers of literary criminality,
and up to Genet, literature of crime in the West will not only
replicate the predominantly male world of Schiller; it will also
consist primarily of masculinity's repressive, anxious monologue
with its own false feminine double.

5

The Tyranny of Form

Defense, Romance, and the Pursuit of the Criminal Text in Godwin's *Caleb Williams* and Kleist's *Michael Kohlhaas*

Both William Godwin's novel of the 1790s and Heinrich von Kleist's novella of the early 1800s provide apt summations of the trends in eighteenth-century criminal literature, and as such they clearly establish their lineage within the Enlightenment tradition. Not only do *Caleb Williams* and *Michael Kohlhaas* utilize the plot of the criminal biography, they also employ a plethora of character types and situations encountered before in the works considered here.[1]

These influences run rampant in Godwin's novel. Like Lillo's innocent apprentice, Caleb is the naive employee of a paternal authority, gradually sucked into "outlawdom" by the criminal machinations of others. Like Justine, he is falsely accused and becomes a fugitive, while the repetitive structure of his quest for a safe haven clearly resembles the shape of Sade's novel. *Caleb Williams* is also an obsessive tale of evasion and pursuit (see Harvey Gross' essay), which moves between different carceral spaces (the mansion, the prison, the robbers' hideout, the urban tenement lodging) in a manner that looks forward to that most famous of all "innocent outlaw" novels—*Les Misérables*.[2] Moreover, while Caleb's story, like Justine's, functions as a vindication of the protagonist's true innocence for the one listener who will

114

believe him, it also eventually proves to be a kind of confession (Rothstein 21). Indeed, Caleb's story possesses many of the features of des Grieux's. Both men are verbose narrators of sensibility whose memoirs at once insist on the narrators' guiltlessness and simultaneously reveal their attraction to crime, which they can neither explain, justify, nor in the end overcome. Other previously encountered criminal figures find their way into the turbulent social world of Godwin's novel. Falkland, Caleb's mentor and nemesis, also resembles Barnwell insofar as he gradually succumbs to murderous violence through an ill-fated wish to protect the honor of two women—a state of affairs which recalls *The London Merchant's* suggestion that women and the desire which they engender are the true source of criminality. Fielding's professional criminal emerges in the character of Gines, the relentless former gang member; like Jonathan Wild, Gines works both with and against the law, and he takes pleasure in inflicting pain on his innocent victim, in much the same way that Wild relishes his victimization of Heartfree. And even the noble robber captain evoked in *The Robbers* reappears in Godwin's portrait of the morally astute but socially disenfranchised Mr. Raymond.

Michael Kohlhaas also sketches out previously seen criminal conventions within the constraints of the novella's narrow focus and compact form. Like Caleb Williams, Kohlhaas too resembles Barnwell. A virtuous and upstanding bourgeois like Lillo's hero, he is drawn into criminal activity by those far more unscrupulous than he. His highly emotional reaction to a personal injustice recalls that of Karl Moor, while his formation of a robber army and his fatal inability to control the actions of his criminal community (which boasts an ambitious insurgent not dissimilar to Spiegelberg) clearly echoes the predicament of Schiller's robber chief. In addition, Kleist provides a unique variation on the confrontation between the outlaw and the priest (as found in *Manon Lescaut, Jonathan Wild, Justine, The Robbers*) in his surprising account of the encounter between Martin Luther and the recalcitrant horse trader. And once again, the corrupt world of the aristocracy—outlined so ironically in *Manon Lescaut*—is an object of critical attack here. As in Prévost's novel, Kleist's aristocrats band together against one who is not of their class, transforming their intended victim into a dangerous outlaw in the eyes of others: just as the Chevalier's rivals collaborate with his own father to criminalize Manon, so do the friends and relatives of the cowardly Junker von Tronka conspire to impede Kohlhaas' appeal for justice and to force him into increasingly serious transgressions. And, although the space of the prison plays a less prominent role than in *Caleb Williams*, the Foucaultian "disciplinary" already hinted at in Sade acquires an added force in Kleist; in *Michael Kohlhaas* a complex legal/governmental bureaucracy both dwarfs and shapes the actions of the individuals—good and evil—who are caught within its official confines.

Also familiar to the reader by now is the exclusive focus in both *Caleb Williams* and *Michael Kohlhaas* on the relations between men, despite the fact that both works boast more female characters than *The Robbers*. In Godwin, the women are mere props in what proves to be a tragic exploration of men's failure to establish meaningful bonds. This emphasis continues the concern with masculinity and the homosocial, which has played such an important part in the discussion thus far, and although Godwin's male characters are less overtly gendered than those of Schiller, the questions of masculine love and of homoerotic longing become, for the first time in criminal literature, objects of direct inquiry.

While *Michael Kohlhaas'* interest in intermale relations is a nonhomoerotic one, the importance of the homosocial is indicated by the overweening presence of all-male gatherings and interviews in the novella. Through this strategy, Kleist schematizes homosociability so that it becomes, not so much an object of scrutiny, as the self-evident gendered grounding to all sociopolitical intercourse. But this is not to say that sexuality does not play a strange role in Kleist's novella, insofar as it seems to play no role at all. In contrast to all of his predecessors, there is no overt gender trouble in the character of Michael Kohlhaas who is the picture of bourgeois heterosexuality. But the nature and object of his passion are certainly odd nonetheless. An intense and emotional man, Kohlhaas is in love, not with his wife, but with justice, and the degree to which he is willing to sacrifice his family to this juridic ideal, suggests an emotional-sexual displacement, which proves symptomatic of the entire world which Kleist describes.

Thus, *Caleb Williams* and *Michael Kohlhaas* display the cluster of interests that have been refined from Lillo through Sade: attention to gender, particularly the possibilities/limitations of masculinity; the uncovering of the contradictory relationship between apparent criminality and apparent compliance; the portrait of the criminal as possible social (tragic) paragon.

At the same time however, Godwin and Kleist further rework and refine the three elements of modernity noted by Gadamer. While these features are immediately apparent, as was the case in the works of Schiller and Sade, *Caleb Williams* and *Michael Kohlhaas* rearrange these concerns into more complex and sophisticated combinations than we have seen thus far—a move that results in a critique of enormous, destabilizing proportions, as will become evident.

Godwin and Kleist consolidate the first and third of Gadamer's modern hallmarks, namely, they integrate the separation from Christian humanism and the alienation of the author from his community into one seamless, contemporary-looking strategy. Both works studiously eschew any appeal to the reader on metaphysical grounds, and in fact, the whole notion of an "appeal" acquires for the first time a recognizably modern, forensic connotation. Here readers are asked to judge the protagonists on the bases of the following criteria: the convincingness of the testimony, the logic and consistency of the reconstruction of events, and the likeliness of the discernible motivations of the individuals involved. This legalistic orientation is announced and maintained in both works by the deployment of a jurisprudential language and by the events themselves—appeals, briefs, affidavits, hearings, and incarcerations—described in the minute detail typical of legal proceedings. Correspondingly, their fictions present themselves as evidential arguments in a criminal trial, and they unfold as formal defenses of the accused—a situation already suggested by the titles of the novel and novella (which bear the names of the alleged criminals).

Through this appeal to the legal, Godwin and Kleist very self-consciously set themselves apart from their reader, whom they reposition into an imaginary courtroom where he or she is expected to render judgment on the accused protagonist. An adversarial relation is necessarily built into this interpretive task, because the present narratives can proceed judiciously only if the narrator and the reader are not of one mind. Consequently, in both books, the narrator functions as a witness/advocate who must convince his juror/reader, while the latter operates under an opposed obligation to exercise a hermeneutics of suspicion, as he or she looks for the holes in the narrative testimony.

Even more striking is the manner in which Godwin and Kleist address the problematization of form that has been developing since *The London Merchant*. These authors extend the dynamic of form/failure in the criminal text beyond a demolition of genre into a far-reaching analysis, which proves even more disruptive and more disturbing than that of any work encountered heretofore. Although Godwin and Kleist do not, in contrast to Schiller and Sade, employ obviously subversive genres, their works create odd fictional hybrids through the mixture of a legalistic defense with other narrative modes, notably the medieval romance. Further, Godwin and Kleist repeatedly call attention to the problem of form by means of a curious stylistic marker—namely, they constantly foreground both the act of writing and the importance of its product, the text. In fact, "texts" play a role of unprecedented importance in both the novel and the novella; in both, the criminal protagonist is himself an author who is pursued and undone by writing. Moreover, as the summary of familiar criminal conventions at the beginning of this chapter signals, Godwin and Kleist represent an unprecedented exemplification of what Harold Bloom has called "the anxiety of influence" (5), insofar as their works seem obsessed with intertextuality and with the power of other texts to shape their own present writerly gestures.

The tension between fictional and nonfictional narrative texts provides the organizing principle of *Caleb Williams*, whose narrator is at once reader, writer, and subject of a veritable profusion of stories.[3] Caleb Williams is a sometime penman of popular tales, and his present, truthful narration is (he reminds us frequently and emphatically) a written memoir, as opposed to an oral recitation. Caleb transforms his master's story into a text that is to elucidate (and therefore serve) his own, and he searches for another text of which the master is himself the author—the latter's true confession that lies, purportedly, in a locked trunk (Simms 352). But if Caleb pursues a text, he is also pursued by one that has been written about him—a sensational criminal biography relates the adventures of "Kit Williams." This fictitious nonfiction (it purports to be true but is really false) follows him wherever he goes; more than any other force in the novel, the pamphlet ensures Caleb's continuing reputation as a dangerous criminal and thereby guarantees his disenfranchisement from whatever community he tries to enter. Thus, Caleb Williams' memoirs represent a textual response to another preexisting text, and as such, it participates in a complex intertextual network (Simms 349)—a written tradition, of which this work is to be the definitive, and presumably final, exponent.

   In Kleist's novella, *Michael Kohlhaas*, there is no less a proliferation of writing (Koelb 1101), although the texts in question are quite different from those in *Caleb Williams*; rather than consisting of true and false narratives, they comprise missives of either private or public nature. These "documents" (Koelb 1102) contain vital information destined for a clearly specified party, and while Caleb spends most of his time pursuing and being pursued by texts, Michael spends his time attempting to deliver texts to the right people. But these communiqués are almost invariably misdirected, and Michael Kohlhaas' tragedy derives consequently from his problematic role as both producer/transmitter and recipient of these messages. He obtains a text that others want (the magic capsule), and he is effectively criminalized, like Caleb Williams, by a text—in this case, one of his own making (his letter to his former recruit, Nagelschmidt).

   Employing a precociously semiotic view of literature as *écriture*, both Godwin and Kleist demonstrate that a text has a power all its own; writing can make or break the individual, be he subject, object, or both at once. Thus, in contrast to the earlier works of the eighteenth century, the interpretive chal-

lenges issued by Godwin's novel and Kleist's novella are only
indirectly concerned with either the (re)definition of criminal
acts and by implication, the nature/character of the criminal (as
in Lillo, Prévost, and Fielding) or with the revision of readers'
interpretations of the criminal's story (as in Schiller and Sade).
Instead, Godwin and Kleist push the problem of criminal representation back to its source. It is the act of writing that now
becomes suspect, and it is at the moment of writing that the
criminal's tragic immolation takes place.[4] Both *Caleb Williams*
and *Michael Kohlhaas* uncover the paradoxical nature of the
author's *textual enunciations about crime*—which possess at once a
peculiar inability to satisfactorily express themselves and an
eerie tendency to *say something else.*

In both fictions, the narrator's gesture of textualizing the
criminal's story bypasses rather than negates his intended defense because his narrative is invaded by foreign literary forms
that penetrate his design and that impose their own rules and
regulations on the subject matter. Under these ironic circumstances, the fictional exonerations of Caleb and Michael render
themselves irrelevant through their meticulous attention to detail and consistency; transformed into text, those very details
recombine themselves to tell stories of a very different nature.
Thus, Godwin's novel and Kleist's novella dramatize how their
narrators of crime succumb to the tyranny of form. Form asserts
an insidious power over the writer, inscribing its own text upon
the tale that he wants to tell.

Caleb Williams establishes narrative reliability by announc-
ing at the outset the motivations behind his narrative act. It is
notable that these motivations seem extremely honorable:[5] "I
am incited to the penning of these memoirs only by a desire to
divert my mind from the deplorableness of my situation, and a
faint idea that posterity may be by their means induced to
render me a justice which my contemporaries refuse. My story
will, at least, appear to have that consistency which is seldom
attendant but upon truth" (5). In contrast to des Grieux's narrative, whose similarity we have already noted, Caleb's recollec-
tions lack the overtly manipulative quality of the former; unlike
the Chevalier, he is not reciting his experiences orally to an

acquaintance whom he wishes to win over/seduce, rather, his is a private written meditation, undertaken both to comfort the teller himself in the present, and to set the record straight for the future.[6]

Not surprisingly, Caleb's insistence on the self-evident nature of his innocence is reflected by his repeated emphasis throughout his account on his helpless plight (Ellis xiv–xv). Pursued all over England for a theft he did not commit, Caleb is terrorized, imprisoned, and socially discredited by his former master, Mr. Falkland, who seems determined, not only to assure his silence, but to punish the young man for discovering his secret crime. Yet despite the fact that Caleb consistently depicts himself in situations of extreme physical and psychological suffering—chained, wounded, ill, and starving; living under fearful and despair-inducing circumstances—until the end of the novel, he is neither physically nor emotionally undermined by his circumstances. Rather these adversities serve to make even keener both his instincts for survival and his sense of his own righteousness: "Blessed state of innocence and self-approbation! The sunshine of conscious integrity pierced through all the barriers of my cell, and spoke ten thousand times more joy to my heart, than the accumulated splendours of nature and art can communicate to the slaves of vice" (192).

Caleb also appears scrupulously honest as far as his own behavior is concerned. He admits his weaknesses, revealing that he does not understand what drove him to spy on his master and confessing that he is not always above morally questionable actions when they ensure his survival; this is, he stresses, an objective account, and he will include all the pertinent facts even if they might disappoint his reader: "I know not whether my readers will pardon the sinister advantage I extracted from the mysterious concessions of my keeper. But I must acknowledge my weakness in that respect; I am writing my adventures and not my apology; and I was not prepared to maintain the unvaried sincerity of my manners at the expense of a speedy close of my existence" (202).

Even more surprising, however, is Caleb's emphasis on the overall guiltlessness of the other criminals whom he encounters during his journeys. Rather than using this opportunity to display his innocence by contrasting himself with these true criminals, Godwin's protagonist establishes solidarity with them. Thus, in contrast to Justine who appears to be the only innocent outlaw cast adrift in a licit criminal society, Caleb stresses that his own predicament is actually a typical social phenomenon. In jail, he is reunited with an honorable peasant who killed his opponent in self-defense, and he befriends Brightwel, a literary-minded convict falsely accused of highway robbery. Caleb reveals that these felons and others like them are law-abiding citizens falsely labeled as malefactors by a legal system that combines injustice with inefficiency: "I soon found, upon enquiry, that three fourths of those who are regularly subjected to a similar treatment [imprisonment] are persons whom, even with all the superciliousness and precipitation of our courts of justice, no evidence can be found sufficient to convict" (189). Thus, according to Caleb, the vast majority of prisoners are in fact innocent men unjustly incarcerated. Moreover, the outlaw's lot is not much better outside prison walls, as Caleb discovers during his discussions with the democratically inspired criminal reformist Mr. Raymond. Raymond extends Caleb's critical portrait of due process when he negatively assesses the average criminal trial's efficacy in meting out judgment:

> Who ever thinks, when he is apprehended for trial, of his innocence or guilt as being at all material to the issue? Who ever was fool enough to volunteer a trial, where those who are to decide think more of the horror of the thing of which he is accused, than whether he were the person that did it; and where the nature of our motives is to be collected from a set of ignorant witnesses, that no wise man would trust for a fair representation of the most indifferent action of his life? (232)

In this manner, Caleb's narrative not only affirms his own innocence, but also points to the guiltlessness of all other criminals. With these views, the narrator suggests that the very notion of criminality is a false one, since it designates, not the victimizers of society but its victims: either the accused have not committed the crime of which they are charged, or their petty offenses are vastly outweighed by the gross manner in which the judicial system has treated them.[7] Thus, although Caleb assures his readers that he was in no way tempted to espouse the radical politics of Raymond and his gang, who have rejected law-abiding society in favor of a successful form of anarchy (in contrast to Schiller's bandits), he also pointedly refuses to condemn them: "I did not indeed feel that aversion and abhorrence to the men which are commonly entertained. I saw and respected their good qualities and their virtues. I was by no means inclined to believe them worse men, or more hostile in their dispositions to the welfare of their species, than the generality of those that look down upon them with most censure" (235). In keeping with the political critiques articulated by Millwood, Wild, the Moor brothers, and Sade's criminal philosophers, Caleb suggests that the real criminals are in fact the most powerful of society's (male) citizenry. Wealthy aristocrats such as Tyrrel and Falkland both abuse their socioeconomic advantages in order to protect their self-defined notions of honor and prestige (Harvey 237).

And if the corruption of the landed gentry is the main target of Godwin's attack, such good, average citizens as Laura and Collins are not above criticism either. Despite the fact that they are essentially virtuous individuals, they have also been tainted by the hypocritical moral values of their milieu. Disturbingly, those very people who should recognize in Caleb qualities which they themselves possess are blinded by an obsession with appearances. Laura and Collins, representatives of bourgeois respectability, refuse to even hear Caleb's side of the story for fear it will upset their comforting belief in appearances: "If you could change all my ideas, and show me that there was no criterion by which vice might be prevented from being mistaken for virtue, what benefit would arise from that? I must part with all my interior consolation, and all my external connections. And for what?" (320).

Read in this fashion, Caleb's self-defense proposes a fiercely republican, proto-proletariat tale of socioeconomic oppression (Gross 407); the so-called criminals of the piece, Caleb included, are innocents who are manipulated directly or indirectly by the powerful to ensure the maintenance of their power. This would seem to be the significance of the inclusion of the Falkland-Tyrrel story. Within the context of Caleb's self-defense, this digression functions as a political parable that foreshadows Caleb's own experience and whose lesson is pointedly anti-aristocratic. It is certainly no coincidence that only the economically and socially weakest members of the community (Hawkins family and Emily) possess the courage to rebel against Tyrrel's tyrannical government.[8] Like Caleb, Hawkins and Emily are falsely accused of criminal acts and unjustly imprisoned, eventually becoming sacrifices to Tyrrel's obsession with control and reputation. But this antiaristocratic polemic applies no less to Falkland himself. Although he opposes Tyrrel, he proves as obsessed with public consideration and with power as his adversary, for he is equally determined to protect his status as first citizen of the community at any cost.[9]

Yet the manner in which Caleb relates the inserted tale of Falkland and Tyrrel corresponds not at all to these republican sentiments. Moreover, because this insertion occurs so early on in Caleb's narrative process and because the narrator insists so forcefully on its importance, the Falkland episode exerts a disruptive influence on the entire story, causing it to veer away from its defensive testimony, toward a revelation of a very different kind of truth.

This shift becomes evident when one considers where Caleb puts the emphasis in the Falkland-Tyrrel incident. Instead of describing Falkland as expected—that is to say, as the true criminal behind the scenes (like Franz Moor)—Caleb paints Falkland in enthusiastic colors as a nobleman extraordinaire, a gentleman of courage and gallantry who adheres to an honor code from an older and better time: "From them [his favorite authors] he imbibed the love of chivalry and romance. . . . He believed that nothing was so well calculated to make men delicate, gallant, and humane, as a temper perpetually alive to the sentiments of birth and honour. The opinions he entertained upon these topics were illustrated in his conduct, which was assiduously conformed to the model of heroism that his fancy suggested" (12). Significantly, Caleb shares these same literary proclivities: "In fine, this [curiosity] produced in me an invinc-

ible attachment to books of narrative and romance. I panted for
the unravelling of an adventure with an anxiety, perhaps almost
equal to that of the man whose future happiness or misery
depended on its issue. I read, I devoured compositions of this
sort. They took possession of my soul" (6).

Although he has just described himself as a man driven by a
disinterested scientific curiosity to discover the truths behind
natural phenomena (and by which he justifies in advance his
relentless surveillance of his master), Caleb also reveals that his
speculative powers turn toward works of fiction, the romance—
the least realistic of narrative forms—in particular. This piece of
information will prove vital. It establishes an unexpected kinship between the innocent victim and his criminal victimizer,
insofar as their aesthetic tastes are concerned. More importantly,
Caleb's reference to the romance provides a key to understanding his account of the Falkland episode, while it also situates
Caleb the writer as a part of a literary tradition of which he is a
direct, impassioned inheritor.[10] Granted, Caleb cites the sources
of his knowledge concerning young Falkland and carefully
explains the organizing logic for his current presentation.[11]
Nonetheless, Caleb's opening description of young Falkland as
ideal incarnation of *courtoisie* signals that his taste for the chivalric romance is already prevailing over his testimony—undermin-
ing what ought to be the most compelling piece of evidence in
his favor (namely, the true criminal character of his master).[12]
Necessarily, the romance will shift the ground of interpretation—asking the reader to judge Caleb and Falkland, not in the
jurisprudential terms of guilt or innocence, nor in the political
terms of oppression and revolt, but rather in the metaphysical
terms of good and evil.

Thus, the manner in which Caleb chooses to tell his story
already threatens to cancel out its criminal subject matter, as well
as its political, antiaristocratic thrust. But it will also accomplish
an even more drastic goal; it will reveal the presence of a very
different "crime." As we shall see, the Falkland episode revolves
around a central contradiction: the implication that Falkland is a
homosexual—an inconceivable suggestion for a work of romance—proves to be inextricably linked to Caleb's portrait of his

master as a tragic hero and to his own partially admitted homoerotic desire.

These paradoxical dynamics permeate the accounts of Falkland's youth. The description of Falkland and Count Malvesi presumably establishes a pattern of action that is repeated in that of Falkland and Tyrrel: a conflict arises between Falkland and another man because of their rivalry for a young woman's favor—a typical romance situation ("Medieval Romance"); the crisis is precipitated by a flirtatious female (Lady Pisani and later, Miss Hardingham) who egotistically awakens jealousy for Falkland in her admirer; Falkland attempts to come to a private understanding with the envious lover in order to avoid a senseless physical combat.[13]

The sexual dynamics of this pattern are, by this time, well known. Like his forefathers des Grieux and Karl Moor, Falkland is both a charismatic man of sensibility and a homosocial mastermind; adored by both women and men, he automatically becomes the first among equals in aristocratic society—be it in Italy or in the gentlemen's assembly in his hometown. Yet Falkland is even less interested in women than Karl Moor was. Without even a token love interest to legitimize his masculinity, his relations with women are consistently cordial but indifferent, while his connections with other men are always invested with a passion bordering on violence. Unlike all the other male protagonists considered in this study, Falkland is presented—quite overtly—at the beginning of the narrative, as a man without a woman. This state of affairs already hints that his difference from (and superiority to) other men lies, not only in his incarnation of knightly virtue, but also in that of sexual orientation. These hints proliferate, even as Caleb's romance stresses the qualitative differences between the hero and his antagonist.

If the Malvesi episode establishes Falkland as a homosocial knight in modern dress, it serves another equally important function, namely, setting up Barnabas Tyrrel as a complete villain. The picture of the impetuous but essentially good-hearted Italian count contrasts markedly with the portrait of the British squire, which follows, and the latter emerges as the true "enemy" to whom Caleb referred in his introduction; he is the demonic origin of the calamities which have blasted Falkland's life and that have destroyed Caleb's existence in turn. Further, inasmuch as Falkland is a latter-day Gawain—the flower of the town's miniature court, a chaste object of female admiration and the only champion who accepts the gage of a most daunting opponent—so is Tyrrel something of a modern Green Knight. Like that chivalric romance figure, he too plays a double role of lord of the manor and invincible opponent; he is a brutish, uncourtly, but powerful warrior whose physical strength borders on the magical and whom no one dares challenge.

In this manner, the romantic idealization of Falkland already under way in the Malvesi story (and underlined stylistically by such epithets as "the god-like Englishman") is further amplified by the present account that portrays the conflict between Falkland and Tyrrel as no less than a mythic struggle between the forces of good and evil. Tyrrel's brute physical strength, for example, acquires preternatural proportions in Caleb's rendition: "His stature, when grown, was somewhat more than five feet ten inches in height, and his form might have been selected by a painter for that hero of antiquity, whose prowess consisted in felling an ox with his fist, and devouring him at a meal" (19). Reversing the gender affiliations between good and evil seen in *The Robbers*, Caleb paints Tyrrel as an overbearingly masculine evil principle who represents the primal, sensual, aggressive, and ultimately deadly strength of the body—a suggestion reinforced by Caleb's comparing him a page later to the earthbound Antaeus (20). Conversely, the diminutive Falkland incarnates the pure, ethereal, spiritual feminine, which nonetheless possesses its own phallic power, as his reported effect on Tyrrel at the dance clearly indicates: "Mr. Falkland uttered these words with the most unruffled temper in the world. The tone in which he spoke had acquired elevation, but neither roughness not impatience. There was a fascination in his manner that made the ferociousness of his antagonist subside into impotence" (25).

Like the poetry of Orpheus, Falkland's very words cause the bestial Tyrrel to fall silent, as though spellbound by a kind of magic exuding from Falkland's speech. Falkland's connection to the Orphic forces of language is further underlined by his intimate friendship with yet another confirmed bachelor—the poetic genius Mr. Clare, who favors him above all the others in the community.[14]

Thus, Caleb invokes the same curious fear of and fascination with a nonbiological "feminine," which was also at work in Schiller and Sade. It is according to this same odd dynamic, that Tyrrel's traditional manhood also becomes both vulnerable to Falkland and suspect insofar as he closely resembles his rival in important ways. We cannot fail to notice that despite all his love for "manly" activities, Tyrrel is also a man without a woman; he is unmarried, entertains no apparent romantic interest in any woman, and like Falkland, is obsessed with the admiration of other men. It is also evident that Tyrrel is all too easily threatened by the gentle virtue of Falkland, and the entire episode is scattered with hints that it is precisely Falkland's ambiguous sexual appeal, which disturbs, enrages, and *moves* Tyrrel. This attraction is already indicated in the dance scene; Tyrrel is, despite himself, momentarily entranced, unmanned ("impotent"), and rendered passively feminine by Falkland's linguistic poise.

The suggestion of a mutual desire and an anxiety about what it portends is expanded in the depiction of Falkland's goodwill visit to Tyrrel's home. During the conversation, Tyrrel seems almost won over, until Falkland tries to touch him: "Saying this, Mr. Falkland offered his hand to Mr. Tyrrel in token of fellowship. But the gesture was too significant. The wayward rustic, who seemed to have been somewhat impressed by what had preceded, taken as he now was by surprise, shrunk back" (32). The fact that a man of Tyrrel's size and strength recoils in fear from physical contact with his undersized opponent points, albeit obliquely, to a sexual sympathy between the two antagonists.[15]

The passionate nature of the antipathy between Falkland and Tyrrel becomes even clearer in their fatal clash over Emily's affections. This conflict seemingly returns the characters to the obligatory circuit of homosocial behavior, whereby men bond with and establish superiority over each other by means of the competition for womanly affection. But it is important to note that this circuit is employed in the most superficial manner possible, and the description of it becomes increasingly strained and strange. Once again in contrast to the Franz-Amalia-Karl struggle, neither Tyrrel nor Falkland possesses *the slightest sexual interest* in the doomed woman—a state of affairs that makes Caleb's passionately sexual rendering of the fire rescue scene suspicious indeed. Given that this highly emotional tone cannot be Collins' (it does not sound at all like his manner of speech), we can only conclude that it is Caleb who has decided to invest this episode with its sensual character: "She flew into his arms with the rapidity of lightning. She embraced and clung to him, with an impulse that did not wait to consult the dictates of her understanding. Her emotions were indescribable. In a few short moments she had lived an age of love. In two minutes, Mr. Falkland was again in the street with his lovely, half-naked burthen in his arms" (46). We will see another scene of passionate embrace later in the novel. But for now, it is important to ask why Caleb suddenly interests himself so profoundly in Emily's feelings and why he then transforms this woman (who is clearly of no interest to Falkland) into an object of sexual desire.

Clearly, this scene points to a complex process of erotic wish fulfillment on the part of Caleb. But is it Falkland's place that he longs to assume in this scene? The fact that Caleb subsequently dwells so ecstatically on Emily's dying moments, when she believes to have become Falkland's wife, suggests indeed, that it is with Emily (the imprisoned, punished desirer) that he identifies (Gold 142)—at least briefly—and that the lovely, unidentified "half-naked burthen" imagined in the rescue scene, is in fact Caleb. This curious moment in the Falkland story points to the unauthorized desires, not only of Caleb's nemesis, but of Caleb himself.

Not surprisingly, the plot of this homoerotic romance recounted by a narrator who seems to be homosexual himself goes horribly awry. Just as this romance violates its heterosexual dynamics, so does the antagonism between Falkland and Tyrrel culminate in a physical confrontation that defies expectation. Good should, but does not, triumph over evil; the spiritual power of language should, but does not, triumph over brute physicality. Instead, the violence of the body shatters the power of the mind. While Tyrrel is subsequently murdered—with the same phallic instrument that penetrated Schiller's Amalia—(by a still-mysterious assailant), Falkland is no less certainly destroyed himself, as Collins notes: "Everybody respects him, for his benevolence is unalterable; but there is a stately coldness and reserve in his behaviour, which makes it difficult for those about him to regard him with the familiarity of affection. These symptoms are uninterrupted, except at certain times when his suffering becomes intolerable, and he displays the marks of a furious insanity" (109).

Unlike Gawain, Falkland does not emerge from his defeat a sadder but wiser man, rather the experience devastates him; overcome by the extent of Tyrrel's ferocity, Falkland loses his mental equilibrium and is thus himself spiritually and psychologically murdered. In this way, the invisible, feminizing wound that Tyrrel inflicts on Falkland proves to be as fatal as the blow that struck down the former. Through this wound, Falkland loses the possibility of meaningful relations with other men—a state of affairs that in turn renders him vulnerable to the penetrating powers of Caleb, his sympathetic helpmate, who would know the source of his trouble.

Caleb's tragic interpretation of Falkland's confrontation with Tyrrel as a frustrated, homosexual romance surprisingly glorifies the contriver of the narrator's sufferings and thereby neutralizes in advance a negative judgment of Falkland once we do learn that he is in fact Tyrrel's murderer. Caleb's subsequent account also suggests that Falkland's body, deprived of its original spirit, has been somehow possessed by the man who destroyed him, for it is certainly the vengeful, powerful squire whom the Falkland of volumes 2 and 3 most clearly resembles.[16] We have only to compare Tyrrel's vengeful determination to persecute Emily with Falkland's obsessive pursuit of Caleb to see both the similarity and the gender ramifications that the similarity predicates—making Falkland more manly but at the same time forcing Caleb to play the feminine part of the fugitive maiden.

More importantly, the romantization of the Falkland story also foreshadows and grounds the structure of Caleb's own testimony.[17] As if to further underline the identity between Falkland's story and his own, without which he literally cannot proceed, Caleb's account of his own life acquires a distinctly romantic cast after this digression. And seen within the romance context, Caleb's story resembles that of Parzival, another callow youth, whose own nobility like that of Caleb has been concealed and who has lived removed from and ignorant of true courtly society. Significantly, the mistakes of the two heroes are inverted mirrors of each other. While Parzival's curiosity fails—for he does not seek explanation of the strange grail ritual nor inquire into the nature of the fisher king's mysteriously incurable wound—Caleb is too curious about his master/host's equally grave and equally secret injury. Parzival is banished from the castle, while Caleb is imprisoned within it, but both must suffer and endure a number of tests to finally, against all odds, assert their nobility.[18]

Seen from this point of view, Falkland more clearly resembles, not Gawain, but Anfortas—an impotent knight who presides over his eternally melancholy household and who hovers agonizingly between life and death.[19] Moreover, the nature and source of Anfortas' physical wound hint, by analogy, that there is more to Falkland's psychological torment than the mere loss of honor. Anfortas' injury is an overtly sexual one; he suffers from an incurable wound in the testicles because he has transgressed the law of the Grail, which explicitly forbids sexual desire (Wolfram von Eschenbach 264). Falkland, as portrayed by Caleb, is also a sexual transgressor, for the objects of his desire are always men—Tyrrel, whom he tries to win over and then kills; and Caleb himself, whom he endeavors to shut up in his own home as his wife/servant.

In this way, Caleb's romance recasts the relationship between himself and his master into a eroticized version of the fellowship between Parzival and Anfortas. Just as Parzival represents a more perfect version of the Lord of the Grail, whose place he eventually assumes, so do Caleb's actions improve upon those of Falkland. Caleb confronts Falkland with the same arsenal

with which Falkland faced Tyrrel, namely, with the rhetorical
power of truth and integrity, and this time the power of the word
prevails. Caleb's accusation, coupled with his courteous apology
to his master, brings forth Falkland's own equally courteous, and
sexually charged, confession: "He saw my sincerity: he was
penetrated with my grief and compunction. He rose from his
seat, supported by the attendants, and—to my infinite astonishment—threw himself into my arms! 'Williams,' he said, 'you have
conquered! I see too late the greatness and elevation of your
mind'" (335). This incredible scene combines elements of sexual
climax seen previously in this study. It relocates the Louisiana
Liebestod of *Manon Lescaut* into the carceral space of the homosocial union between Barnwell and Trueman. It employs the
orgasmic language of sensibility encountered in Fielding's depiction of the Heartfrees' anguish. And it is reminiscent, perforce, of Amalia's ecstatic rush into the arms of her execu-
tioner/lover Karl Moor.

By bringing Falkland to trial, Caleb affirms the very qualities that young Falkland once represented, and thus by defeating
Falkland, he defeats Tyrrel and thereby completes young Falkland's mission; he fulfills what his master tried and failed to
accomplish. At the same time, Falkland—penetrated, not by an
actual phallus or a phallic instrument, but indeed by the narrator's rhetoric—surrenders himself to Caleb with a passionate
abandon that replicates Emily's actions in the rescue scene.
Falkland accepts and embraces his feminized powerlessness as
Caleb's love object, although (because?) this act literally annihi-
lates him.[20] The power ramifications of this move should not be
overlooked. Through these maneuvers, the servant both surpasses and possesses the master by incarnating the best of the
master's originally virtuous and lost identity, just as Parzival
eventually exceeds Anfortas in knightly virtues. The true homosocial genius of Godwin's novel thereby reveals himself to be
none other than Caleb himself, who through a homoeroticism
that he never acts upon gradually establishes himself as his
master's authority.

Curiously, however, this second, frustrated homosexual romance turns out no better than the first. Caleb's romantic (in

both senses of the word) impulse has not completely erased his original wish to present a proof of his innocence before an objective jury of readers, although he seems to realize what his romance has done to his story only as it approaches termination:

> The writing of these memoirs served me as a source of avocation for several years. . . . I had a melancholy satisfaction in it. . . . I conceived that my story, faithfully digested, would carry in it an impression of truth that few men would be able to resist; or at worst that, by leaving it behind me when I should no longer continue to exist, posterity might be induced to do me justice, and seeing in my example what sort of evils are entailed upon mankind by society as it is at present constituted, might be inclined to turn their attention upon the fountain from which such bitter waters have been accustomed to flow. But these motives have diminished in their influence. I have contracted a disgust for life and all its appendages. Writing, which was at first a pleasure, is changed into a burthen. (314)

Caleb restates his opening argument and affirms the politically didactic nature of his account, but this declaration sounds both hollow and telling; Caleb's disgust for "life's appendages" and his awareness of his writing as burden rather than pleasure reveal that he is finally beginning to understand what his written story might mean, for it is the very pleasure of the text that has betrayed him by indicating precisely toward what "appendages" he is so fervently attached.

Caleb's surprising self-condemnation at the end of his testimony reveals that he is unable to dispense either with the legalistic framework, which first gave rise to his narrative, or with the desire, which has been unwillingly voiced in the romantization of his tale. Under the pressure of literary coherence, Caleb's text turns his own intention on its head, transforming the self-defense into self-indictment. Without his knowing it, Caleb's testimony proceeds inevitably toward his confession of his love for Falkland; this constitutes the true "crime" exposed here.

Generically opposed signs of this love are everywhere. Certainly, Falkland and Caleb "play house" not only as father and son (Ellis 176; Storch 192) but as husband and wife (Gold 146), for Caleb's overriding concern to share and thereby remedy the

personal troubles of his master is as much a spousal as it is a filial
reaction. Most significant of all is Caleb's obsession with the
trunk containing Falkland's own text. As a hollow, "feminine"
(Frye 194), Grail-like vessel containing a mysterious and desired
truth, the trunk indicates Caleb's "masculine" wish to open or
penetrate Falkland's secrets and thereby to know him completely
(with all that that image implies); but at the same time *trunk* also
denotes Caleb's "feminine" desire to be penetrated by the phallic
body that possesses the case.[21] Under the romance influence,
Caleb's defense mode becomes even more sexually resonant; his
fugitive scenario reverses the roles that he assigns to himself and
his master in the romance but still allows him to play out a fantasy
of desire from a different, "innocent" perspective (Sedgwick 92)—
as the object of desire rather than as the desirer. But perhaps the
most striking proof of Caleb's love is his return to "extravagant
adulation" (DePorte 163) for Falkland at the end of his narrative,
once the object of desire/desirer is safely out of the way.

Consequently, the opposing narrative modes that Caleb
employs place him in an impossible quandary, which is simultaneously artistic, political, and sexual: just as he is the pursued,
victimized, penniless woman in his defense, so is he the powerful, aristocratic questing man in his romance, while Falkland is
both his male pursuer/tyrant and his female object/victim. Seen
in this light, the writing process itself furnishes the contradictory means by which Caleb seeks to resituate, recuperate, and
consummate his love for Falkland. A Barthian "writer of pleasure," Godwin's narrator has renounced the bliss of physical
jouissance "in order to have the right and the power to express it,"
and consequently "the letter *is* his pleasure" (Barthes, *The Pleasure of the Text* 21). With Barthes in mind, we can understand the
sexual significance of Caleb's nested narrative and of the series
of texts referred to in the novel; put together, they all struggle
toward a displaced masculine/feminine erotic reciprocity.[22]
Through the virile act of writing—a sexual act whereby the
phallic pen inscribes what it will on the blank and passive paper
(Gilbert and Gubar 6)—Caleb gains the illusion of possessing
the obscure object of his desire at the same time as he is textually
possessed by him, for he places Falkland's story *inside the body of*

his own text. By making Falkland a subject of his own story, he can at least imagine him as the instrument of his pleasure, just as Falkland (as Caleb sees him) has the illusion of possessing Caleb through the biography of Kit Williams. And why else would Caleb long for a manuscript that lies locked in Falkland's trunk? Thus, Caleb's text reveals "itself in the form of a body split into fetish objects, into erotic sites" (Barthes, *The Pleasure of the Text* 56).[23] This textual "corpus" both replaces and lays bare the very masculine/feminine body that it does not want to want to possess or be possessed by.

Yet Caleb suppresses the sexual self-discovery that his own text inaugurates in order to rescue his story from ambiguity at any cost, even that of his own self-justification. His self-condemnation is the price that Caleb is willing to pay for coherence—in order not to tell a "half-told and mangled tale." But this act of renunciation, which amounts to self-annihilation ("I have now no character" [337]), is worse than futile. The tale of unauthorized desire remains half-told nonetheless, because neither the defense nor the romance can ever articulate the nature of Caleb's relationship to Falkland. Godwin effectively shows us that there is no available narrative form that does not falsify by reducing the characters to a series of inadequate dichotomies, which destroy the couple they are meant to describe (Cixous and Clément 64).

The very existence of Caleb's double narrative suggests, of course, that both presented "realities" are equally true: Falkland is indeed both a hero and a villain, a masculine murderer and the feminine victim of murder, both innocent and guilty, just as Caleb himself is both an oppressed victim and a wily survivor, a knight and a rebel; one part Parzival and one part escaped felon and master of disguise, at once masculine desirer and feminine desired.[24] Thus, far from being homophobic (Sedgwick 116), *Caleb Williams* presents homoerotic love as both the logical outcome to homosocial patriarchy (Sedgwick 1) and as its doomed, desired nonopposite. At the same time, the novel points to the indescribability of this relationship within the constraints of patriarchal, homophobic writing—at once "beg[ging] us to utter the word *homosexual*" and "at the same time . . . frustrat[ing] our desire to do so" (Bredbeck xii). In marked contrast with *The*

Robbers, where the absence of any real affection between men constitutes the tragedy, it is rather the authentic presence of an intermasculine love, which can never find adequate expression (in life or on paper) and which destroys itself in its very literary articulation, that makes up the compelling, poignant calamity of *Caleb Williams*—a story that textualizes itself into that very contemporary transgression known as sex crime.

Through the figure of the sexually deviant writer/criminal, Godwin revises the linkage between art and crime made by Diderot's would-be genius Rameau. In contrast to the works reviewed thus far—where criminality presents itself as at least potentially artistic (as the self-consciously theatrical performances of Millwood, des Grieux, Jonathan Wild, Franz Moor, and Juliette clearly suggest)—it is art that now emerges as being distinctly, necessarily illicit in character.[25] Seen from this perspective, the discovery of Godwin's outlaw writer looks forward to that of his descendant, author/thief Jean Genet. One hundred fifty years later, the criminal creator of *The Thief's Journal* will confront the same problem encountered in *Caleb Williams*: the writing of unauthorized desire necessarily becomes a "crime," and yet it may never be transgressive enough to surmount the tyranny of form. The conclusion to this study will suggest that, for Genet as for Godwin, not just literary form, but literature itself—the entire patriarchal homophobic/homosocial Western tradition—operates as an implicitly tyrannical force, exerting its influence and exacting its price from any reader/writer/desirer who would resist it.[26]

Michael Kohlhaas operates on the basis of the same formal contradiction employed by Godwin—but with very different results.[27] Unlike Caleb's problematic depiction of Falkland, there is no apparent contradiction between romance and defense modes here because both narrative versions see Kohlhaas in much the same light: as a heroic character whose personal failure conceals a true triumph over his antagonists. Thus, from the outset, the romance is actively enlisted in exonerating the protagonist of any wrongdoing.

Having announced the prodigious nature of the title figure in a manner reminiscent of fairy tale, Kleist's narrator organizes the plot according to the usual romance pattern; he presents a series of adventures that advance toward the fulfillment of a quest. So that he may present his case before the Kurfürst and thereby obtain justice, Michael must overcome an astonishing array of obstacles, each of which is recounted quickly yet forcefully in dramatic scenes that condense the courtly romance's episodic progression toward its goal (Bahktin 151). And we should note that, seen within the romance context, Michael does carry out his mission; he eventually succeeds in presenting his case, wins it, and subsequently retrieves his horses in their original good condition.

Other romance motifs present themselves in Kleist's narrative. Michael confronts the discourteous knight (again, this is a variation on the brutish Green Knight) who will not let him pass through his territory without a struggle; he, in return, assails and destroys the knight's castle. The standard encounter with a wise man who will educate the hero and thereby facilitate his quest (Frye 195) is also reproduced here in the guise of Michael's meeting with Martin Luther. Equally noteworthy is the presence of the supernatural. Kohlhaas defeats his ultimate enemy[28] — the Kurfürst of Saxony, who has protected Wenzel von Tronka [in chivalric terms, von Tronka's liege lord] — with the help of magical "text."[29] A mysterious gypsy fortune-teller predicts the demise of the Elector's dynasty and passes the written information to Kohlhaas, who swallows the piece of paper at the block. With this devoured literary talisman, the spirit of the executed Kohlhaas triumphs eerily over the men who conspired against him, even beyond the grave, for his descendants, the narrator tells us, continue to flourish, while those of the Elector of Saxony presumably die out.[30] And as if in recognition of Kohlhaas' nobility, the Elector of Brandenburg elevates Kohlhaas' sons to knighthood.

This understanding of *Michael Kohlhaas* as a chivalric hero is seemingly borne out by the second narrative strand of the novella — the revisionist history — which yields an analogous reading, symbolically, if not logically. Like Caleb, Kleist's narrator also makes a claim for testimonial reliability by admitting to his protagonist's failings, but at the same time, his repeated emphasis on the hero's righteousness diminishes Michael's criminality and makes him into an exemplary, if fallible, individual. Although the task of proving Michael's innocence should present a greater challenge than did Caleb's, the narrator convincingly argues that the protagonist's illegal acts were committed under extreme duress and that these dire circumstances excuse and justify otherwise reprehensible actions.

This revisionist agenda is apparent from the very beginning. Although Kohlhaas is a victim of a humiliating injustice, his many attempts to redress this wrong—unlike those of Karl von Moor—are at first, not only legal, but measured and carefully considered (Fink 77; Kuhns 77). The narrator insists that the terms of his grievance are reasonable, and a detailed legal explanation is given of the reasons why the verdict should, under all circumstances, favor the plaintiff:

> With the aid of a lawyer with whom he was acquainted, he drew up a statement in which he gave a detailed description of the outrage committed against him and his groom Herse by Junker Wenzel von Tronka. He demanded punishment of the Junker in accordance with the law, the restoration of the horses in their former condition, and compensation for what both he and his groom had suffered. The evidence in the case was clear. The fact that the horses had been retained unlawfully threw a decisive light on everything else, and even if it were assumed that the horses had only chanced to fall ill, the horse-dealer's demand that they should be returned to him in a healthy state would still stand [*würde . . . noch gerecht gewesen sein*]. (127)

Even when the complaint is dismissed due to the pressure which Tronka's relatives exert on the Dresden court, Kohlhaas' responses remain restrained and fair-minded. After two more unsuccessful attempts to obtain legal redress (an appeal through the Stadthauptmann, Heinrich von Geusau, to the Kurfürst of Brandenburg, and one through his wife to the Landesherr himself, in which she is fatally wounded by the lord's guards), the frustrated horse dealer takes the matter into his own hands. Even at this point, he offers the Junker one more chance to redeem himself. When this measure also fails, the hero resorts to vigilantism, but the narrator shows Michael Kohlhaas comporting himself in ways that belie the apparent brutality of his activities, as his description of the invasion of Tronka castle makes clear: "It was as though the avenging angel of heaven had descended on the place. . . . Kohlhaas entered the hall, seized Junker Hans von Tronka, as he came towards him, by the jerkin and hurled him into a corner, dashing his brains out against the stones. As his men overpowered and dispersed the other noblemen, who had drawn their swords, he demanded to know where Junker Wenzel von Tronka was" (139). Endowing the protagonist's actions with an angelic aura, the narrator distracts us from the more disturbing details of the raid (Herse the groom kills the warden and steward, as well as their families, and throws their corpses out the window) and then swiftly changes the subject to an account of Kohlhaas' writ "in which he called upon the country to withhold all aid and comfort from Junker Wenzel von Tronka, against whom he was engaged in a just war; instead he required every inhabitant, not excepting his relatives and friends, to surrender the Junker to Kohlhaas on pain of death and the certain destruction by fire of whatever they possessed" (140–41).

Like Caleb, Michael Kohlhaas also employs the power of the written word to bring his enemy's criminality to the attention of a world that has thus far only condemned *him*. But Kohlhaas' document produces an even more dramatic effect than Caleb's. Through textuality the former transforms his criminal words into law—a transformation which endows him with the authority to call for the assistance of the public, not as witnesses to the justness of his claim, but as coenforcers of his legal ordinance. The "Kohlhaas Mandate" thus reverses the roles that the horse trader and the Junker have been playing (for now it is Tronka who is the lawbreaker, and Michael who is the law enforcer) and simultaneously insists that the population ratify this decree through personal action. With this reversal, the bourgeois Michael Kohlhaas emerges as a political martyr of a corrupt, unjust German society, and the rest of the novella seemingly advocates the kind of civil disobedience covertly advanced in *The Robbers*—a reading shored up by the dramatic depiction of two mass protests provoked (unwittingly) by Kohlhaas against the powers that be.[31]

In sum, the Kleistian narrator's juxtaposition of two narrative modes within a single frame appears to function very differently than it does for Caleb Williams. Rather than laying bare the problematics of the accused's self-defense, here the romance forms a vital component of the revisionist historian's vindication of a maligned figure from the past. It is particularly thanks to its romance dimension that the history successfully rewrites Michael Kohlhaas' character—enabling him to be seen as a synthesis of chivalric and middle-class ethics. Kleist's hero is both knight and revolutionary, criminal and ideal citizen, tragic sacrifice and triumphant rebel, whom we should exonerate on both moral and political grounds. Consequently, the protagonist's personal failure and demise should be regarded as the stuff of a larger moral and political victory that has empowered our actual present (Wexelblatt 126). And it is no coincidence that the written word should play such a major part in this process; Kleist's novella acquires by analogy the magically subversive, truthful power of the magic capsule and implies literature's ability to both predict that liberated future and help that future to come to pass.

Or does it? If, as Kleist's narrator implies, Kohlhaas is both a good man and an innocent victim, who is to blame for his sufferings? On closer inspection of Kleist's novella, this question proves difficult to answer. Although the narrator establishes Wenzel von Tronka as Michael's nemesis, he simultaneously suggests that Michael is the victim, not just of one person, or even of one class, but of a complex network of power relations in which he and everyone else are enmeshed and from which none can escape.

Behind the fictional realities presented in *Michael Kohlhaas* by both the romance and the defense/revisionist history, lies a third narrative tendency very different from either of these. This strand threads its way through the narrative in the many, seemingly irrelevant, digressive descriptions in the novella of minute power struggles that play themselves out between individuals. These struggles take place on such a tiny scale and are so banal that it is tempting to disregard them, but the narrator's increasing emphasis on these insignificant maneuvers reveals the extent to which they dominate the dynamics and determine the outcome of human interaction within the tale. This third strand is present, albeit subtly, from the beginning of the novella. The narrator goes into great detail in the account of the initial encounter between Kohlhaas and the Junker because the credibility of Kleist's defense of Kohlhaas obviously depends on establishing his clear victimization by the Junker. But the very meticulousness of the account of this crucial scene renders the key point maddeningly unclear, for while it is obvious that Kohlhaas has been victimized, it is virtually impossible to say by whom.

Under normal circumstances, one would hold Tronka, as master of his household, solely responsible for what happens there, but the narrator forestalls such a straightforward judgment by implying that it is in fact the servants, the warden and the steward—apparently jockeying for position in their master's favor—who actually devise the plan to take the horses away from Kohlhaas: "The warden, looking at the Junker, said that Kohlhaas would at least have to leave something behind as surety that he would get the permit. The Junker stopped again in the castle gateway. . . . The steward muttered into his beard. 'Of course,' said the warden, 'that is the most practical solution'" (117–18). Although the Junker's presence during this conversation suggests his tacit approval of the proceedings (he stands listening to his servants' discussion), he does not directly order his inferiors to undertake any specific action; neither does he seem at all in control of the situation but rather looks to his servants for an appropriate reaction to Kohlhaas, so that he might not lose face in front of any of them. Similarly, the warden and the steward search for a sign from their master as to what they should do; their actions are not part of a premeditated plot against Kohlhaas; rather they are engaging in a competitive improvisation designed to please the master, who, as they have already noticed, has admired Kohlhaas' horses.

Who then is guilty of perpetrating the first injustice on Kohlhaas? Given the information that the narrator provides us, this is uncertain. The question is further complicated by what follows. The decision, made at Tronka castle during Kohlhaas' absence, to work the horses in the fields and thereby ruin them, represents the true source of Kohlhaas' complaint against the Junker, but Tronka says nothing at the time of Kohlhaas' return to establish his involvement in this act and later swears to his cousins that he had nothing to do with this decision; the Junker claims that it was a malicious act on the part of the warden and the steward—a charge that might be true, given the earlier portrayal of the two men, although they are both conveniently dead and cannot give an alternative version of the events.

A similarly ambiguous pattern is present in the report of Elizabeth's disastrous attempt to deliver Kohlhaas' petition to the Elector of Brandenburg. Again, the individual's encounter with an authority/superior is distorted by the intervention of official underlings who are themselves engaged in an ambiguous power relation with the authority figure in question. Once more, the very detail of the narrator's description reveals the ambiguity of these people's dealings with one another: "It seemed that she had thrust herself forward too boldly towards the Elector, and through no fault of his, a rough and over-zealous member of his bodyguard had struck her a blow on the chest with the shaft of his lance" (136). As in the case of Kohlhaas himself, Elizabeth is clearly the innocent party here, but the question of blame is unsolvable. As in the scene with the Junker, the presence of the authority figure—this time, the Kurfürst— suggests his tacit approval of the guard's actions, but he did not specifically order the guard to strike the woman, and therefore he cannot be held personally responsible. Like the Junker's servants, the guard was apparently only adhering to an unwritten code of behavior, which he believes is expected from him by his superior—a code that the superior neither overtly affirms (by giving the order) nor denies (by punishing the guard).

From these scenes it is apparent that, contrary to first impressions, the narrative does not teach a revolutionary political lesson after all. *Michael Kohlhaas* does indeed invoke the Promethean image of a courageous individual whose rebellion against an unjust power is both doomed and valid. But at the same time, the narrative surreptitiously supersedes this thesis with a far more disturbing proof. Kleist's novella covertly demonstrates that the individual's struggle for personal justice is of necessity already intertwined with other people and their power relations to such a degree that it is virtually impossible for one person to deal uniquely with another; instead, each relationship between two individuals is already circumscribed, qualified, and colored by other preexisting rapports, which are themselves confused by each other, and so on.

In such a sociopolitical environment, the protagonist's self-imposed task—the procurement of justice through the restitution of goods—must prove impossible. Kohlhaas cannot obtain justice, regardless of the possibility that what he wants may or may not be unreasonable, but because he lives in a world where a specific person can never be held personally responsible for a particular action; as Luther unwittingly reveals during his interview with Kohlhaas, guilt and innocence are irrelevant terms that human beings can never profitably use: "Who but God can call him to account for appointing such servants?" (153).

Luther is correct to reject guilt and innocence as viable concepts in human relations but not for the religious reasons he gives. It is practically—not morally or metaphysically—impossible to assign blame or responsibility to any one person in a society that functions as bureaucratically as this one does, because no one ever decides or takes an action alone but always in concert with and/or in reaction to the machinations of others. Kohlhaas' mistake, as Luther observes, lies in his "incomprehensible" unwillingness to play by the rules of his society; it would have served Kohlhaas' interests far better to have simply taken the horses back and restored them himself to their previous condition (154)—thereby protecting his own position in the network of power.

In support of this contention, Kleist's narrative focuses increasingly on the small power struggles between individuals, struggles that yield the arbitrary, sometimes nonsensical, decisions that propel Michael Kohlhaas' fate. It is significant in this context that after the turning point meeting with Luther, Kohlhaas ceases to be the focal point of the action, and the narrator's attention shifts almost entirely to the wranglings between the various representatives involved in his case. In the rest of the novella, Kohlhaas will be seen only briefly and only the most cursory information can be obtained about his thoughts and feelings. Correspondingly, the characters of the novella also see Kolhaas as marginal and without importance, for he has become a political pawn in a complicated chess game. The Luther interview marks this turning point in the narrative and demonstrates in a shocking way how purely power-oriented relations between people in this world are. It is ironically fitting that this demonstration should emerge from Kohlhaas' fictional encounter with a "real" revolutionary hero—a man who changed the face of the world through his adherence to a new religion, which, as its name signifies (Protestant), is a religion of dissent and rebellion. But what surfaces from this conversation is neither the religious fervor of this famous reformer nor the revolutionary nature of his politics, but rather the dubiousness of his motivations for involving himself in the affair at all.

Although he may in fact sympathize with the now-criminal Michael Kohlhaas, Luther also clearly uses him to further his own quest for power. This is evident in the minister's use of a proclamation to win Kohlhaas' attention (shrewdly placed, we are told, in every town *and village* in the electorate)—a move that contributes both to his fame and virtuous public image. Is he really so surprised when Kohlhaas, a good Protestant, appears on his doorstep, or does he already see in the Kohlhaas affair a way to promote his own prestige?

It is also clear that during the interview, Luther eventually decides that supporting Kohlhaas is a good idea, but he does so only for his own purposes. He makes no concessions to the horse dealer whatsoever until after having assured himself of the modesty of Kohlhaas' claims (which both surprise and relieve him) and then withholds the last favor (his blessing through Communion) in order to guarantee his continuing influence over the horse dealer. Having done all this, he writes a letter to the Elector of Saxony, which paints another picture entirely of the outlaw: "Public opinion, he noted, was on the man's side in a highly dangerous degree. . . . and since if this present proposal were rejected he would undoubtedly, with malevolent animadversions, make it known to the people, the latter might easily be so far won over that the authority of the state would become powerless against him" (156).

Although he has seen for himself how paltry Kohlhaas' requests are, Luther builds up the horse dealer into a threat against national security. We should also note that nowhere in the letter does this religious leader allude to the religious, ethical, or moral issues at stake in the Kohlhaas case, nor does he appeal to any of those concerns on the part of the Elector. Instead, Luther outlines the enormous political danger that Kohlhaas represents—thereby implicitly denying the rectitude of Kohlhaas' claims and any sympathy he, as a man of God, might have with the case: "He concluded that . . . the situation would best be remedied if Kohlhaas were treated not so much as a rebel in revolt against the crown, but rather as a foreign invading power" (156). By stressing the subversive force that Michael Kohlhaas represents, Luther cleverly augments his own prestige with the Kurfürst by creating the impression that only he knows how to deal with this dangerous criminal.[32]

Throughout his involvement in the affair, Luther plays both ends against the middle; angry and disapproving of Kohlhaas during the interview, he manipulates him into a position very much against his own interest (Kohlhaas agrees merely to demand safe passage to Dresden so that he might present his case); only then does Luther relent and offer his help. Luther subsequently uses this opportunity to both criticize the influential Tronka family and to make political recommendations directly to his sovereign. Thus, on one hand, Luther subverts governmental authority by helping Kohlhaas, while at the same time reinforcing it (with himself as key adviser to the Elector) by portraying Kohlhaas in such a dangerous light that he all but guarantees the horse dealer's eventual undoing by the Saxon authorities. Luther's Machiavellianism is signaled again at the end of the novella; he sends a personal letter to the condemned Kohlhaas and has one of his ministers give him Communion at the scaffold—again ensuring that he is involved in the affair, as a critically distanced (appearing at Kohlhaas' execution would be undignified as well as politically problematic), but all-pervasive moral authority.

The Luther interview marks the end of Michael Kohlhaas' own story, and after his letter to the Elector, the novella's action flies apart into fragmented minivignettes. There is a good reason for this. The revelation that Luther is engrossed in his own quest for political power (one which has, apparently, nothing to do with his religious aspirations and which he uses one of the "faithful" to help him further) stops the narrative in its tracks. Luther is the ostensible moral authority in *Michael Kohlhaas*; he is the first judge to whom the title character appeals and the only judge whose opinion really matters. The overwhelming evidence that Luther cannot transcend self-interest and the obsession with power strongly suggests that no one else in Kleist's world can be expected to behave any better. What more can happen after this point?

It is consequently no surprise that the action disintegrates into description. The discussion between the Elector of Saxony's ministers upon receipt of Luther's letter presents yet another variation on the dynamics of power in the novella. The Kurfürst's advisers reveal that they care nothing at all about the merits of Kohlhaas' case; rather each uses the situation as a way to protect and possibly strengthen his position of power vis-à-vis his sovereign. In this manner, their relationships to each other and to the Kurfürst are identical to those between the steward and the warden vis-à-vis the Junker. But again it is important to note that the power relation operates in two directions; the ostensibly powerful Kurfürst is in fact no more free a man than his so-called inferiors, for he is himself caught in a tangled web of conflicting responsibilities to his advisers (Foucault, *Discipline and Punish* 202). Unwilling to actually wage war on Kohlhaas because of his relationship with the Tronkas (which precludes his treating Kohlhaas as a foreign power), the Kurfürst decides to accept Luther's suggestion of amnesty, only later to override it, when the Tronkas trap Kohlhaas with the letter from Nagelschmidt.

In this manner, the actions that the narrator depicts surrounding the Kohlhaas case cease to have anything to do with protagonist. The novella now scrutinizes struggles for power, which occur on increasingly high levels of governmental and political planes—as the "friendly competition" between the electors of Saxony and Brandenburg makes clear. But the decisions these officials make assume a bureaucratic life of their own and follow their own peculiar procedural logic, regardless of individual desire. This is manifest toward the end of the novella, when the Emperor reveals that even he is unable to call back the case brought by the Imperial Prosecutor against Kohlhaas in the High Court of Brandenburg. The Emperor himself is powerless in the face of his own legal bureaucracy.

Thus, the crucial, yet apparently simple task of assigning guilt in the actions taken against Michael Kohlhaas becomes hopelessly obfuscated as more and more "official" individuals become involved for reasons that are in no way connected to the protagonist. This holds true, not only for such professed enemies of Kohlhaas as the Tronka family and their associates, but even for those who might be considered sympathetic to Kohlhaas' case.[33] Even the so-called good characters are motivated by obscure political interests, as the career of Governor Geusau indicates. The seeming selflessness of his attempt to get Kohlhaas' case heard is belied by his eventual promotion to chancellor and his desires to further the power of Brandenburg (and thereby his own). Seen in this light, the success of the trial in Dresden does far more for Geusau than it does for Kohlhaas, as their final positions at the end of the story dramatically imply— with Geusau on horseback beside the Elector of Brandenburg and Kohlhaas on his knees at the block.

Further, the narrator emphasizes the ubiquitousness of such officialdom by consistently identifying characters only according to their official title. This device makes it all but impossible to keep track of the individual characters and stresses the importance of the function over the identity of the person filling that capacity. The end result is telling. Through this strategy of naming, the narrator stresses both the interchangeability of persons and the key importance of those functional titles within a complex hierarchy.

Thus, rather than asking readers to measure the alleged criminal's guilt against that of another person whose guilt itself proves problematic (*Caleb Williams*), Kleist's narrator demands that we gauge Michael's innocence against a whole network of personal relations that become so intertwined that it becomes virtually impossible to assess and place blame. While Kleist's narrator never denies Kohlhaas' claim to innocence, his narrative convincingly demonstrates that this question is, in the reality of things, totally irrelevant. The novella gradually trivializes its own defense of Michael Kohlhaas' innocence by both expanding the number of potentially guilty parties to include almost everyone with whom Kohlhaas deals and suggesting that they too are engaged in and are victimized by power struggles they cannot possibly escape. Therein lies the significance of the Kurfürst subplot; even the two electors' attempt to take a vacation from politics by making fun of the fortune-teller turns itself into a competition for power that gradually and dramatically brings one of them down.

All that matters, as is seen repeatedly in the novella, is the ability to maneuver effectively within this network of power relations—to safeguard and possibly enhance one's role, without going too far or risking too much. It is Michael Kohlhaas' refusal to do just this that dooms him. His insistence on justice on his terms, (i.e., the restitution of his goods in their proper condition) and his refusal to barter the mysterious capsule for his life condemn him. In this context, the judgment rendered by the state is significant. Kohlhaas is sentenced to death for "breaking the peace of the Empire"; he dies, not because he has murdered or robbed, but because he has disrupted the normal order of things.

Kohlhaas' "disruption" is a crime because he exists in what Foucault has called a "disciplinary society"—a regime that comprises a series of mechanisms that organize, hierarchize, and normalize human behavior in order to ensure docility. This explains why Kleist's narrator emphasizes the importance of the hierarchy of titles, functions, and law courts; these categories comprise the only sociopolitical values that count in the world depicted here. Further, in such a society, power becomes a disembodied principle that produces relationships of power between individuals without, however, investing anyone with power (Foucault, *Discipline and Punish* 202–3)—which accounts for the curious fact that although practically everyone in the novella is interested in power, no one actually seems to possess any.[34] And within such a system, crime itself takes on a different identity: "What is specific to the disciplinary penalty is nonobservance, that which does not measure up to the rule, that departs from it. The whole indefinite domain of the noncomforming is punishable" (*Discipline and Punish* 178–79). Thus, Kohlhaas' crime is, finally, nothing more or less than the refusal to conform.

Furthermore, texts play a particularly important role in this technique of social control, for narrative itself is now enlisted in order to more effectively perform the meticulous scrutiny of individuals that discipline demands. Deployed by the Panoptic machine, narrative becomes a mode of social regulation, which by documenting personal histories, convicts the offender the moment he veers from the norm: "Slow formation is shown in a biographical investigation. The introduction of the 'biographical' is important in the history of penalty. Because it establishes the 'criminal' as existing before the crime and even outside it . . . it marks the author of the offense with a criminality all the more formidable and demands penitentiary measures that are all the more strict" (*Discipline and Punish* 252). Biography now becomes a technique of power that reifies all citizens into "cases" and records their lives, not in order to glorify, but in order to manipulate and dominate them all the more efficiently (*Discipline and Punish* 191–92). What has Kleist's novella been, if not just such a disciplinary case study?

Caleb becomes so entranced by the romance that he is forced to imitate it both in the story of his oppressor and in his own. Likewise, the narrator of Michael Kohlhaas' history gradually becomes so enthralled by the minute reportage of discipline that the hero of the novella is, in the last analysis, not a man at all, but the surveillance machine whose permutations not only oppress, but also shape, and determine the lives—not just of the victim—but everyone else in it, from the bottom up. The very movement of the novella away from its protagonist and toward the procedures around him testifies to the weird irresistibility of the minute techniques by which disciplinary power asserts itself, and this analysis accounts for the work's strange sense of stasis.

One might well argue that the novella gradually ceases to be a story at all and becomes instead a series of technical descriptions—a taxonomy of a structure of power, which organizes everything according to its own particular shape.

But while Kleist's narrator, like Caleb, also succumbs to the tyranny of form, the form that overcomes him does not belong to a classically literary genre but rather to a new kind of writing which is an integral instrument of power in the society he depicts.[35] Seen from this perspective, the Kleistian narrator's meticulous reportage not only reflects, but also extends and perpetuates the oppressive mechanisms which he, in telling the story of Michael Kohlhaas, has ostensibly sought to resist and escape. The very penning of the tale perpetuates the injustice perpetrated against Michael Kohlhaas in the first place—that of casting him outside the protection of the state, as Michael himself tells Luther (152), for certainly Kleist's narrative marginalizes the character who should be at its core. Yet at the same time, the novella ironically corrects the hero's statement about himself; Kohlhaas has not in fact been situated outside the state, rather he is trapped *inside*, and like everyone else, he can never break loose. For Michael Kohlhaas, even more than for Caleb Williams, the visible world is a penitentiary (Ellis 159), which continually surveys and surely punishes.

In this way, Kleist gives us, not a retrospective critique and present paean to political progress, but a chilling picture of the mechanisms of the modern state, the presence of which his own text furnishes the most convincing proof.[36] In Kleist, the outlook for literary writing is even bleaker than it is in Godwin, because here, transgressive writing is only a possibility that can never be realized, even partially. The would-be transgressive writer is doomed from the start to reinscribe the power structure which he tries to rebel against, and thereby he extends discipline's domination. Thus, in *Michael Kohlhaas*, criminality ceases to present the great "danger" that it provided in earlier eighteenth-century literature; rather it is the threat to the individual issued by the social *machine infernale*, which is the fearful subject of fascination here and which will obsess all writers and readers of criminal literature thereafter.

With Godwin and Kleist, we reach the culmination of Enlightenment literature's critical and creative use of the criminal protagonist as an occasion for both ethical and aesthetic self-reflection. For Lillo, Prévost, Fielding, Schiller, and even Sade the criminal character provides a way to rethink society and to open new creative formal possibilities for literature; through the criminal, all envision either implicitly or explicitly (and even if briefly) a different kind of world—a better, more honest, more just one. The lawbreaker is seen, at least potentially, as attractive, as a subversive social force who at the same time may uphold those values that a democratic society holds most dear, while he or she challenges us overtly or covertly to rethink the demarcations of masculine and feminine. In corresponding fashion, these authors are able to widen the scope of heretofore narrow genres: the bourgeois tragedy envisions values which are at once antibourgeois, antimercantilist, and profemale; the confessional novel of sentiment simultaneously celebrates the pleasure of lawbreaking and reveals the masculinist tyranny of the aristocratic class; the prose satire moves beyond mock-heroic and the attack on vice in society and points to the limitations of its own narrator; the Sturm und Drang *Trauerspiel* becomes a study in male patterns of aggression, and the libertine novel, an ethically engaged *mise en question* of the gendered categories and bases on which we make moral pronouncements.

For Godwin and Kleist, the situation shifts; like Schiller and Sade, they focus on the predicament of a falsely accused criminal protagonist, but the lack of difference between innocence and guilt exercises even more drastic effects on their enterprises. Both narratives uncover the means by which they are easily undermined by mechanisms of power that invade from within and without their own literary tradition, subjecting them to discursive procedures that neutralize the resistance to power that engendered them in the first place. Here the criminal text's "failure" is not, in and of itself, liberating, for Caleb and the Kleistian narrator break generic laws only to have other formal laws imposed upon them. Consequently, these authors do not invite us to read beyond but rather to read/write *against* their works' "failures" as well as the tradition from whence they come.

Seen from this perspective, the hermeneutic challenge issued by *Caleb Williams* and *Michael Kohlhaas* brings us to the end of an era even as it heralds a new, important understanding of the reader, not just as an interpreter, but as a potential writer as well. The very insistence in *Caleb Williams* and *Michael Kohlhaas* on intertextuality summons us, not only as receivers, but as creative transmitters of Western tradition, and they remind us that the war against the tyranny of form is a struggle in which we ourselves are inevitably implicated and from which no writing is exempt. And with this implication, Godwin and Kleist lay the problematic, modern ground for a far more complicated relationship between reader and author—as common textual producers in an intricate network of signs.

Equally important, the radical problematization of criminal narrative in Godwin and Kleist carries with it a rethinking, not just of genre, but of literary aesthetics and the end that literature should aim to achieve. *Caleb Williams* and *Michael Kohlhaas* transport us far beyond the classical tenets of *dulce et utile*, to a frontier where artistic failure and artistic success become, in fact, one and the same thing. As I have tried to show, the complexity with which Godwin and Kleist demonstrate the aporias in which they are caught and the fact that they allow us to read/write these aporias from so many different points of view produce an experience which is most emphatically not a failed one. Thus, Godwin and Kleist exploit their own texts' insufficiency in order to demonstrate that literary art must actively court and embrace "failure," for if writing is by nature tyrannical, then literature can only free itself and succeed by failing. Ergo, it is *through the failure of the written word* that the literary works of Godwin and Kleist appeal to us so completely and achieve no end other than the creation of a dangerous adventure through which we repeatedly "pass . . . like a test" (Gadamer, *Truth and Method* 62): "What we call emphatically an experience thus means something unforgettable and irreplaceable that is inexhaustible in terms of the understanding and determination of its meaning" (60).

Certainly, the formal impasses that *Caleb Williams* and *Michael Kohlhaas* dramatize (and by dramatizing, transcend) anticipate Friedrich Schlegel's advocacy of romantic "fragmentariness" (182), and the resolutely anticlassical, contorted formal permutations that romanticism employs in an ongoing attempt to liberate literary expression from the tyranny of form. But more important is their precocious incarnation of that "tragic" attempt to achieve "the zero level" of writing, which Roland Barthes regards as the determining feature of all modern literature since romanticism: "Thus is born a tragic predicament peculiar to Literature.... Each one [act of writing] is an attempt to find a solution to this Orphean problematics of modern Form.... Whenever the [modern] writer assembles a network of words *it is the existence of Literature itself which is called into question*" (*Writing Degree Zero* 62; my emphasis). Through their self-conscious indictment of writing, *Caleb Williams* and *Michael Kohlhaas* already display the eternally self-revising concerns which we recognize almost two centuries later as typical of avant-garde art.

6

Conclusion

Resistance, Metaphysics, and the Aesthetics of Failure in Modern Criminal Literature

The ensuing literary movements of the nineteenth and twentieth centuries clearly bear the legacy of the eighteenth century's artistic experiments with criminality in general, and they owe a particular debt to Godwin and Kleist. Three points bear stressing here. First, the modern criminal protagonist often retains the artistry and creative genius that Rameau's nephew ascribed to him two hundred years earlier. Honoré de Balzac's outlaw genius Vautrin, the unstoppable Fantômas of French popular fiction, Alessandro Manzoni's grandiose archvillain L'Innominato, and the *Wunderkind* perfumer of Patrick Süskind's 1987 novel *Perfume* (set, not coincidentally, in eighteenth-century France) represent only a few examples of the degree to which modern visions of the criminal are still very much allied to the questions of aesthetics raised by Diderot and to the glamorous aura that criminality acquires in the texts discussed in this study.

Second, it is also important to recognize that, after Godwin and Kleist, literary representations of the criminal never look quite the same again. Like Caleb Williams and Michael Kohlhaas, the criminal from here on will be seen predominantly as the lonely individual striking out at a monstrous system, against which he is no match; his crimes usually fade into the back-

154

ground and his actual guilt or innocence is far less relevant than is his often-doomed struggle against something more huge and more insidious than he could ever be. He is, regardless of his actions, an underdog with whom readers can all sympathize, whatever his guise: the murderer-seducer of *Faust*, the criminal saints of Fyodor Dostoevsky, the vital, doomed McMurphy of Ken Kesey's *One Flew Over the Cuckoo's Nest*, and the outlaw "console cowboys" of William Gibson's cyberpunk fictions.

A third important point: the landscape/architecture against which the modern criminal's story unfolds changes radically as well. In the texts studied here, the scenes gradually shift away from the urban center as modern Babylon (London and Paris in *The London Merchant*, *Manon Lescaut*, and *Jonathan Wild*) toward a more varied, provincial geography that, although it may include the capital city, does not focus uniquely upon it; this continues to be true for criminal literature of the nineteenth and twentieth centuries. This spatial shift in fictional representations of the criminal toward wide, open spaces is an important one; this move testifies once again to the usefulness of the Foucaultian model of *discipline* — an ever-widening, self-decentralizing network of power, which no longer needs the population concentration of the city to effect its technology.

This process of geographical decentralization is in turn integrally connected to an another spatial phenomenon — namely, the fact that the carceral becomes, increasingly, the focal point for fictional representations of crime. The prison plays an obvious role in *Caleb Williams*, while the penal system as a whole informs the dynamics of *Michael Kohlhaas*. Similarly, the threat of the carceral dominates modern criminal fiction; either the action takes place in a prison as books ranging from *The Count of Monte Cristo* to *The Kiss of the Spiderwoman* testify and/or the imminent possibility of incarceration motivates the actions of the main characters from such divergent creations as *Les Misérables*, *Crime and Punishment*, and *The Lost Honor of Katharina Blum*.[1]

But where do these narratives take us and what kind of ethical claim do they make? In his important study of the nineteenth-century novel, D. A. Miller convincingly argues that the *police*—his catchword for the Foucaultian network of discipline *in toto* (viii)—is subtly reinforced through the narrative formulas of most realistic fiction.[2] Specifically, in his analysis of *David Copperfield*, Miller notices that the title character only escapes the penitentiary and its threat by incorporating within himself the mechanisms of social control (220).

This paradoxical pattern, whereby the deviant or potentially deviant protagonist frees himself (and more rarely, herself) precisely by becoming less free—that is to say, by resigning himself to and embracing within himself the power structure—is an extremely powerful one in literature of the nineteenth and twentieth centuries.[3] We can see that this formula is already employed in the later selections considered here; the sudden changes of heart undergone by Juliette, Karl Moor, Caleb and Falkland, and Michael Kohlhaas point in the direction of Miller's pattern, although these transfigurations are problematized to such a radical degree that it is ultimately impossible to regard them as such. But certainly this pattern of redemption/social internalization all but entirely dominates the criminal's story in the nineteenth-century novel: despite their enormous differences, such characters as Julien Sorel, Jean Valjean, Tess of the D'Urbervilles, and Raskolnikov are all "transfigured" by a recognition of their criminal deeds as such, and their transfigurations lead them to submit to the authority of social "justice" without a murmur. But what does this spiritual metamorphosis signify, if not an internalization of the very social mechanisms that have brought them to this pass? Seen from this point of view, many of the most revered canonical texts of the nineteenth century use the criminal, ostensibly, to criticize society, but that criticism is itself undermined and neutralized by the story's plot and form that—to borrow D. A. Miller's argument—exert such a strong disciplinary force that they reify rather than subvert the tyranny of form, which both Godwin and Kleist so energetically lay bare and in so doing, resist.

This is, for example, the insidious mechanism at work in Victor Hugo's "masterpiece," *Les Misérables*. At first glance, this book seems to glorify criminality through the depiction of an impressive pantheon of outlaw characters, presided over by that ultimate romantic overreacher—Napoleon. Moreover, the ostensible hero, Jean Valjean appears to be a clear descendant of the criminal protagonist as he is portrayed by the authors studied here. A virtuous and virginal man of feeling (Barnwell), Jean Valjean is also a hardened criminal (Jonathan Wild, Coeur du Fer), a rebel against society (Karl Moor), a loving father (Michael Kohlhaas), and a wily ex-con on the lam from a relentless police that knows no end to the pursuit (Caleb Williams). And Hugo also employs the problematic dichotomy of true and false criminality, which has been at work since Schiller—carefully distinguishing Jean Valjean from such real criminal professionals as Thénardier and his gang.

Yet the narrative sweep of *Les Misérables* is ultimately misleading; far from testifying (as its size might indicate) to a romantic, chaotic, artistic freedom, the book ultimately suggests that the protagonist's triumph over the police is dubious, to say the least. How free is Jean Valjean, if he must spend his entire life hiding from Javert? How free is anyone who, in the very attempt of avoiding a prison sentence, moves from one self-created prison to another? Nowhere is the reality (and perpetuity) of Valjean's imprisonment more clear than in the final sections of the book: "The tunnel ended in a bottleneck, logical enough in a prison but not in a sewer. . . . But when he reached it, Valjean stopped short. It was an outlet, but it offered no way out" (1090). The famous sewer scene (and the last sentence in particular) allegorizes Jean Valjean's entire story, which has been characterized by just such a series of closed escape hatches; like the sewer bottleneck, the alternate lives which he has tried to live as M. Madeleine, Blanc, and Fauchlevent also prove to be outlets which offer no way out, for Valjean always retains his true identity as a "convict" (1147). Admittedly, his false escape from the tunnel into the custody of Javert supposedly leads to his true escape from his pursuer—a capture that ironically precipitates the suicide of the captor. But is this escape any more authentic than the others? To the contrary, it becomes obvious that Hugo's hero can never be free, and worse, Hugo suggests that he *should* never be free. Both Jean Valjean and his horrified son-in-law conclude that the protagonist must sacrifice his one intimate

relationship—that with his adopted daughter Cosette—and re-
tire once again into a self-imposed carceral obscurity.[4] In this
manner, Jean Valjean represents a perfect exemplification of D.
A. Miller's theory of disciplinary internalization; Hugo's protagonist proves to be his own most effective jailer.

Far more flagrantly than *Michael Kohlhaas*, Hugo's magnum
opus exerts the power of discursive discipline at its most encom-
passing. Not only do all eventually succumb to discipline within
the text (including Javert, whose suicide in this context looks less
like a defeat than an affirmation of the powers that be), but more
importantly, the book itself does so, without any apparent
awareness of the irony of its own narrative proceedings.[5] Thus,
Les Misérables gives us a criminal hero of epic proportions, but
the epic space that holds him (in both literal and penal senses of
the word) is a place where all rebellions fail and where even the
most socially deviant can be "normalized" by the diminutive
power of realistic portraiture.[6]

This exercise of diminution is practiced on everyone in *Les
Misérables*, living and dead.[7] But this operation is performed
with particular violence on the female characters, and it is in
Hugo that we see a male author's nullification of physical
feminine presence (chap. 4) at its most skillful. Having served
her function as a paternalizing figure, Cosette grows up into a
silent, beautiful cipher, while Hugo's potential criminal heroine,
the androgynous, desiring Éponine, fares even worse.[8] The
author's simultaneously voyeuristic and dismissive glance at the
naked bosom of the recently expired *gamine* unites the phallic
and the disciplinary into the simultaneously dismissive and
penetrating gaze of policeman Javert:

> The dead bodies dragged off the barricade formed a dreadful heap a
> few paces away, and among them was an ashen face, a pierced heart
> and the breast of a half-naked woman—Éponine.
>   Javert glanced sidelong at the dead body and murmured in a
> voice of profound calm: "I think I know that girl." (1039)

Hugo's approach to the criminal differs considerably from
that of Balzac, perhaps the most important innovator of literary

criminality in the nineteenth century. In contrast to the ostensibly heterosexual (but, in truth, nonsexual) Valjean, the homosexual Vautrin (Hunt 91) fulfills Rameau's dream of the sublime
criminal artist (Balzac 125), recapitulates the sexual ambiguity
of Jonathan Wild, Franz Moor, and Falkland (we are told emphatically that he does not like women), and presents a sublime
appearance which fascinates both women and men.[9] And
Vautrin plays an important role in *Old Goriot*—the novel of *The
Human Comedy* in which he makes his splashiest appearance.
Here the self-styled "pupil of Rousseau" (Balzac 223) hovers on
the margins of what is apparently a bildungsroman, serving as
the evil genius who both repels and attracts Eugène Rastignac,
Balzac's variation on the man of sensibility. Interestingly, in
opposition to the rest of Madame Vauquer's residents, Balzac
leaves Vautrin a mystery, thereby making him into the one
forceful exception to the otherwise flawless omniscience of the
narrative (Denommé 314–15). Yet, paradoxically, he is the only
individual in the world of Balzac's novel to offer a meaningful
course of action, as Rastignac himself recognizes near the end of
the book: "He [Rastignac] saw the world as an ocean of mud into
which a man plunged up to the neck, if he dipped a foot in it.
'Worldly crimes are mean and ignoble!' he said to himself,
'Vautrin was greater than this. He had seen society in three great
aspects: Obedience, Struggle, and Revolt; or in other words, the
Family, the World, and Vautrin" (271).
    It is significant that Vautrin is the only person mentioned in
this otherwise impersonal triad of social realms. With these remarks, Balzac's youthful hero does something very odd; he makes
it clear that the true hero of the piece is not himself but rather the
very man who was arrested by the police a few pages earlier.[10] It is
Vautrin who emerges as Rastignac's ideal man because he has
demonstrated the courage to choose revolt both against the family
and the world—a choice that Rastignac admires in this passage,
but that he cannot bring himself to make, as the novel's sardonic
closing lines make clear (304). Thus, *Old Goriot* suggests that
Vautrin's essential indescribability is in fact an essential indicator of
his exemplary nature; like his distant progenitrix, Manon, he
resists qualification *by the narrative* just as he resists qualification by

society *within the narrative*, and he therefore escapes the realist confines of Balzac's fictional project.[11]

The fact that Vautrin proves to be the true hero is profoundly ironic on two levels; first, this changeover exposes Rastignac's moral weakness and reveals the formulaic emptiness of the so-called novel of education. More importantly, the fact that the most virile man in *Old Goriot* is a pederast indicates the degree to which Balzac radicalizes the problem of the homosocial—and the implicit critique of patriarchy—signaled by Lillo and explored with increasing virulence till Godwin.[12] Taking up Godwin's linkage of the outlaw, the artist, and the homosexual, Balzac goes one step further. Through Vautrin, Balzac further refines an understanding of the heroic as necessarily both politically subversive and sexually deviant[13] (as well as aesthetically adept), as he ironically rewrites the dynamics of the bildungsroman into a perverse human comedy that has recognizably tragic overtones.

However, Vautrin is something of an exception, and even he is rehabilitated in a later Balzac novel.[14] For the most part, the power of the redemption/internalization formula persists also in twentieth-century literature. Despite its expressionist fireworks, *Berlin Alexanderplatz* forces its antihero to reform and even *L'Étranger*'s existential protagonist undergoes a spiritual—albeit existential—transfiguration which "frees" him to welcome his capital punishment. An even more extreme version of this scenario manifests itself in the legions of reformed criminals who (like Vautrin, Arsène Lupin of the popular French series by the same name, and Dim in *A Clockwork Orange*) eventually go so far as to *become* the police—thereby both retaining their deviant, criminal glamour and at the same time, shoring up the moral correctness of the social structure that has punished them. This identity between apparently opposing, gendered social forces is pointed up more than once in the plays of Bertolt Brecht—no more effectively than in the *The Good Person of Szechuan* where the "upstanding" business*man* and the "depraved" *female* prostitute are in fact the same person.

Thus, while the modern criminal protagonist still may retain the glamorous aura that imbued the Chevalier des Grieux, the disciplinary machine constantly surveys and menaces his movements and more importantly, it constantly threatens to pull the criminal's story back into itself—making the criminal a fantasy of freedom, which is then eventually rehabilitated into an acceptance of things as they are. Ultimately, the artistic representation of criminality in the West has not left either Godwin or Kleist very far behind.

Only a few twentieth-century writers have both understood and further refined the problematic, crucial place Godwin and Kleist carve out for representations of the criminal in Western literature, and I will conclude this study of with a brief discussion of three of those writers. In the introduction, I stressed the particular relevance of eighteenth-century art as the passageway of modernity for us, thinkers of the late twentieth century. It is within this context that the post–World War II writing of Jean Genet, Anthony Burgess, and Peter Handke seems especially illuminating. These authors have taken the representation of criminality further in the directions already trailblazed by the seven artistic creations already discussed, and at the same time, they have marked out complex connections to the literary tradition that has come before them. Genet, Burgess, and Handke revise the fictional use of the autobiographical mode that we have seen in *Manon Lescaut* and *Caleb Williams*, and all three authors continue the dialogue between the criminal and religious authority, which is present more or less explicitly in all of the artistic creations studied here. Moreover, all three are engaged in the development of a criminal discourse—an artistic language which celebrates criminal subjectivity and thereby seeks to make us rethink our systems of values on the level of the word. Through this experimentation with linguistic structure, these authors take up the battle against formal tyranny on the front discovered by Godwin and Kleist; like their Enlightenment predecessors, they recognize that the obstacle to be overcome is *writing itself*. At the same time, these writers further refine the cheerful, alternative criminal voices of Jonathan Wild and Sade's libertines; they simultaneously articulate and problematize a utopian view of criminality as an arena wherein free will is still possible.

Most important of all is the fact that the works of Genet, Burgess, and Handke self-consciously and persistently court artistic failure as a means to open up textual representation to new possibilities; as self-willed failures, they are therefore profoundly connected to the aesthetic projects analyzed in this study of Enlightenment creations.

The lyrical, disjointed, and digressive language of *The Thief's Journal* (1949) rejects formal/ethical/sexual boundaries in a series of stylistic maneuvers that mirror the willful illegal border crossings that Genet undertakes throughout the narrative, as well as the physical border Genet necessarily violates in his transgressive sexual practices. Moreover, the journal wittily dismantles (while at the same time acknowledging its debt to) both the spiritual confession on the model of Augustine and the fictional criminal autobiography on the model of *Manon Lescaut* (with whose title character Genet briefly identifies [80]) and *Caleb Williams*. Genet's "confession" rejects all of the narrative directions seen before; it is neither an admission of sin (Augustine) nor a defense (Prévost), and it is manifestly uninterested in questions of its own sincerity (Godwin). Rather the journal is a self-announced fiction representing both an act of defiance and an act of seduction undertaken by an unrepentant masculine/feminine sinner/criminal. Indeed, this very recalcitrance is what will allow Genet to claim sainthood:[15] "I call saintliness not a state, but the moral procedure that leads me to it. It is the ideal point of a morality which I cannot talk about since I do not see it. It withdraws when I approach it. I desire it and fear it. This procedure may appear stupid. Yet though painful, it is joyful. . . . Will anyone be surprised when I claim that crime can help me ensure my moral vigor?" (215). Thus, Genet both radically reworks Augustine and glories in the very criminal narrative process that caused Caleb to condemn himself. Through this reworking, Genet proclaims himself priest and criminal—because he is the one, he is able to be the other—and he archly deems the journal itself to be the procedure that canonizes him; unlike the church father, he redeems himself through and because of crime and unlike Godwin's protagonist, he revels in the homosexual desire that proclaims his "guilt."

   While he pits his criminal, homosexual values against those
of his readers—considering and then discounting all the pat
sociological answers for his own criminality—Genet forces us
both to rethink the purpose of narrative (Meitinger 65) as well
as confront the limitations of language:

> If I attempt to recompose with words what my attitude was at the
> time, the reader will be not more taken in than I. We know that our
> language is incapable of recalling even the pale reflection of those
> bygone, foreign states. The same would be true of this entire journal
> if it were to be the notation of what I was. I shall therefore make clear
> that it is meant to indicate what I am today, as I write it. It is not a
> quest of time gone by, but a work of art whose pretext-subject is my
> former life. It will be a present fixed with the help of the past, and not
> vice versa. (71)

There are good reasons for this distrust of language in the
service of history. In order to remain resistant, Genet's story has
to invent its own language and its own manner of unfolding; it
cannot become a history, for history will reify it, and it cannot not
use "our language" because this language will impose its own
values on it. The journal can be meaningful only insofar as it
enacts a present, ongoing resistance against society and its
institutions: "In embellishing what you hold in contempt, my
mind, weary of the game that consists of naming with a glamorous name that which stirred my heart, refuses any qualification" (109).
   Yet such wholesale refusal exacts a high price, for Genet's
apparently gleeful exercise in defiance eventually reveals itself
to be something quite different. In fact, *The Thief's Journal* is
increasingly haunted by its own possible futility to such a degree
that in the last quarter of the book, the author says that he hopes
never to write again (205). Oddly, it seems that Genet's overtly
homoerotic composition has proved as much of a burden (and as
little a comfort) to him as Godwin's covertly homosexual romance becomes for Caleb. Why should this be? First of all, Genet
comes to doubt the very aesthetic expressibility of criminality—
as though literature, by its very nature, falsifies whatever it
wants to enshrine. Like those writers who have come before him,

Genet struggles with the problem of making the criminal and the work of art coexist, and as he proceeds, the author/hero seems less and less certain that they can. Although crime seems to need art to fully become itself ("It is only after a theft, and thanks to literature, that the thief chants his gesture" [218]), Genet repeatedly (and humorously) exposes the means by which literature itself betrays crime,[16] only to conclude: "The utilization of crime by an artist is impious. Someone risks his life, his glory, only to be used as ornament for a dilettante" (213).

Although Genet is careful to distinguish himself from such artists, he seems to sense that such a critique can easily be leveled at himself. This observation reveals the second dilemma of the journal, namely, the problem of Genet's operative term *betrayal*—a word that unites the aesthetic, criminal, and homosexual agendas of Genet's book: "Sometimes, the consciousness with which we have pondered a reputedly vile act, the power of expression which must signify it impels us to song. This means that treachery is beautiful if it makes us sing. To betray thieves would be not only to find myself again in the moral world, I thought, but also to find myself once more in homosexuality" (22). But if betrayal is to be true to its meaning, it must betray everything and everyone indiscriminately. Thus, Genet's own acts of betrayal (on all fronts—including literary, sexual, and moral) may in fact betray *him*, while his work of art about betrayal may betray itself as well as its author.

Under the weight of these two related difficulties—the just (both aesthetic and judiciary) rendering of crime by art and the control of betrayal both within and around the text—*The Thief's Journal* turns increasingly in toward itself, picking apart its intentions and goals, returning obsessively to its lost El Dorado of interiority—the now-defunct penal colony of Guiana (255–56). Yet while Genet dreams of a narrative as self-enclosed as a penal colony in which his criminal characters are all subjects equally, he suspects that such a project must fail and become the "pursuit of the Impossible Nothingness" (94). He can overturn literary/linguistic tradition, but he must continue to work with it; he must, in the end, have recourse to "our" language, just as, in the end he cannot do without "our" acclamation, for the world of the prison is not outside but inside "our" world: "The Prison—let us name that place in both the world and the mind—toward which I go offers me more joys than your honors and festivals. Nevertheless it is these which I shall seek. I aspire to your recognition, your consecration" (268). In this way *The Thief's Journal's* aesthetic/ethic of betrayal betrays itself and turns back with longing to the world it earlier dismissed with contempt.

Is *The Thief's Journal* a failure because of this betrayal of betrayal? Yes, but it is important to remember what "failure" means for Genet.[17] Two complementary images arising at the end of the book provide the best indicators of what the notion signifies: the palace of mirrors that traps Stilitano and the piece of lace paper, created, surprisingly, by the "butch" Armand. Both images—the rigid, yet ultimately fragile, glass edifice that reflects only the lost self (to the amusement of the crowd) and the even more fragile cutout snowflake, so delicate that it can be blown away with one breath—derive from scenarios that dramatize the failure and the unconquerability of their main actors, and by implication, of Genet's artistic project as a whole. The virile homophobic Stilitano cannot find his way out of the carnival maze; he is enraged and humiliated by the jeering onlookers (whom he cannot see), but when he emerges with the help of Roger, he is transfigured and laughing (266). Similarly, the macho Armand is discovered as being a closet lace maker, but he exits the bar (the scene of his unmasking) like a triumphant hero (258).

Thus, Genet presents both Stilitano and Armand as wounded heroes of a failure, which has an unmistakably feminizing quality, insofar as his beloveds are reborn and transfigured by the same feminine powerlessness at work in Schiller and particularly in Sade. But in an important reversal of Sade, Genet's version of perverse writing valorizes, not the criminal masculine, but the criminal feminine. He displays the humiliations of his beloveds as the wounding instruments of their martyrdom; as such they are the emblems both of a femininity which they can approximate but never incarnate and of pederast sanctity—ordeals which glorify their magnificent ability to survive them.[18]

Taking its cue also from the spectacular homoerotic failure of *Caleb Williams*, *The Thief's Journal* "fails" as narrative and lovingly embraces the failures of the book's characters. Unpacking itself as artifice, Genet's book simultaneously celebrates itself as artistic process and denigrates itself as artistic product and points toward the vision of a criminal world that is no longer deviant but resplendent with gender possibilities: "What is inscribed under Jean Genet's name, in the movement of a text that divides itself, pulls itself to pieces, dismembers itself, regroups, remembers itself . . . bombards and disintegrates these ephemeral anomalies so that they can be recomposed in other bodies for new passions" (Cixous and Clément 84). Genet's journal shoulders that burden of the criminal/homosexual text and transforms/translates/betrays it into the beautiful, making failure into a beginning rather than an end: "Heroized, my book . . . has become my Genesis" (268).

The tension between criminality and aesthetics is articulated in a quite different way in Anthony Burgess' now-notorious novel *A Clockwork Orange* (1962), on which Stanley Kubrick has based his equally notorious (though stylistically and thematically quite different) film. Here a criminal utopianism emerges, apparently despite the author, who in his most recent preface (1986), claims that the public has completely misunderstood the novel, because the final chapter was edited out (due to editorial coercion) in the original American publication (Burgess vi). Because of this "misdemeanor" (Burgess' telling expression [vii]), *A Clockwork Orange* has been misread as a paean to violent crime, and in an authoritative voice reminiscent of Prévost's Man of Quality, Burgess, in the preface, insists upon the novel's evident morality (vii). Interestingly, the author implies that the narrative follows exactly the kind of transfiguration scenario that was discussed earlier in this chapter, when he notes that his hooligan protagonist finally does "grow up" (vii) and sees the error of his ways.

The author's anxious preface to the book, which he would disinherit if he could, conveniently introduces the problematics of *Clockwork*. It is ostensibly a satire[19] and its debt to *Jonathan Wild* is apparent, insofar as this work, too, undertakes the exposure of bogus greatness—a task made even more evident here by Burgess' use of the name "Alexander" for his protagonist. Like Fielding's novel, Burgess' narrative unfolds as regress in the form of progress; it too traces the fall of a modern-day prig and leads, if not to the block, then to its twentieth-century disciplinary equivalent, the criminal hospital laboratory.

Despite this satiric thrust, Burgess' book remains dangerous—as he himself seems to recognize. This is in part due to the complex nature of the main character, who in contrast to Jonathan Wild, truly is the man of taste he claims to be. Alex's character is a compendium of contradictory qualities; his high art proclivities, as well as his concern with fashion and with theatricality, make this character as much a descendant of Prévost as of Fielding, while as a writer of memoirs, he resembles Caleb. Moreover, his cool interest in witnessing and performing sexually charged acts of "ultra-violence" links him clearly with Sade. We should note, moreover, that Alex's fictional world represents a combination of the Schillerian and the Sadian. It is (in contrast to the film) a relentlessly, obsessively masculine world, and its flat, talky, claustrophobic scenery incorporates a series of increasingly constraining architectures reminiscent of Sade. The book's landscape comprises an array of "prisons"—from the apartment "block" where Alex lives to the cells he inhabits at the public penitentiary and at F. Alexander's house to the hospital rooms at the Ludovico Center and at the hospital where he is treated after his attempted suicide. The parade of various professionals (the writer, the scientist, the warden, the priest), all proclaiming platitudes in very much the style, is also reminiscent of Sade's procedure in *Justine*.[20]

Yet, the real "danger" of *Clockwork* lies elsewhere. It is a satire that "fails" even more dramatically than does that of Fielding, because it seduces in a manner far more radical than Sade; the book captures rather than reports (in a way that perhaps no other piece of contemporary literature has) the joy of breaking the law and the blissful state of the mind which imagines violence inflicted upon others.

The pleasure of crime manifests itself less in the narrative's formal structure (for the reasons just discussed) than in the exuberant linguistic artistry of the narrator/hero, whose use of the almost incomprehensible teen language *nadsat* imbues the most gruesome criminal acts with heroic grandeur. Again, the Barthian "pleasure of the text" is at work here: "So he did the strong-man on the devotchka, who was still creech, creech, creeching away in very horrorshow four-in-a-bar, locking her rookers from the back, while I ripped away at this and that and the other, the others going haw haw haw still, and real good horrorshow groodies they were that then exhibited their pink glazzies, O my brothers, while I untrussed and got ready for the plunge" (28). Like Genet, Alex seduces his reader through language, making him (and even her) an accomplice, a brother, a "droog."

Burgess' own commentary to the contrary, his novel makes it clear that Alex's tragedy lies, not in the fact that he is a master of "ultra-violence," but in the fact that, unlike Genet, he fails to recognize that he carries within him the structures of discipline. It is, after all, his Napoleonic insistence on his gang's conformity to rigid standards of behavior (such as cleanliness and proper barroom etiquette) that precipitates his downfall from a modern robber captain to convict, to experimental subject, and finally, in the restored final chapter, to docile adult. Furthermore, even though it is ostensibly Alex's reformed self telling this story, the fact that he has taken up the criminal language that was once his own in order to recount it, suggests that his reformation is problematic at best. By telling his story in *nadsat,* Alex reverts to his former self and he becomes an accomplice of his own story. Thus, if Caleb uses textuality to displace pleasure, it is through textuality that Alex relives, reaffirms, and passes on to us the pleasures of criminal subjectivity.

In this manner, the "clockwork" of Burgess' narrative—its formulaic plot (bad boy gets cocky and gets his comeuppance) and comic-strip characters (Three Stooges-like gang members, brutish prison guards, scotch-belting prison chaplain, maniacal clinical research scientist)—circulates around but does cannot alter the heart of the story, the "orange."[21] The refrain "What's it going to be then, eh?," which repeats itself throughout the narrative and opens the reincluded last chapter, ironically returns us to the beginning of the novel, and to that night of "ultra-violence" where Alex, the once and future criminal genius, leads us on an infinitely recuperable series of criminal adventures, which culminate in music and in orgasm. *A Clockwork Orange* invokes and realizes the Sadian dream, even as it revises Sedgwick's homosocial into a grimly logical homo-antisocial view of intermale relations. Burgess' book uses satiric failure, not only to reinscribe criminal mystique in contemporary terms, but also to envisage a world where masculine crime (dreaming about it, doing it, and/or remembering it) reinvents itself into its own language, thereby becoming at once pleasure, freedom, power, and art in an otherwise mechanical society.

As for Genet and Burgess, criminal acts represent a touchstone for Peter Handke whereby otherwise totally automatized, alienated male individuals regain some kind of vitality and connection to their surroundings. But Handke differs from both Genet and Burgess in his insistence on the universality of criminal consciousness — an insistence made manifest by the fact that none of his criminals are professionals; either they merely dream of committing a crime (*A Moment of True Feeling* and *Short Letter, Long Farewell*), or they are one-time killers (*The Goalie's Anxiety at the Penalty Kick* and *Across*) whose acts derive from no perceptible motivation. For these characters, criminality seems both a state of mind and a social given that predetermines their relationships with others even before and whether or not any actual crime has been committed. They are all modern Phaedras — criminals before and despite the fact.

Nowhere is Handke's internalization of criminality more radical than in his 1983 novella *Across* (*Der Chinese des Schmerzes*). While *Michael Kohlhaas* unfolds as a taxonomy of disciplinary mechanisms seen on the outside — in the tangible form of bureaucracy — and *Caleb Williams* reveals a guilt that derives from the crime of sexual deviance, *Across* does the exact inverse. Handke's narrative dramatizes (precisely with its lack of drama) discipline felt from inside, and it tells of a crime committed by a perpetrator who feels himself to be criminal, without feeling guilty (at least in any traditionally recognizable fashion).

The internalization of the criminal and the disciplinary in

late twentieth-century experience announces itself in the opening pages of the book. First, Andreas Loser surveys the scene of
his Panopticon-like housing complex (with the penal-sounding
name Oak Colony), where almost everything and everybody are
visible.[22] His act of viewing testifies to the actual normalization
of daily human life into routines exercised within specific,
carefully articulated, viewable spaces and to his own participa-
tion in this creation of disciplinary order:[23] "A trolleybus turns
into the circle. . . . People get out, schoolchildren, locals, for-
eigners (who occupy the few wooden houses); all are in a hur-
ry. . . . They make their way in a cluster across the little canal
bridge, followed by a few teenagers on their bicycles, which they
left at the bus stop this morning. All together they enter the
Colony" (3–4). With a few changes of detail, Handke could just
as well be describing the concentration camp detachments returning to Buchenwald.[24] Second, even as the book opens,
Andreas is filled with a Foucaultian sense of his own criminality.
He already considers himself a social deviant, for he possesses,
in his mind, a clear, criminal history (*Discipline and Punish* 252)—
a documented predilection for violence—which dates from
childhood, and which has made him a visibly marked man:
"That slap showed me up as a criminal. The look on the boy's face
. . . has said to me down through the years: Now I know you, now
I know what kind of man you are, and I won't forget it" (10).

Formally, *Across* can scarcely be called a narrative at all,
although the book bears superficial resemblances to the standard novella—small focus, tragic atmosphere, concentrated action. Handke's extremely static reportage—which one moment
imitates the flat, informational tone of a local guidebook and the
next, resembles the opaque, yet metaphysically resonant, object-
descriptions of Stéphane Mallarmé's poetry—literally freezes
the action into a series of vignettes, which we are obliged to study
in isolation, like individual paintings in a gallery or like a film
which we must look at frame by frame.[25] As its odd division titles
indicate, the entire book is a series of dispassionate views: city
panoramas, architectural exteriors, landscapes, the interiors of
rooms—all of which conspire to make it appear that *Across* tells
no story at all.

This "storylessness" is disturbing, precisely because we expect a plot to automatically evolve from an act that patriarchal literature of the West has traditionally considered to be significant.[26] Andreas Loser murders an unidentified man who was spray-painting a swastika on a Salzburg city wall (we do not know why). The murder scene contains a variety of symbolic elements that should, but do not quite, lend the actions a mythic significance. Andreas' pursuit of his victim on a mountainous path is reminiscent of Oedipus; the victim may be old (he has white hair) and therefore may be a symbolic father; furthermore, he may be a former Nazi, and therefore this violent confrontation may represent a crisis whereby Austria's present must meet and kill off its fascist past (Caviola 392). Somehow, it seems, this should be the beginning of a well-known criminal tragedy.

These significations are fragmented by other details, however, which point to a very different mythology altogether—that of contemporary, disciplinary society. It is no coincidence that this Oedipal crossroad is literally surrounded by institutional symbols: the hospital, the old-age home, the student dormitory, the crushed french-fry carton from the new McDonald's. This institutional backdrop reinforces the abnormality of what takes place, making both the pursuer and the pursued into deviants of equal stature. Thus, in a reverse of the archaeological task— which carefully sifts through the past to reproduce the intact original (a task which is the avocation of the protagonist)— Handke's writing carefully buries Oedipus and his father, by overlaying them with two recognizable archetypes from our present: an alienated schoolteacher and a (equally alienated?) defacer of public property. Like Genet, Handke is also interested in developing a new legend of criminality, but his mythology is the very opposite of the Genetian "beautiful"; it is, rather, the modern iconography of the mundane.

This new myth, the author suggests, is the one that readers ought to be interested in, but he provides few hints as to how to read it, and the subsequent happenings in *Across* do little to help us. Andreas momentarily feels a surge of energy after the murder, but (and?) discovers (gradually? suddenly?) that the murder has in fact intensified his own feelings of nonexistence.

The crime has also opened up a new space for and within
Andreas, a space that is particularly significant in light of the
disciplinary architecture that encloses the book. Appropriately,
it is a building's physical point of transition between out and in—
the threshold—which becomes internalized in Andreas, representing both his state of mind ("the unfilled space within" [87])
and his story (129).

What is the nature of this threshold? It is perhaps a gate, an
entryway that will inaugurate spiritual renewal. According to
the priest who attends Andreas' weekly card game,[27] the threshold is a bridge to both individual and collective salvation, precisely because it has been forced to reside within the individual:

> What may be less evident is that the threshold is itself a zone, or
> rather, a place in is own right, a place of testing or of safety. . . .
> According to modern doctrine, of course, there are no longer any
> thresholds in this sense. . . . "But," . . . [a modern teacher asks]
> "where nowadays are we to find the destroyed thresholds, if not in
> ourselves? By our own wounds shall we be healed. . . ." Every step,
> every glance, every gesture, says the teacher, should be aware of itself
> as a possible threshold and thus recreate what has been lost. This
> threshold consciousness might then transfer attention from object to
> object, and so on until the peace relay reappears on earth. . . . Thus,
> thresholds as seats of power may not have disappeared; they have
> become conceivable, so to speak as inner powers. (66–67)

While Andreas suspects that the significance of the threshold
(which is also the favorite object of his archaeological study) may
be illusory, there is throughout *Across* the paradoxical suggestion
that even if this threshold does not exist, it certainly ought to:
"Then we all watched the television news together, and after-
ward someone cried out: 'But some sort of immortality must be
possible!'" (128).

The problematic identity of the threshold is reinforced by
Handke's suggestion that Andreas' criminal act both liberates
and entraps him—turning the scholarly commentator into a
storyteller in his own right, but removing him from the boundaries of human relationships (especially those with women),
even as he comes to recognize their value. In keeping with this
ambiguity, Handke's book does not end with any recognizable

criminal formula. Neither transfigured nor destroyed, neither discovered nor pursued, the protagonist returns to work, and he recounts (but does not confess) the murder to his son, and it is in that possibly ensuing dialogue that the issue of his guilt will be raised or not, that the Oedipal scene may or may not be rewritten, and the value of his "threshold story" (of which this work is literally the pretext) will be affirmed or denied.

With this refusal of closure, *Across* presents itself very literally as the threshold that it meant to describe (Caviola 392)—not as narrative movement but precisely as a zone between narrative possibilities. As in Genet and Burgess, the very act of telling the criminal's story exercises a potentially utopian function—it proclaims a freedom—but Handke self-consciously suppresses this telling, as if aware of the limitations, which the very articulation of such criminal utopianism implies: "The narrator opened his eyes, unfolded his hands, uncrossed his legs, sat up straight, breathed deeply, and he looked imploringly over his shoulder into empty space, as though waiting for someone or remembering someone; or as though collecting himself for a very different story. (A story meant: it was, it is, it will be—it meant future)" (129–30).

In this manner, even more radically than his predecessors, Handke resists qualifying criminality at the same time as he recognizes that crime is an inevitable result of our psychosocial present, and of our political, explicitly patriarchal Western history. *Across* lays bare its own inability to tell the criminal's story through a series of stop-action linguistic pictures that constantly, as though aware of their insufficiency, point onward and inward (rather than outward) toward truer, but as yet inexpressible, versions of themselves. Understood in this context, the "Epilogue"'s portrait of the canal bridge belatedly explains the meaning of Handke's title; *Across* epitomizes a deferred hope that our inner powers may lead us somewhere, although neither Handke nor his reader ever crosses this bridge.

The nonnarrative of criminality in *Across* encapsulates in a way that we cannot fail to recognize the predicament of the late twentieth century. Like Handke's protagonist (and like Handke himself) we are all either imprisoned or liberated by the threshold (or both); as modernists, we purport to have successfully rejected the metaphysics of the West, but we are unable at present to take the next step into an as-yet-undefined other zone. We cannot yet *tell the story* of that transition; we can only *describe* the space we are in—a place where we are all "criminals"—and grope for a spiritual transformation that eludes us even as it hovers on the horizon of our thought as a necessity. Can we still say that murder (or crime in general) is "wrong"? And if we can (for Andreas ultimately decides that it is, although he [and Handke] rejects all the familiar ways of dealing with that decision) on what basis do we make this judgment, and what do we do with it?

It is both ironic and appropriate that Handke's use of the criminal and his highly abstract internalization of late-twentieth-century experience returns us to precisely the domain that the authors of this study tried so hard to abandon—namely, that Christian metaphysical realm, the emancipation from which marks one of the characteristics of modern art (see the discussion of Gadamer and modernity in chap. 1). It is for this reason, however, that *Across* represents such an important moment in the literary dialogue of criminality as it has evolved since the eighteenth century. What happens, Handke asks, when social mechanisms become so radically internalized that they become the very givens of consciousness? Do not these mechanisms then become spiritual rather than social/political concerns? Is this not the meaning of the inwardly transposed threshold? These are vital questions, and it is to this intellectual horizon—where politics, history, psychology, and religion meet and where, as Genet prophesied, criminality, sainthood, and art merge—that Handke leads and leaves us, teetering on the edge of possibilities as yet unthought and unspoken, but which challenge us to make them flesh.

Notes
Works Cited
Index

Notes

1. Introduction: Hermeneutics, the Eighteenth Century, and the Challenge of Criminal Literature

1. I am aware that in making this statement I seem to provide what is, according to Felicity Nussbaum and Laura Brown, "perhaps the least convincing . . . argument against the alteration of the critical status quo [in eighteenth-century studies]" (*New 18th Century* 13). Yet, while I applaud in particular these scholars' pluralistic project of presenting "systematic and strongly argued modes of inquiry in confrontation with another" (17), I simply cannot dismiss the importance of aesthetic value (in Gadamer's sense), nor can I assume that there is no real difference between the various types of writing produced during the course of the eighteenth century. What makes the eighteenth-century literary works of this study so important to my mind is the fact that they *themselves*— through their self-construction and presentation—"encourage us to rethink our assumptions" (13–14), not just about crime, but about art, ethics, and sexual identity as well.

2. See Nussbaum and Brown's excellent historical overview of English eighteenth-century studies in the introduction to their book. I would add that the resistance to theory which they see as the bane of English (1) is also applicable to German studies in the eighteenth century—for which the category is still, more often than not, *Goethezeit*—a designation which reveals the ongoing prejudice that this period produced only one "great" male artist.

3. It is this point of view which allows Thomas Beebee to persuasively argue that the very "perversity of [French and German] translations" of *Clarissa* allows the work's larger meaning to emerge (Clarissa *on the Continent* 4). He suggests that it is through the national-linguistic differences between Richardson's novel and its adaptations by Prévost and Michaelis, that the original work can be more fully understood, giving "us insight into it" (205)—an argument that points, in my opinion, to a kind of dialectical commonality existing between works from different countries, produced during the same time period.

4. There are undoubtedly differences between Gadamer and Foucault. The former is interested in texts—in the written tradition as a whole—and in the experience of art in particular, while the latter concentrates on a variety of discourses in what we usually think of as a sociological domain. Foucault is also—at least in his formal writings—often more suspicious than Gadamer of the process by which we understand the past, in much the same way as is Habermas (from whom Foucault is careful to distinguish himself [*Foucault Reader* 377–78]). But in his analysis of the Habermas-Gadamer debate, Paul Ricoeur has convincingly argued that there are striking similarities between hermeneutics and what he calls the "critique of ideology." He contends that there is a "place for one in the structure of the other" (*Hermeneutics and the Human Sciences* 64) and that hermeneutics turns toward the critique of ideology in many important ways (91–93).

5. Hubert Dreyfus and Paul Rabinow argue that Foucault's work can only be understood as having moved definitively beyond hermeneutics, especially that of Gadamer, but I think the authors seriously distort Gadamer's theoretical position by making his work into an unproblematic continuation of Heidegger's strategy of "deep interpretation" (xxiii). In so doing, they fail to take into account both the very real difficulty of understanding, which Gadamer repeatedly alludes to (and which the denseness of his style dramatizes), and the degree to which Gadamer sees that process as always inherently dangerous. This sense that the quest for truth is always both jeopardized and jeopardizing corresponds, in my opinion, very well to the sense of danger which permeates Foucault's corpus.

6. Foucault has been considered the enemy of the "subject" as traditionally constituted by phenomenology, but such an interpretation is something of a misunderstanding, as he explains when discussing his past and present approach to the problem in a January 1984 interview:

Q: But you have always "refused" that we speak to you about the subject in general?
A: No I had not "refused." . . . What I refused was precisely that you first of all set up a theory of the subject—as could be done in phenomenology. . . . What I wanted to know was how the subject constituted himself, in such and such determined form. . . . On the other hand and inversely, I would say that . . . now I am interested, in fact, in the way in which the subject constitutes himself in an active fashion. (Bernauer and Rasmussen 10–11)

Foucault does not say that the subject does not exist but that it is a form rather than a substance (10) and that it therefore changes from relation to relation. Moreover, as both Garth Gillan and Thomas Flynn note in their essays, Foucault grows increasingly concerned with the development of a personal practice of ethics, and this emphasis on individual "practice of the self" (and its classical Greek roots) clearly links him with Gadamer's philosophical recuperation of the Western ethical tradition.

7. James Bernauer's incisive discussion in *The Final Foucault* of Foucault's paradoxical desire to both escape and care for the self is reminiscent of Gadamer's description of the essentially ecstatic experience inaugurated by art (a game in which we both lose and find ourselves [*Truth and Method* 111–13]). Bernauer also explicitly establishes the complex connection between the French philosopher and Christian hermeneutics (of which Gadamer is undoubtedly a product [Bernauer and Rasmussen 69–71]).

8. Gadamer is extremely wary of the notion of interpretational authority, as it risks imposing a false understanding of the humanities as a kind of objective science (*Truth and Method* 6). Hélène Cixous expresses an analogous (if more violently expressed) view when she argues in her closing dialogue with Catherine Clément that the concept of intellectual mastery is a dangerous one: "The one who is in the master's place, even if not the master of a knowledge, is in a position of power. The only way to bar that is to execute the master . . . eliminate him, so that what he has to say can get through, so that he himself is not the obstacle, so it will be *given*" (Cixous and Clément 140).

9. Despite its complex generic affiliations, most critics agree that *The Beggar's Opera* is essentially a comedy (see, for example, William Empson's reading). Because of this, Gay's presentation of criminality is not ultimately a subversive one, and the play becomes, as Ronald Paulson has noted, a comedy of manners that dramatizes rather than satirizes "social classes on the move upward" ("Mock-heroic Irony" 63). Further, I am wary of including Gay's musical piece in a discussion of otherwise literary texts. Peter Lewis' "The Beggar's Rags" makes the important observation that the work is not a literary drama (despite the fact that it was created by a poet) but rather a ballad-opera (142–43) that maneuvers within the related confines of comedy, burlesque, and satire.

10. Among those noting the Christian moralist sphere of Defoe's work is Alberto Rivero, who reads *Roxana* as a self-conscious reversal of Christian narrative patterns and emblems in "The Restored Garden and the Devil as Christ." See also Paul Alkon's intelligent discussion of this point of view in *Defoe and Fictional Time*.

11. James Maddox notices the importance of guilt and also makes an intriguing comparison (which I wish he had developed) between the character of Roxana and that of Hawthorne's tortured sinner-preacher in *The Scarlet Letter* (675). See "On Defoe's *Roxana*." Likewise, Robert W. Uphaus argues that *Roxana* is concerned with the problem of virtue (see

his "Fear of Fiction" 190).

12. *Roxana's* simultaneous yoking of gender dynamics to questions of predestination and free will would also seem to connect it in interesting ways to Racine's *Phèdre*.

13. Compare with Ruth Angress' view in "Kleists Abkehr von der Aufklärung."

14. Such otherwise excellent revisionist volumes as *Sexual Underworlds of the Enlightenment*, for example, apparently assume that the Enlightenment and the eighteenth century are more or less synonymous. See the introduction to this collection of essays by George Rousseau and Roy Porter.

15. See for example Porter and Teich's *Enlightenment in National Context* for a discussion of national and linguistic boundaries. See the books by Jacob, Rousseau, and Clive, respectively, for ideological boundary discussions.

16. See for example Frühwald and Martino, eds., *Zwischen Aufklärung und Restauration* (1989); Vajda, ed., *Le Tournant du Siècle des Lumières 1760–1820* (1982); Mortier's "La Transition du 18e au 19e Siècle" (1982); and Alan Bewell's *Wordsworth and the Enlightenment*.

17. This reevaluation is already under way, as recent studies testify. See Bewell's *Wordsworth and the Enlightenment* and William R. Paulson's *Enlightenment, Romanticism, and the Blind in France*. Still, much remains to be done.

18. Rameau's concept of "sublime crime" clearly reflects Edmund Burke's notion (which echoes Aristotle's theory of the effects produced by the tragic) that the sublime only arises upon contemplation of the terrible, which in turn evokes the accompanying reactions of astonishment, admiration, reverence, and respect—precisely those emotions which the nephew posits as the effects of great evil. Notably, Burke himself implies a connection between sublimity and crime. He cites the *Iliad*'s description of the effect of a fugitive murderer on an astonished crowd as a perfect example of the sublime (57–58). Burke's example suggests that the experience of the sublime is grounded, not merely on the terrible, but on the criminal specifically. Furthermore, as Thomas Weiskel notes, Burke's description implies an "empathic identification on the part of the spectators" (89). The onlookers both sympathize with the criminal rather than condemning him, *and* they participate imaginatively in the crime itself.

19. Leonard Davis argues that this was precisely the case of the early novel in England, noting that "there seems to have been something inherently novelistic about the criminal or rather the form of the novel seems almost to demand a criminal content" (125).

20. In his essay on the literature of crime as narrative system, Maximillian Novak rightly observes that the line between literary and

nonliterary narratives of crime was often obscure in the eighteenth century (particularly in England), and I would add to his statement, that the division between artistic and popular representations of criminality in the twentieth century is equally, if not more, hazy. But nonetheless, I think there *is* a line (albeit an elastic one), as Novak himself seems to suggest when he discusses the relationship between *Caleb Williams* and the biography of Eugene Aram. See Novak's "'Appearances of Truth.'" This unspoken suspicion also lurks in Lüsebrink's well-researched study of popular, historical criminal narratives of eighteenth-century France. Although the author claims to expand the canon of what is called literature, he carefully brackets canonical texts of the Enlightenment (Lüsebrink 6), arguing that he is interested primarily in the social effects of these narrative documents—an act which implies that the *belles lettres* of the period may be operating on bases quite different than those of popular productions.

21. Novak also suggests that the reverse is true ("'Appearances of Truth'" 37).

22. For the purposes of this argument, I am uninterested in the heated debate surrounding the actual authorship of the drama. See D. J. Connacher's excellent summary of the opposing theoretical positions in *Aeschylus'* Prometheus Bound: *A Literary Commentary.*

23. This strategy is even more reminiscent of *Prometheus Bound*, in which Zeus himself never appears.

24. This is in contrast to Aeschylus' hero. While Prometheus' rebellion also fails, there is the clear promise at the end of the play that he shall be vindicated and finally released from bondage. Moreover, his creation, man, is saved—thereby pointing to the ultimate triumph of his endeavors.

25. This is precisely the argument put forth by D. A. Miller in his important study *The Novel and the Police*—which I will discuss further in the Conclusion. While I find his readings of nineteenth-century English novels to be in many ways convincing, I do not believe that this model applies to the works examined here.

26. Compare with Lüsebrink (249–51), who traces an increasingly prorevolutionary tone in the popular criminal literature of France. Similarly, George S. Rousseau and Roy Porter observe a kind of productive ambivalence at work in Enlightenment writing—an ambivalence that on one hand doubts the possibilities of "radical praxis" and on the other affirms the dynamism of thinking as an "expression of being." See *The Languages of Psyche.*

27. In their intriguing work *The Politics and Poetics of Transgression*, Peter Stallybrass and Allon White rightly take exception to Julia Kristeva's contention that literature's formal subversion is equivalent to political change (201). But it seems to me that their dismissal of *any*

possibility in this direction represents an equally distorted view of the function of art. Art does no more (and no less) than challenge its audience to think; the rest is, and always will be, up to us.

---

2. Economy and Extravagance: Criminal Origin in Lillo's London Merchant and Prévost's Manon Lescaut

---

1. The strong Christian philosophical orientation of both texts has been recognized by several critics, particularly in the case of *The London Merchant*. See Stephen Trainor's enlightening discussion of Puritan sermonic formulas, Richard E. Brown's analysis of Christian mercantilist and Hobbesian economic philosophies, and Paul Hazard's reading of *Manon Lescaut*.

2. Elaine Pagels neatly summarizes this connection in her discussion of Augustine: "Augustine . . . traces how sin, transmitted from the primal parents through sexual reproduction infected their offspring. . . . So Cain, when another form of carnal desire, envy, overcame his rational judgment, murdered his brother" (114).

3. The following readings of *The London Merchant* and *Manon Lescaut* attempt to resolve the critical splits that have plagued both works. In the case of Lillo's play, critics have argued and continue to dispute its nature as amoral sentimental drama or a clear-cut religious morality play (or most recently, as clear expression of bourgeois ideology—Laura Brown, *English Dramatic Form*). See George Bush Rodman's and Raymond B. Haven's opposing views. In her essay "The Evil of Goodness," Roberta Borkat astutely notices a disjunction between "the announced moral aims of the play and the actual effects of the events within it" (291), but she dismisses this discrepancy as part of the paradox of moral sentimentalism. I argue that, far from being an incidental flaw in the play's construction (as Borkat implies), this apparent disjunction between the moral and the immoral lies at the heart of the play and plays a vital role in shaping is meaning.

Manon Lescaut's critical history is somewhat more complicated, for radically opposed attitudes have been prevalent from the beginning. Even immediately after the novel's publication, reactions were extremely mixed—either touting the novel as a sensitive, moral parable or damning it as a subversive and immoral production (Deloffre and Picard clvii–clxxvii). Twentieth-century evaluations range from romantic readings, which see the Chevalier as a misguided but ultimately compelling idealist who, despite his real flaws, affirms the transcendent values of the heart over and against societal law (see Jean-Luc Jaccard; Rita Winandy; Elaine Showalter; and William Mead) to structuralist and deconstructive assessments, which stress the duplicity of the Chevalier and question the possibility of any valid interpretation of the novel (see Naomi Segal; Sylvère Lotringer; Herbert Josephs; and especially Lionel Gossman). I contend that the Chevalier's duplicity coupled with the moral limitations of the narrator (whom I consider as a literary character separate from the author) do in fact inaugurate a meaningful moral reading of the novel.

4. Thoroughgood's observation that "it is the industrious merchant's business to collect the various blessings of each soil and climate" (3.1.25–27) provides a good example of this mixture of commercial and religious imagery.

5. Trainor intriguingly argues that Barnwell has already fallen because he is guilty of the sin of "spiritual pride" (512), but he neglects to explain how this preliminary fall is connected (or if it is) to the evil influence of Millwood. Does he mean that Barnwell would have become a criminal without her?

6. Laura Brown (161) suggests that Lillo's nonpresentation of this scene allows him to keep "his paragon as pure as possible."

7. See Eve Sedgwick on Luce Irigaray, 26.

8. Thus, Millwood is not guided by pure self-interest, as Richard Brown argues (98).

9. Compare with Flores' view (97).

10. Compare the dynamics of this conversation with that of Roxana's discussion with *her* London merchant in Defoe's novel (185–97). Roxana's passionate plea for female independence is easily countered by her lover, who insists that marriage is not only moral but practically advantageous to the woman.

11. Richard Brown concedes that there is no refutation to Millwood's arguments here (101). Indeed, only physical death can silence Millwood, for no one else in the play can.

12. In this context, we might reread Millwood's refusal to repent at the gallows in a more positive light. See Lawrence Price for such a reading.

13. Deloffre and Picard are highly sensitive to the rich complex of rhetorical registers that the Chevalier employs throughout his narrative—among them Christian, Jansenist, tragic, and comic vocabularies. See their introduction to *Manon Lescaut.*

14. That the Chevalier's performance is indeed richly rewarded by Manon's sexual favors is slyly indicated by the brief temporal reference which the Chevalier includes in his account of their arrest by the police: "We were still in bed when an officer from the Lieutenant of Police entered our room with half a dozen Guards" (90). Thus, this adventure in malfeasance procures, not only des Grieux sexual fulfillment, but also the theatrical pleasure of demonstrating his male prowess to a male audience.

15. The connection between crime, theatre, and Eros is also demonstrated in reverse, for if malfeasance does not promise immediate gratification with the beloved, then des Grieux's description of his criminal activity changes radically. He ceases to play the leading role, and he relates the episode quickly and indifferently. No longer wishing to be the hero of the drama in these instances, the Chevalier cleverly removes dramatic interest from these confrontations, reduces them to banalities, where others are forced to play unattractive leading parts.

16. As Nancy Miller has already forcefully argued that the Chevalier describes his mistress only in terms of an array of feminine stereotypes (*The Heroine's Text* 74), I question to what extent, if any, Manon's personality is recuperable. Such a conclusion is implied in Bernadette Fort's remark that, not only is Manon's voice obliterated, but her message is suppressed in favor of the addressee (176). The attempt to replace the admittedly displaced character of Manon Lescaut within the novel seems especially suspect given the findings of recent criticism that itself commits the very sin of des Grieux's narration. Namely, it too reduces Manon to an array of stereotypes—from the twentieth, rather than from the eighteenth, century. Given this state of affairs, I have limited my discussion of Manon herself to observations that give insight, not into her character, but into that of the Chevalier, who is the central character and dominating voice of the narrative.

17. This lack of description as regards Manon Lescaut has been remarked by a number of critics, among them Paul Hazard, Frederic Deloffre and Raymond Picard, Jean-Luc Jaccard, Vivienne Mylne, and Walter Rex.

18. The events immediately following further undermine des Grieux's claim to innocence and honorable intention. It never occurs to him to marry Manon after their sexual union until after the lovers are at the point of financial ruin. Only then does the Chevalier think of reconciling with his father and of attaching himself to Manon legally. He tells us that his mistress reacts coldly to this idea because she knows that the Chevalier's father will never sanction their relationship and that therefore she might lose her lover. The Chevalier's analysis is corroborated by what follows, for it is only after this discussion (which points to the Chevalier's possible abandonment of his mistress in order to return to the bosom of his family) that Manon strikes her deal with B.... While the Chevalier sees the affair with the *fermier général* as a clear case of betrayal—which is the *only* sexual infidelity that occurs in a story—what he has already told us about her anxiety suggests that this is not so. Given her fears of abandonment, Manon's subsequent actions may be motivated, not by the desire to be unfaithful but by desperation on the part of a young woman totally without economic resources and estranged from her family (Donahoe 121–23).

19. Other examples abound. When Manon applies what she has learned from her experience with the elder G... M... to the attentions of his son, the younger G... M..., again the Chevalier finds her at fault. When she proposes to des Grieux that she reject this suitor outright, instead of praising her show of fidelity, the Chevalier refuses to allow such a demonstration and again reveals an essentially negative appraisal of Manon's character: "But you know very well . . . [*tu sais assez, toi, friponne*], I added with a laugh, how to get rid of a disagreeable or tiresome suitor" (129).

20. Des Grieux's reaction to Manon's staged rejection of the Italian prince is another case in point. Although the Italian prince behaves vulgarly (again it is the appellation *grossier* that inaugurates des Grieux's negative evaluation of this individual), the Chevalier does not condemn him and even lends him his tacit support. Finally, although he once despaired at ever having assurance of Manon's love, the Chevalier is displeased with this *pièce de théâtre* (whose erotic flavor and humiliation of a sexual rival mirrors des Grieux's staging of the G... M... embezzlement) because he does not find it in good taste.

21. Nancy Miller is undoubtedly right to include des Grieux in her discussion of female impersonation in the eighteenth-century novel, but she is wrong to interpret the Chevalier's shenanigans as, in any fashion, *submissions to the father*. As she seems to suspect at the end of her essay, the male narrator's "narcissism" is profoundly connected to a struggle for power with other males. See "'I's' in Drag: The Sex of Recollection."

22. In this sense, Prévost seems to anticipates the awareness of (and ambivalence toward) the connection between Christianity and homosexuality, which is developed later in the century by Voltaire and Diderot. See Michel Delon's essay "The Priest, the Philosopher, and Homosexuality in Enlightenment France."

23. This is, then, not a reconciliation with, but a triumph over, the "father." Similarly, Maurice Daumas argues that des Grieux spends the entire second part of the novel challenging and eventually replacing his own father. See "Une Lecture de *Manon Lescaut*" in *Le Syndrome Des Grieux*, 93–117.

24. Far from having a failed frame structure, as several critics have argued, the frame to Manon Lescaut is a circular one. Likewise, I cannot accept Donahoe's contention that "the moral acuity of the Avis simply no longer matters" (135).

---

3. Greatness, Criminality, and Masculinity: Subversive Celebration and the Failure of Satire in Fielding's *Jonathan Wild*

---

1. Such a view of the work is commonplace but is perhaps most

clearly expressed by John Preston in his comparison of Fielding's satire with Gay's *Beggar's Opera*. Preston contends that Fielding regularly does "the expected thing" with his irony, which clarifies and simplifies the matter at hand; but above all, the author uses the irony to reinforce orthodox morality. More recently, Michael McKeon and John Bender have also seen the novel as essentially conservative, although the former notes the author must struggle to keep his critique on course.

   2. As David Nokes convincingly shows the considerable changes made in the manuscript (25), I am treating the 1754 edition separately and have not included in my discussion Fielding's intriguing preface to the 1741 *Miscellanies*.

   3. Critics have usually been content to discuss *Jonathan Wild* in terms of comedy and satire, without distinguishing between the two. A. E. Dyson compares satire and comedy as moralizing versus normalizing forms but then dismisses satire altogether as an important feature of Fielding's corpus, while Robert Hopkins conflates the two genres, arguing that *Jonathan Wild* is at once a comic masterpiece and a satire, without clarifying how these two functions interrelate. Ronald Paulson sees the work both as innovative picaresque novel and satire, but he also recognizes that the work represents an exception to the general fictional practices of Fielding, and it is unclear whether he finds the satiric world of the novel to be effective or not (*Satire and the Novel in Eighteenth-Century England* 73–83.)

   Other scholars have focused on the multitude of sources Fielding uses for mock-heroic purposes, but while they testify to the author's erudition and point to the many levels of literary parody in the satire, they do little to elucidate the peculiar narrative structure that informs the novel. See Bernard Shea; William J. Farrell; and William R. Irwin. Allan Wendt's groundbreaking article, "The Moral Allegory of *Jonathan Wild*," suggests that both Wild and Heartfree are objects of the author's ironic scrutiny. However, Wendt does not discuss the novel as satire and consequently does not explain how the novel develops this ironic strategy through its problematic formal properties or how the text's double irony inaugurates an un-ironic understanding of the whole.

   Uncertainty as to how Fielding's satiric irony operates has also led to debate on the stance of the narrator in the text and to questions as to which passages in the book can and should be read ironically and which should be taken "seriously." This concern reaches a crisis point in Michael McKeon's tantalizing reading of the satire, which has been in turn severely (and I think, unfairly) criticized by Treadwell Ruml in his 1989 article. Although McKeon observes that Fielding's mock-heroic is so self-subversive and unstable that it threatens to "assume a force of its own and overturn its original premises" (384), he later dismisses the importance of this subversive force with the conclusion that that work is simply a reflection of ideology. Fielding is able to restabilize the narrative, and thus, in McKeon's opinion, the author insists unproblematically on the validity of conservative, sociopolitical values (392–93). John Bender returns to an earlier position—arguing that the author's ironic attack is directed against Walpole and as such is clear.

4. In other words, this is a parody both of traditional classical history and of modern history, specifically the criminal biography. See McKeon 383.

5. "The idea of a supreme Being, infinite in power, goodness and wisdom, whose wisdom, whose workmanship we are, and on whom we depend; and the idea of ourselves as understanding rational beings; being such as are clear in us, would, I supppose, if duly considered and pursued, afford such foundations of our duty and rules of action as might place morality amongst the sciences capable of demonstration: wherein I doubt not but from self-evident proposition by necessary consequences, as incontestible as those in mathematics, the measures of right and wrong might be made out to anyone" (Hume 334).

6. See Glenn W. Hatfield (107–8) and William R. Irwin (44–55) for opposing readings of the concept introduced in this passage. McKeon alone recognizes the extraordinary complexity of the introduction's irony and notes that while it lampoons the unheroic rogue (Wild) who cannot meet the standard of greatness, the passage also subverts the standard of greatness itself (384).

7. This argumentation is reminiscent of Hume's discussion of the irreducible and inexplicable nature of belief, that "something felt by the mind, which distinguishes the ideas of the judgment from the fictions of the imagination. It gives them more weight and influence; makes them appear of greater importance; enforces them in the mind; and renders them the governing principle of our actions" (Hume 614).

8. This tonal shift can be observed elsewhere. In Heartfree's soliloquy in book 3, for example, the style moves into a combination of sentimentality and Boethian stoicism—an appropriate choice given the hero's imprisonment: "How mean a tenure is that at the will of fortune, which chance, fraud, and rapine are every day so likely to deprive us of, and often the more likely by how much the greater worth our possessions are of! Is it not to place our affections on a bubble in the water, or on a picture in the clouds!" (127).

9. See Clément's discussion of silent movie actresses in Cixous and Clément's Newly Born Woman.

10. These gestures all represent Wild's exercise of freedom, and in this context, the division between Wild's moral imprisonment and Heartfree's moral liberty is by no means as clear-cut as David L. Evans argues.

11. In this sense, Wild is not a failure, as Dircks argues (79), and he

transcends his status as what Nokes sees to be an "authorial puppet" (16).

---

4. Criminal Kin: Gendered Tragedy, Subversion of Inversion, and the Fear of the Feminine in Schiller's *Robbers* and Sade's *Justine*

---

1. Harald Steinhagen has observed the intellectual affinities between Schiller and Sade, and his own comparison of Franz Moor's character with that of Juliette in Sade's 1797 novel by the same name suggests generic as well as philosophical connections between *The Robbers* and the *Justine* cycle. I have chosen the 1791 *Justine*, which is the first version of the story published by Sade (as opposed to the 1787 *conte philosophique*, which was never published during the author's lifetime), as well as his very first publication. This novel provides a more intriguing and more timely analysis with *The Robbers*, Schiller's first play, than the later, greatly expanded and significantly altered *Nouvelle Justine* of 1797. See Alice Laborde's comparative analysis of the three *Justine*s, 41–129.

2. Much has been made in Schiller criticism of the polar opposition between the two Moor brothers, and consequently, scholarship on *The Robbers* has concerned itself primarily with pinning down the philosophical/psychological stereotypes that Franz and Karl embody rather than analyzing them as individual characters. Jürgen Schlunk goes so far as to reduce the brothers to two columns of opposing characteristics; more recently Richard Koc's Freudian reading—astute though it is—also remains on the surface of these characters, dismissing the Moor brothers as aspects of "one son's . . . ambivalent self-conflicting feelings" (91). The detailed character analysis that has been done tends to focus on Karl (see Wiese; Mann; and Leidner for positive assessments; Linn for negative readings).

3. In "Le Récit d'Initiation dans le Roman libertin," Claude Reichler argues for the centrality of "initiation" and entrance into the world in the libertine novel (101)—both hallmarks of the standard novel of education.

4. This is a typical libertine device according to Reichler ("On the Notion of Intertextuality" 213).

5. Jonnes notices the marginalization of mothers in Schiller's early drama but does not discuss its significance (145–46).

6. In this manner, Karl upholds the Lockean notion of inalienable natural rights, which ground all legal relations between men (Cassirer 249–50).

7. There is also a Rousseauian return to origins suggested here, insofar as this scene reenacts the ritual of the *Heerkaiserwahl* common among the ancient Germanic tribes.

8. Franz essentially (and wittily) agrees with his brother's critique

of a hypocritical, oppressive society, when he remarks: "There are certain conventions that men have made, to rule the pulses that turn the world . . . admirable devices to keep fools respectful and to hold down the mob [*unter dem Pantoffel halten*], so that clever people can live in better comfort" (32; 1.1).

9. In addition to Amalia's defiance, Franz's henchman Hermann betrays Franz, not once but twice, first by telling Amalia that Karl and the count are alive, and second by bringing the old man food in prison, while Daniel refuses to kill the disguised Karl and reveals Franz's secrets.

10. See Spiegelberg's account of the nunnery episode (72–73; 2.3).

11. Karl's removal from the robber band is consequently *not* the product of a moral transfiguration, as Hans-Günther Thalheim would have it (105).

12. Therein lies the necessary insufficiency of masculine identity under patriarchy. As Carole-Anne Tyler suggests in "Boys Will Be Girls," the particular man must always fail in his quest to incarnate masculinity because "no one has or can have the phallus and the omniscience, omnipotence, and wholeness which it signifies" (41).

13. See Koc's lucid discussion of multiple father-sons in the play. However, he neglects to discuss the priests as father figures—which are of key importance, in my view—and does not comment on the role of the many brother mirror relationships in shaping the drama's meaning (93–97).

14. See Tyler's corrective reading of the Freudian father's desires (45).

15. Seen from this point of view, *The Robbers* cannot be seen as a religious play. For a traditional reading of this question, see Alan Leidner's discussion of Wiese, May, and Müller (61–62).

16. And Daniel is further feminized in the recognition scene with Karl, which clearly replays Odysseus' recognition by his old nurse (117; 4.3).

17. In this generic paradox, even the most "manly" of men in Schiller's play become more feminine than the play's only woman does (Tyler 50–51).

18. Relatively little has been written specifically on *Justine*, but the controversy as to its merit points to the work's importance and difficulty. See Nancy Miller's "Justine, or the Vicious Circle" and Jane Gallop for opposing viewpoints.

19. These masculinizing possibilities are already implied in Roland Barthes' discussion of the oddly open power dynamics of libertine ritual. In particular, he notes that the (usually female) libertine victim ceases to be a victim (and becomes a master) as soon as he or she is able to find pleasure in the experience. See *Sade, Fourier, Loyola*.

20. Angela Carter notes that Sade's women are so "masculine" that "it is easy to mistake them for female impersonators" (104), while Tyler observes that the Juliette of Sade's mature novel by the same name is the "archetypal phallic woman" (48). In light of these arguments, David Morris' contention that "power in Sade is ultimately genderless" seems erroneous, although Morris does admit the "shiftiness" of gender in connection with the power to inflict pain (325).

21. As such, Sade's criminals form a carnival procession, not unlike that of the promiscuous masquerades so common in the eighteenth-century popular imagination. See Terry Castle, "The Culture of Travesty," 159.

22. Despite these democratic overtones, the episodes of the novel move roughly from the bottom to the top of a rigid hierarchy—from common criminals (a dishonest usurer and a roving group of bandits) to aristocrats, medical doctors, members of the clergy, the ostensible guardians of legal justice—judges themselves, and finally back to Juliette, with whom the defense of crime has begun.

23. In the first half of the novel, Justine refuses to take advantage of the opportunities for criminal complicity presented her by Du Harpin, Dubois, and Coeur de Fer, Count Bressac, and Rodin, although they would not mistreat her sexually and might even reward her if she complied with them. This repeated refusal in the first half of the novel delivers her into the hands of those who will abuse her physically regardless of her behavior—the monks, in the central episode of the novel, and in the second half, the counterfeiters, the decapitating monseigneur, and the judge.

24. The novel also gradually tightens the connection between murder and sexual gratification; the monks take pleasure by physically abusing and then killing; the counterfeiter is gratified because he may or may not kill; the blood-letter, because he gradually kills; the decapitator, because he executes; the judge, because he tortures and then condemns to execution.

25. The honest judge M. S... and Juliette's lover M. Corville are the exceptions who ostensibly prove this rule.

26. Compare with Angela Carter, who argues that Justine's virtue consists in the repression of pleasure (47).

27. The name "Thérèse" is probably a play on the 1788 pornographic novel *Thérèse philosophe* by de Montigny, but the name clearly functions as an ironic religious emblem as well (Praz 98–99).

28. For reasons that will become evident, I do not agree with Josue Harari's assessment of the role of libertine discourse in Sade's writing, which he argues, serves no communicative function (155–60).

29. Justine tells her tale to most of the novel's major characters— Bressac, Father Clement, M. Guernande, Roland, Dubois, and Judge

Cardoville. Only Rodin does not hear the history, but he "reads" her story on a much more physical level—namely, in the massive physical injuries which he cures—and thereby guesses the most important elements of her history.

30. Simone de Beauvoir argues that the libertine's stance is already vulnerable, because it is inherently contradictory and isolates him in a "lonely immanence," which he cannot overcome if he is to remain a libertine. For example, Rodin's wish to vivisect his daughter in order to further mankind is a wish that completely contradicts his philosophy of pure self-interest ("Must We Burn Sade?" 58).

31. Both Nancy Miller and Peter Cryle see the ending as essentially unproblematic (Miller claims the novel's moralistic finale is merely formulaic, while Cryle maintains it is merely ironic), but to my mind the use of this formula is key to the novel's meaning. My reading extends and sheds light on Jean Paulhan's astute observation that the novel's "surprise ending" poses an important problem in interpreting Sade (12).

32. In the construction of masculinity and femininity, physiology is not destiny (Morris 315), rather it is gender which inscribes its "truth" onto the body, be it male or female.

33. I disagree with Paglia who maintains that "Sade's evasive sodomy is a ritual of riddance to evade maternal [female] power" (246). Even Sade's monastic monster, Clément, seems to sense the inevitable danger of feminization; his Lockean defense of perversion can be read at the same time as an ironic, feminized undercutting of his own self-consciously misogynist libertine practice (see his speech 601).

34. Béatrice Didier sees Sade's writing as a linguistic revolt in favor of all that does not fit (98), while Angela Carter argues that "the inversion of regular practice transforms the significance of the practice" (76). In *Justine* at least, Sade suggests that simple, inversive revolt—by word or deed—does not succeed.

35. In his corrective analysis of Foucault's reading of *La Nouvelle Justine*, Georges van den Abbeele signals Sade's importance in the *oeuvre* of the late French philosopher. But I suspect that Foucault's most valuable comments on Sade might be found in the study that does not focus on the eighteenth-century author at all—namely, in *Discipline and Punish*. There is repeated emphasis in *Justine* on the regimentation of the libertine's sexual program, the self-discipline of the libertine, and on his scrupulous training of his victims into appropriately docile bodies.

36. Donnes implies that something similar occurs in Schiller's emphasis on the public versus private role of the father, although he sees the "recognition of the [Foucaultian] mechanisms of power" (154) articulated in the later play *Kabale und Liebe*, rather than in *The Robbers*.

37. Similarly, Paglia notes that "Sade has spectacularly enlarged female character" (247).

38. This masculinism (subconsciously?) informs Peter Cryle's apt description of Sade's writing as "hard" and his observation that the "libertines want to have maximum impact on the bodies of their victims" (294).

39. And this is why, I suspect, contemporary popular criminal fictions, both literary and cinematic, are as unrelentingly masculine as they are.

---

5. The Tyranny of Form: Defense, Romance, and the Pursuit of the Criminal Text in Godwin's *Caleb Williams* and Kleist's *Michael Kohlhaas*

---

1. The narrative dynamic that informs *Jonathan Wild* guides Kleist's narrative, for the latter presents itself as an objective, "true" history of Kohlhaas' criminal career, beginning (as does *Jonathan Wild*) with the protagonist's first foray into crime and ending with his death on the block. The awareness of a popular criminal tradition is even more overt in *Caleb Williams*, which specifically refers to the criminal biography as a genre and to *Jonathan Wild* in particular and has Caleb both imitate that kind of writing as an author and appear in a criminal pamphlet as the hero.

2. James Thompson is on the right track when he refers to the importance of punishment in *Caleb Williams* (179), but sympathetic as I am to his Foucaultian analysis of novel—based on the notion of surveillance—I find that his argument falls short of the mark. First, the Foucaultian notion of the carceral, where "the guilty are kept isolated from one another, yet under constant surveillance by the authorities" (Thompson 189) does not in any way reflect the actual prison scenes as described by Caleb, which—typically, as will be seen—provide yet further opportunities for intense male-bonding; these carceral scenes are indeed far more reminiscent of the kind of relaxed prison socializing seen in *Jonathan Wild* than they are of Foucault's disciplinary space. Further, Caleb's "anguished isolation" is not as total as Thompson argues (183), for Godwin's hero repeatedly establishes emotional relationships with criminal characters; it is only from the "innocent" characters (among whose number he wishes to count himself) that he is alienated. Second, I agree with Eric Rothstein, whom Thompson criticizes (187), in observing that Falkland does indeed have personal power, which he uses and takes pleasure in using (in contrast to the strangely powerless officials of *Michael Kohlhaas*)—a state of affairs at odds to the transformation of power into an impersonal network under discipline.

3. Leland Warren's useful essay is the first on *Caleb Williams* to discuss the importance of writing in a postmodern theoretical context,

although I disagree with his contention that writing is somehow secondary to speech in the novel. See "*Caleb Williams* and the 'Fall' into Writing." See also Karl N. Simms' reading.

4. According to this reading, Caleb and the Kleistian narrator both resemble the Barthian mythologist who "'wishes to protect reality' against the 'evaporation' with which it is threatened by the alienating speech of myth," but who discovers that "he has himself contributed to its disappearance." See Jean Genette on Roland Barthes in *Figures of Literary Discourse*.

5. This reading unites three strands of Godwin criticism—the political, aesthetic, and sexual (see Ken Edward Smith's summary of critical trends). Until very recently, few studies of *Caleb Williams* have analyzed the novel's much-discussed conflict in a literary-generic context (while Dean Thomas Hughes cites the importance of romance, like Harvey Gross, he uses the concepts of romance and novel more or less interchangeably), and with the exception of Alex Gold's insightful Freudian reading, sexuality in Godwin's novel has been studiously ignored. Donald Wehr's article situates the novel within the eighteenth-century literary tradition, and Kate Fergusson Ellis implies (but does not explore) the book's violation of the Gothic erotic procedures (which involve the interplay between male and female) by focusing on men and on "opposing ideals of masculinity" (151). Michael DePorte may be right when he argues that the Gothic is ultimately not very important in the novel (159).

Andrew Scheiber comes closest to understanding what the book is about formally; he observes that *Caleb Williams* portrays "the inherent tensions of the novel form itself" (265) but again does not tie this in with the significance of the book's subject of investigation. Similarly, Karl Simms argues that the novel is about "the fact of textuality" (359) and how this fact assaults "the problem of History" (361).

6. This is also a recognizable eighteenth-century maneuver. See Gary Kelly's discussion of the influence of Rousseau's *Confessions* on Godwin.

7. This point is reinforced by the fact that all the offenders in Caleb's prison are accused of petty thievery and by the fact that the members of Raymond's band pride themselves on being thieves and not murderers (220).

8. The other gentry seem for the most part indifferent to Tyrrel's outrageous abuse of privilege.

9. Mr. Clare warns Falkland of the younger man's weaknesses during his deathbed speech (37).

10. Thus, if Caleb's version of the Falkland story employs "themes . . . familiar to any reader of Richardson" (Wehrs 499), it is only insofar as these eighteenth-century *topoi* also replay standard romance conventions.

11. Caleb goes to great lengths to legitimize his procedure in the relating of the Falkland story: "I shall interweave with Mr. Collins' story various information which I afterwards received from other quarters, that I may give all possible perspicuity to the series of events. To avoid confusion in my narrative, I shall drop the person of Collins, and assume to be myself the historian of our patron" (11).

12. While Collins clearly rejects the chivalric ideal that has guided Falkland, it is clear from the way Caleb tells the story and from the way he shapes his own narrative, that he does not reject these ideals himself; his decision to quote Collins directly at the end of the narrative obviously distances him from Collins' point of view and suggests that the original, orally transmitted story has been reshaped by the writer (Rothstein 20). Scheiber is correct to insist on the power that Falkland's story exerts over Caleb's own tale (256), but I disagree with his contentions that Falkland has a voice of his own, accessible to us through Caleb's narrative and that this voice represents the voice of British society. Rather it is Collins who represents the spokesman for society here and elsewhere in the novel, and this voice both admires Falkland but rejects the chivalric ideal for which he stands.

13. Thus, Falkland incarnates all the features of a typical romance knight ("Medieval Romance").

14. Seen within the romance context, Mr. Clare becomes an Arthurian figure, an older, wiser, kingly authority who presides in the background over the depicted community—a sense especially evident in the scene at the gentlemen's assembly where Falkland reads his poetry to an enthusiastically attentive court (Frye 195).

15. This looks very much like "homosexual panic," as Sedgwick understands it (89).

16. This transference between Falkland and his nemesis is already implied by the fact that in order to destroy Tyrrel, Falkland must resort to physical force, the principle that Tyrrel represents, and in so doing he "becomes" Tyrrel.

17. Thus, the Falkland story not only provides "a moral lexicon for what is to happen later" (Rothstein 22) but a structural framework as well.

18. For all the stress on his victimization, Caleb's account of his adventures (which contain in and of themselves a certain structural repetitiveness typical of the courtly romance) also stresses his resourcefulness, prowess, courage, and cunning (i.e., his multiple escapes from prison, from the robber band, from Gines; his talent for the most varied disguises; his poetic, technical, and scholarly powers). His tale is then as much a tale of ingenuity and eventual triumph (romance) as it is a tale of suffering (defense).

19. Unable to die because of his proximity to the Grail and unable

to live as a normal man, Anfortas' "life is but a dying" (Wolfram von Eschenbach 126) till he can be released by a younger, more perfect version of himself who will take then assume his place as Lord of the Grail.

20. Compare with Kenneth Graham who reads the trial scene as a "meeting that overcomes jealous self-absorption and enacts change" (223).

21. This urge may well be the wish to merge with the father, as both Storch and Ellis have argued, but it is a mistake, I think, to deny its connection to homoeroticism.

22. In other words, despite Gold's protestations to the contrary, this *is* indeed a "story about sexual passions between men" (145).

23. This explains the highly sexual (and generically ambiguous) nature of the "written *lacunae* which *pervade* the work" (Simms 359; my emphasis).

24. Compare with Gold who sees Caleb as victim and Falkland as tyrant (145).

25. Joel Black forcefully argues that this shift from the "criminal-as-artist mode of representation to the artist-as-criminal mode" is a general literary phenomenon (44), and while I disagree with him that this is a "post-romanticism" occurrence, I think he is right to see this shift as a Foucaultian reordering of the criminal into acceptable forms (46).

26. Hence, the "power of ideology" (Graham 225) operates within rather than on narrative.

27. As in the case of *Caleb Williams*, critics have long recognized the paradoxical character of *Michael Kohlhaas*—perhaps the most daunting representative of Kleist's notoriously difficult narrative corpus. As in the case of Godwin, many critics have looked to historical sources for clues as to the novella's meaning (see Clifford Bernd, Malte Dießelhorst, Rolf King; Robert Wexelblatt). Several recent studies have taken a jurisprudential direction and have sought to justify or condemn the hero on the grounds of sixteenth- and eighteenth-century legal theory (see Joachim Bohnert; Hartmut Boockmann; Joachim Rückert). But these appeals to historical materials yield little that contributes to understanding Kleist's text, and as my analysis will suggest, these studies are themselves symptomatic of the kind of reading that the novella is actually criticizing. More successful have been studies that have discussed the novella in terms of literary *topoi* and genre—especially tragedy (John Cary; Charles Passage; Richard Kuhns, although these studies do not ultimately help us understand the way narrative functions in the text) and comparatist studies, which point to the modernity of Kleist's fictional vision (see Eric Marson on Kafka; J. M. Lindsay on Camus). The most radical articulation of the interpretative problems attending *Michael*

Kohlhaas has come from Helga Gallas, whose Lacanian reading sees the text as a skeletal reenactment of the Oedipus myth—a skeleton structure that Kleist amplifies in so many contradictory ways, that a coherent reading of the text is impossible. I will argue that those contradictions are, in the end, red herrings; it is not a question of resolving them (and in the romance context, many of them are already resolved) but of moving into a world where such contradictions have lost their relevance.

28. Frederic Jameson emphasizes the transferability in the romance of evil from one character to another (119).

29. Much has been made of the incongruity of the gypsy fortune-teller episode within a realistic fiction (see Richard Kuhns 80; Charles Passage, "*Michael Kohlhaas*" 190; Luke and Reeves' introduction to their translation of the novella 31), which presents no anomaly when read within the context of the romance's miraculous world (Bahktin 155). See also Michael Lützler's pragmatic reading (222).

30. Clayton Koelb likens the devouring of the literary talisman to the act of Holy Communion (1104).

31. Michael's pursuit of Tronka causes the Wittenburg townspeople to turn against the Junker; the citizens seem to recognize that the law-abiding aristocrat, and not the law-breaking horse dealer, is the true cause of all their woes: "The people in their thousands were besieging the Junker's house, which had been barricaded with beams and posts, demanding with frenzied clamour his expulsion from the town" (145). And later the narrator demonstrates the subversive power of Michael Kohlhaas' behavior even more dramatically in the horse identification scene. The detailed description of the escalation of individual actions into a mass riot emphasizes the violence of the burghers' negative feelings toward the aristocrats, feelings which seethe beneath the surface, waiting for the slightest excuse to surge forth: "Master Himboldt cried out: 'Down with the murderous tyrant!' and as the people, incensed by this scene, pressed together and forced the guard back, he threw the Chamberlain to the ground from behind, tore off his cloak and collar and helmet, wrenched his sword out of his hand and with a savage sweep of the arm hurled it away across the square" (179).

32. Thus, while Luther may indeed have realized that Kohlhaas is right and the court is wrong (Bohnert 427), he at no time uses this perspective to help the protagonist.

33. The Tronka family decides to trap the horse dealer with the bogus Nagelschmidt letter, not in order to avenge itself on Kohlhaas, but to unseat the Chancellor, Count von Wrede, who is a political enemy and whose high-handed letter to them demanding that the Chamberlain (Kunz von Tronka) approach Kohlhaas directly has threatened the family's status. There is also a struggle within the family; Hinz and Kunz detest their cousin Wenzel but must support his claim in order to protect

their own credibility and power.

34. This power phenomenon appears consistently in Kafka—notably in *The Castle* and *The Trial.*

35. Therein lies the profound irony of Kleist's frequent use of the novella—the "new" and strange narrative form, which is by nature characterized both by a tension between a host of genres (history, romance, *conte philosophique,* tragedy [Wiese 3]) struggling for ascendancy. The novella would seem to be the perfect place to explore both complex struggles for power and the problem of talking about them—as Kafka and Camus are later to recognize. But Kleist exposes the fallacy of the novella's "newness," for it is in fact no more able to tell a new story than the more traditional forms that coexist within it.

36. Compare with Eric Marson's contention that Kleist is interested "in the processes of law for their own sake" (22).

---

6. Conclusion: Resistance, Metaphysics, and the Aesthetics of Failure in Modern Criminal Literature

---

1. I am bracketing—because of its immensity—the whole domain of prison literature, which has become a genre in and of itself.

2. D. A. Miller suggests that such fictions are particularly insidious because they give the novel reader (and it is unclear whether he means a nineteenth-century audience, a twentieth-century one, or both [x]) an illusion of private freedom, and consequently, a feeling of superiority, which prevents the reader from taking action against society (x–xiii).

3. This narrative formula also appears to be a modification in the typical procedure of popular criminal narrative, as Lincoln Faller understands it; he observes that in the criminal biographies of eighteenth-century popular culture, the criminal almost always repents on the block and becomes, ironically, a standard for the very society which he earlier stood against (79–90).

4. Marius' condemnation of his father-in-law is important (see book 6, chap. 2) and renders problematic his change of heart when he discovers that Valjean saved him at the barricades.

5. Jacques Dubois' insightful reading of Javert points in several important directions. First, he notices the degree to which Javert's pleasure is tied up in the exercise of his duties (15) and second, the extent to which Javert is in fact Valjean's double (17). Third, he makes the intriguing suggestion that Javert is in fact a master of irony whose last testament (a series of minuscule prison reforms—which again testify to his "disciplinary" outlook) reveal a kind of cynical self-consciousness that allows him to momentarily escape the fate that the author intended for him.

6. We have only to think of the diverse "resistances" offered by Énjolras, Gavroche, and Éponine to see the degree to which the individual is repeatedly and devastatingly crushed by the social mechanism in Hugo's novel.

7. Guy Rosa's essay "Jean Valjean: Réalisme et irréalisme des *Misérables*" argues that the characters of the novel are designated, reified into a general indistinction (224), because such misery constitutes that which is not narratable within the confines of bourgeois realism (226). But while he maintains that Hugo's silence vis-à-vis his characters testifies to his rejection of realism (226), I believe that the exact opposite is true.

8. Read from this angle, the metaphorical androgyny which Hugo assigns to Jean Valjean (Grossman 97) actually resembles the covert misogyny of cross-dressing dynamics as discussed by Tyler. Insofar as Valjean is a far better "mother" than Fantine is, Hugo also seems to be suggesting that "only men can become real women" (Tyler 51).

9. Tellingly, Vautrin explains to Rastignac, "I am what you might call an artist" (125), and his satiric social observations clearly echo those of Diderot's nephew (see *Rameau's Nephew*). I fully concur with Berthier's assessment of the two criminal heroes and his insistence on the importance of their sexual orientation (172).

10. Robert Denommé takes this idea even further, arguing that Vautrin is ultimately, the true hero of the entire *Human Comedy*. See "Création et Paternité" 325–26.

11. Because of this, Denommé contends that Vautrin is a modern Daedalus, a criminal architect-father who seeks to escape the confines of society through the construction of multiple identities and the enlistment of surrogate sons into his plans (313).

12. Vautrin's manly energy and power is referred to throughout the novel (Berthier 156).

13. This would explain the highly exaggerated gender typing that Balzac uses throughout his novels; he sets up what Martha Niess Moss calls "the essential polarity of masculinity and femininity" (37) only to knock it down all the more dramatically. See also Paglia's intriguing discussion of female androgyny in Balzac (406–7).

14. Namely, Vautrin is rehabilitated in *Splendeurs et Misères des Courtisanes*, where he becomes an informer. See Hunt 361–62. Seen from this point of view, Vautrin is not, in the end, the lonely *Übermensch* that Alfred Glauser would have him be (see "Balzac/Vautrin" 592) and is ultimately a failure, as Nilli Diengott has argued in "Goriot vs. Vautrin" (71), but for different reasons. Berthier too admits that although Vautrin's very choice of sexual orientation (and he emphasizes that it is indeed a *choice*) keeps him operating as a subversive force within society, Vautrin fails sexually, because his love is always unrequited (174–76).

15. See Sartre's brilliant discussion of the relationship between

criminality and sainthood in "The Eternal Couple of the Criminal and the Saint" in *Saint Genet*.

16. One of the more incisive examples of this exposure is when Genet summarizes the artistic use of the robber band and thereby reminds the audience that criminality always risks becoming falsified by literature, to the point where even real criminals are taken in by the representational image: "Many literary men have often dwelt on the idea of bands. . . . You then imagine rough bandits united by a will to plunder, by cruelty and hatred. . . . In prison, every criminal may dream of a well-knit organization, closed but strong, which would be a refuge against the world and its morality: this is only a reverie" (98).

17. Georges Bataille misunderstands the nature of the "failure" involved in Genet's *oeuvre* (226), as Derrida has already noted in his brilliantly unreadable reaction to Genet in *Glas* (see 219, column 4). I also disagree with Bataille's view that Genet is indifferent to communication (227–30). Both of these postures seem to be radical strategies deployed to rethink aesthetics and the claim that art can/should make on its audience.

18. Genet's "feminine" imitates, pays homage to, but does not replace woman, in much the same way as the saints reiterate but cannot match the goodness of God. Ultimately, the feminine in *The Thief's Journal* is exemplified by a woman—namely, Genet's mother, a figure who is of great importance throughout. See Mary Ann Frese Witt's excellent analysis of the maternal in "Mothers and Stories."

19. It is also a complex parody of Dostoyevsky's *Crime and Punishment*, according to Robert Bowie.

20. Like Sade's characters, those of Burgess also possess "no inner life, no introspection. Their actions sum them up completely" (Carter 25).

21. The novel is then, neither a "running lecture on [Christian] free will" (182) nor a determinist fantasy-nightmare—as Stanley Edgar Hyman paradoxically argues.

22. Compare with Alice Kuzniar's Lacanian reading of Handke's recent works in "Desiring Eyes." Although her discussion of the "gaze"'s changing function from Sartrian to Lacanian in *Across* is insightful (362–63), the argument does not account for the role of the criminal and for the odd, emotionless tone of the narration.

23. The following citation corresponds almost perfectly to Foucault's description of the typical disciplinary space and to the role of writing within it: "This . . . segmented space, observed at every point, in which the individuals are inserted in a fixed place, in which the slightest movements are supervised, in which all events are recorded, in which an uninterrupted work of writing links the center and periphery, in which power is exercised without division . . . in which each individual is

constantly located, examined and distributed" (*Discipline and Punish* 197).

24. Andreas' study also bears the mark of discipline; he keeps specific objects on his desk that "call him to order" whenever he risks becoming too entranced by his private, personal research (14–15).

25. This self-conscious emphasis on visual surface has trapped the few critics who have actually tackled *Across* into relatively simplistic positions vis-à-vis the meaning of the work—seeing it either as a religious epiphany (Peter Hamm), as a purely formal exercise in signs (Susan Bernofsky), or as metaphorical autobiography (Rolf Günter Renner).

26. Robert Gross, conversation on 21 July 1991.

27. By having the priest attend the card game, Handke neatly (and humorously) revises the role of religious authority, by taking him away from the prison cell (and or deathbed) and making him a man like other men at a tavern where he expresses—not the "truth"—but an informed (and beautifully stated) opinion. Thus, Handke's priest resembles one of the guests in Plato's *Symposium* far more than he does one of Christ's disciples.

Works Cited

Primary Sources

Aeschylus. *Prometheus Bound.* Trans. David Grene. Ed. David Grene and Richmond Lattimore. New York: Modern Library, 1942. Vol. 1 of *The Complete Greek Tragedies.*

Balzac, Honoré de. *Old Goriot.* Trans. Marion Ayton Crawford. Penguin Classics. London: Penguin, 1951.

Burgess, Anthony. *A Clockwork Orange.* New York: Ballantine, 1986.

Burke, Edmund. *A Philosophical Enquiry into the Origins of the Ideas of the Sublime and the Beautiful.* Ed. James T. Boulton. Notre Dame, IN: Notre Dame UP, 1976.

Defoe, Daniel. *Roxana.* London: Penguin, 1987.

Diderot, Denis. *Le Neveu de Rameau. Oeuvres Romanesques.* Ed. Henri Benac. Paris: Garnier, 1962. 395–492.

———. *Rameau's Nephew and D'Alembert's Dream.* Trans. Leonard Tancock. Penguin Classics. Middlesex, Eng.: Penguin, 1966.

Fielding, Henry. *Jonathan Wild.* Ed. David Nokes. Middlesex, Eng.: Penguin, 1982.

Genet, Jean. *The Thief's Journal.* Trans. Bernard Frechtman. New York: Grove, 1964.

Godwin, William. *Caleb Williams or Things as They Are.* Ed. Maurice Hindle. London: Penguin, 1987.

Handke, Peter. *Across.* Trans. Ralph Manheim. New York: Farrar, 1986.

Hugo, Victor. *Les Misérables.* Trans. Norman Denny. London: Penguin, 1976.

Hume, David. "Concerning Human Understanding." *The English Philosophers from Bacon to Mill.* New York: Modern Library, 1939. 585–689.

Kleist, Heinrich von. *Michael Kohlhaas.* Ed. Klaus Müller-Salget. Frankfurt am Main: Deutscher Klassiker Verlag, 1990. Vol. 3 of *Sämtliche Werke.* Ed. Ilse-Marie Barth et al.

———. *Michael Kohlhaas. The Marquise of O and Other Stories.* Trans. David Luke and Nigel Reeves. London: Penguin, 1978.

Lillo, George. *The London Merchant*. Regents Restoration Drama Series. Lincoln: U of Nebraska P, 1965. Introd. by William H. McBurney. Reprint of 1731 publication.

Locke, John. "An Essay Concerning Human Understanding." *The English Philosophers from Bacon to Mill*. New York: Modern Library, 1939. 235–402.

Prévost, Abbé de. *L'Histoire du Chevalier Des Grieux et de Manon Lescaut*. Ed. Frederic Deloffre and Raymond Picard. Classiques Garnier. Paris: Garnier, 1965. Reprint of 1731 publication.

———. *Manon Lescaut*. Trans. Helen Waddell. Hyperion Library of World Literature. Westport, CT: Hyperion, 1978.

Sade, Alphonse de. *The Complete Justine, Philosophy in the Bedroom and Other Writings*. Trans. Richard Seaver and Austryn Wainhouse. New York: Grove, 1965.

———. *Justine*. Ed. Annie Le Brun and Jean-Jacques Pauvert. Paris: Pauvert, 1986. Vol. 3 of *Oeuvres Complètes*. Reprint of 1791 publication.

Schiller, Friedrich. *Die Räuber. Dramen 1*. Ed. Herbert Kraft. Frankfurt am Main: Insel, 1966. 7–130.

———. *The Robbers and Wallenstein*. Trans. F. J. Lamport. Penguin Classics. Middlesex, Eng.: Penguin, 1979.

Schlegel, Friedrich. *Charakteristiken und Kritien 1*. Ed. Hans Eichner. Munich: Schöningen, 1967. Vol. 2 of *Schlegel: Kritische Ausgabe*. Ed. Ernst Behler.

von Eschenbach, Wolfram. *Parzival*. Trans. Helen Mustard and Charles E. Passage. New York: Vintage, 1961.

Secondary Sources

Adorno, Theodor. *Aesthetic Theory*. Trans. C. Lenhardt. London: Routledge, 1984. Published in German in 1970.

Alkon, Paul K. *Defoe and Fictional Time*. Athens: U of Georgia P, 1979.

Angress, Ruth. "Kleists Abkehr von der Aufklärung." *Kleist Jahrbuch* (1987): 98–114.

Backscheider, Paula. *Daniel Defoe: Ambition and Innovation*. Lexington: U of Kentucky P, 1986.

Bakhtin, M. M. *The Dialogic Imagination*. Trans. Emerson Cary and Michael Holquist. Austin: U of Texas P, 1981.

Barthes, Roland. *The Pleasure of the Text*. Trans. Richard Miller. New York: Hill, 1975.

———. *Sade, Fourier, Loyola*. Paris: Editions du Seuil, 1971.

———. *Writing Degree Zero*. Trans. Annette Lavers and Colin Smith. London: Cape, 1967.

Bataille, Georges. *La Littérature et le mal*. Paris: Gallimard, 1957.

Beauvoir, Simone de. "Must We Burn Sade?" *120 Days of Sodom*. Trans. Austryn Wainhouse and Richard Seaver. New York: Grove, 1966. 3–64.

———. *The Second Sex*. Trans. H. M. Parshley. New York: Modern Library, 1952.

Beebee, Thomas O. *"Clarissa" on the Continent: Translation and Seduction*. University Park: Pennsylvania State UP, 1990.

Bender, John. *Imagining the Penitentiary*. Chicago: U of Chicago P, 1987.

Bernauer, James, and David Rasmussen, eds. *The Final Foucault*. Cambridge: MIT Press, 1988. Includes essays by Bernauer, Garth Gillan, and Thomas Flynn.

Bernbaum, Ernest. *The Drama of Sensibility*. Harvard Studies in English 3. Boston: Ginn, 1915.

Bernd, Clifford A. "Der Lutherbrief in Kleists *Michael Kohlhaas*." *Zeitschrift für deutsche Philologie* 86 (1967): 627–33.

Bernofsky, Susan. "The Threshold is the Source." *Critique* 23.1 (1990): 58–65.

Berthier, Philippe. "Balzac Du Côté de Sodome." *L'année Balzacienne* (1979): 147–77.

Bewell, Alan. *Wordsworth and the Enlightenment*. New Haven: Yale UP, 1989.

Bickel, Gisele. *Jean Genet: Criminalité et transcendance*. Saratoga, CA: Anma Libri, 1987.

Black, Joel. *The Aesthetics of Murder*. Baltimore: Johns Hopkins UP, 1991.

Bloom, Harold. *The Anxiety of Influence*. New York: Oxford UP, 1973.

Bohnert, Joachim. "Kohlhaas der entsetzliche." *Kleist Jahrbuch* (1988/89): 404–31.

Boockmann, Hartmut. "Mittelalterliches Recht bei Kleist: Ein Beitrag zum Verhältnis des *Michael Kohlhaas*." *Kleist Jahrbuch* (1985): 84–108.

Borkat, Roberta. "The Evil of Goodness." *Studies in Philology* 73 (1979): 288–312.

Bowie, Robert. "Freedom and Art in *A Clockwork Orange*. Anthony Burgess and the Christian Premises of Dostoevsky." *Thought* 56.223 (1981): 402–16.

Brady, Patrick. "Other-Portrayal and Self-Betrayal in *Manon Lescaut* and *La Vie de Marianne*." *Romanic Review* 64 (1973): 99–110.

Bredbeck, Gregory W. *Sodomy and Interpretation*. Ithaca, NY: Cornell UP, 1991.

Brown, Laura. *English Dramatic Form, 1660–1760: An Essay in Generic History*. New Haven: Yale UP, 1981.

Brown, Richard E. "Rival Socio-Economic Theories in Two Plays by George Lillo." *Tennessee Studies in Literature* 24 (1979): 94–110.

Butler, Marilyn. "Godwin, Burke and *Caleb Williams*. *Essays in Criticism* 23.3 (1982): 237–57.

Carter, Angela. *The Sadeian Woman*. London: Virago, 1979.

Cary, John R. "A Reading of Kleist's *Michael Kohlhaas*." *PMLA* 85 (1970): 212–18.

Cassirer, Ernst. *The Philosophy of the Enlightenment*. Princeton NJ: Princeton UP, 1951.

Castle, Terry. "The Culture of Travesty: Sexuality and Masquerade in Eighteenth-Century England." Rousseau and Porter, eds. 156–80.

Caviola, Hugo. "Ding-Bild-Schrift: Peter Handke's Slow Homecoming to a 'Chinese' Austria." *Modern Fiction Studies* 36.3 (1990): 381–94.

Cixous, Hélène. "The Laugh of the Medusa." Marks and Courtivron, eds. 245–64.

Cixous, Hélène, and Catherine Clément. *The Newly Born Woman*. Trans. Betsy Wing. Minneapolis: U of Minnesota P, 1986.

Clive, Geoffrey. *The Romantic Enlightenment*. New York: Meridian, 1960.

Connacher, D. J. *Aeschylus' Prometheus Bound: A Literary Commentary*. Toronto: U of Toronto P, 1980.

Cory, Odille. *Subjectivity and Sensitivity in the Novels of the Abbé Prévost*. Paris: Didier, 1972.

Coulet, Henri. Préface. *Manon Lescaut* by Prévost. Paris: Garnier-Flammarion, 1967. 14–25.

"Crime." *Encyclopédie ou Dictionnaire raisonné des sciences, des arts, et des métiers*. 1754 ed.

"Crime." *Oxford English Dictionary*. 1961 ed.

Crocker, Lester G. "Enlightenment Studies: The Last Ten Years." *Greene Centennial Studies: Essays Presented to Donald Greene in the Centennial Year of the University of South Carolina*. Ed. Paul J. Korshin and Robert R. Allen. Charlottesville: UP of Virginia, 1984. 351–76.

———. "The Enlightenment: What and Who?" *Studies in Eighteenth Century Culture* 17 (1987): 335–47.

Cryle, Peter. "Time Out in Erotic Narrative: The Recreative Pause in Sade and Restif de la Bretonne." *French Forum* 15.3 (1990): 277–99.

Daumas, Maurice. *Le Syndrome Des Grieux: La relation père/fils au XVIII siècle*. Paris: Éditions du Seuil, 1990.

Davis, Leonard J. *Factual Fictions: The Origins of the English Novel*. New York: Columbia UP, 1983.

Deloffre, Frederic, and Raymond Picard. Introduction à *Manon Lescaut*. *L'Histoire du Chevalier Des Grieux et de Manon Lescaut*. By Prévost. Ed. Deloffre and Picard. Classiques Garnier. Paris: Garnier, 1965.

Delon, Michel. "The Priest, the Philosopher, and Homosexuality in Enlightenment France." *Eighteenth Century Life*, Special Issue on Unauthorized Sexuality 9 (1985): 122–31.

Denommé, Robert T. "Création et Paternité: Le Personnage de Vautrin dans *La Comédie Humaine.*" *Stanford French Review* 5.3 (1981): 313–26.

DePorte, Michael. "The Consolations of Fiction: Mystery in *Caleb Williams.*" *Papers on Language and Literature* 20.2 (1984): 154–64.

Derrida, Jacques. *Glas.* Trans. John P. Leavey, Jr., and Richard Rand. Lincoln: U of Nebraska P, 1986.

———. *Of Grammatology.* Trans. Gayatri Spivak. Baltimore: Johns Hopkins UP, 1976.

Didier, Béatrice. *Sade: Une écriture du désir.* Paris: Denoël/Gonthier, 1976.

Diengott, Nilli. "Goriot vs. Vautrin: A Problem in the Reconstruction of *Le Père Goriot*'s System of Values." *Nineteenth Century French Studies* 15.2 (1986): 70–76.

Dießelhorst, Malte. "Hans Kohlhase/Michael Kohlhaas." *Kleist Jahrbuch* (1988/89): 334–56.

Dircks, Richard J. *Henry Fielding.* Boston: Twayne, 1983.

Donahoe, Joseph I., Jr. "The Death of Manon Lescaut: A Literary Inquest." *L'esprit créateur* 11 (1972): 129–46.

Donnes, Denis. "Pattern of Power: Family and State in Schiller's Early Drama." *Colloquia Germanica* 20.2–3 (1987):138–62.

Dreyfus, Hubert L., and Paul Rabinow. *Michel Foucault: Beyond Structuralism and Hermeneutics.* 2d ed. Chicago: U of Chicago P, 1983.

Dubois, Jacques. "L'affreux Javert." *Hugo dans les Marges.* Ed. Lucien Dällenbach and Laurent Jenny. Geneva: Editions Zoé, 1985. 9–34.

Dyer, D. G. "Junker Wenzel von Tronka." *German Life and Letters* 18 (1964/65): 252–57.

Dyson, A. E. "Satiric and Comic Theory in Relation to Fielding." *Modern Language Quarterly* (1957): 225–37.

Ellis, Kate Ferguson. *The Contested Castle: Gothic Novels and the Subversion of Domestic Ideology.* Chicago: U of Illinois P, 1989.

Empson, William. "*The Beggar's Opera*: Mock-Pastoral as the Cult of Independence." *Some Versions of the Pastoral.* Norfolk, CT: New Directions, 1950. 195–250.

Evans, David L. "The Theme of Liberty in *Jonathan Wild.*" *Papers on Language and Literature* 3 (1967): 302–13.

Falk, Eugene. *Renunciation as Tragic Focus.* Minneapolis: U of Minnesota P, 1954.

Faller, Lincoln B. *Turned to Account: The Forms and Functions of Criminal Biography in Late Seventeenth and Early Eighteenth-Century England.* Cambridge: Cambridge UP, 1987.

Farrell, William J. "The Mock-Heroic Form of *Jonathan Wild.*" *Modern Philology* 63 (1966): 216–26.

Felsenstein, Frank. "Newgate with a Mask On." *Zeitschrift für Anglistik und Amerikanistik* 28.3 (1981): 211–18.

Fink, Gonthier-Louis. "Das Motiv der Rebellion in Kleists Werk." *Kleist Jahrbuch* (1988/89): 64–88.

Flores, Stephan P. "Mastering the Self: The Ideological Incorporation of Desire in Lillo's *The London Merchant*." *Essays in Theatre* 5.2 (1987): 91–102.

Flynn, Thomas. "Foucault as Parrhesiast: His last Course at the Collège de France." Bernauer and Rasmussen, eds. 102–18.

Fort, Bernadette. "Manon's Suppressed Voice: The Uses of Reported Speech." *Romanic Review* 76.2 (1985): 172–91.

Foucault, Michel. *Discipline and Punish: The Birth of the Prison*. Trans. Alan Sheridan. New York: Pantheon, 1977.

———. *Foucault Reader*. Ed. Paul Rabinow. New York: Pantheon, 1984. This volume contains the essay, "What Is Enlightenment."

———. *The Order of Things: An Archeology of the Human Sciences*. Trans. Richard Howard. New York: Random, 1965.

Frühwald, Wolfgang, and Alberto Martino, eds. *Zwischen Aufklärung und Restauration*. Tübingen: Niemeyer, 1989.

Frye, Northrop. *Anatomy of Criticism*. Princeton, NJ: Princeton UP, 1957.

Gadamer, Hans-Georg. *Philosophical Hermeneutics*. Trans. David E. Linge. Berkeley: U of California P, 1976.

———. *The Relevance of the Beautiful and Other Essays*. Trans. Nicholas Walker. Cambridge: Cambridge UP, 1986.

———. *Truth and Method*. New York: Seabury, 1975.

Gallas, Helga. *Das Textbegehren des Michael Kohlhaas: Die Sprache des Unbewußtseins und der Sinn der Literatur*. Reinbek: GmbH, 1981.

Gallop, Jane. *Intersections*. Lincoln: U of Nebraska P, 1981.

Gay, Peter. *The Enlightenment: An Interpretation*. New York: Knopf, 1967.

Genette, Jean. *Figures of Literary Discourse*. Trans. Alan Sheridan. New York: Columbia UP, 1982.

Geyer-Ryan, Helga. "Family and Politics in the Drama of 'Sturm und Drang.'" *1789: Reading Writing Revolution*. Ed. Francis Barker et al. Proceedings of the Essex Conference on the Sociology of Literature. July 1981. London: U of Essex P, 1982. 218–25.

Gilbert, Sandra, and Susan Gubar. *The Madwoman in the Attic*. New Haven: Yale UP, 1979.

Gillan, Garth. "Foucault's Philosophy." Bernauer and Rasmussen, eds. 34–44.

Glauser, Alfred. "Balzac/Vautrin." *Romanic Review* 79.4 (1988): 585–610.

Gold, Alex, Jr. "It's Only Love: The Politics of Passion in Godwin's *Caleb Williams*." *Texas Studies in Literature and Language* 19.2 (1977): 135–60.

Golden, Morris. *Fielding's Moral Psychology*. Amherst: U of Massachusetts P, 1966.

Gossmann, Lionel. "Male and Female in Two Short Novels by Prévost." *Modern Language Review* 77.1 (1982): 29–37.

Graham, Kenneth W. "Narrative and Ideology in Godwin's *Caleb Williams. Eighteenth-Century Fiction* 2.3 (1990): 215–28.

Green, Frederick. *Literary Ideas in 18th Century France and England.* New York: Ungar, 1935.

Gross, Harvey. "The Pursuer and the Pursued: A Study of *Caleb Williams.*" *Texas Studies in Language and Literature* 1.3 (1959): 401–11.

Grossman, Kathryn M. "Narrative Space and Androgyny in *Les Misérables.*" *Nineteenth-Century Studies* 20.1/2 (1991/92): 97–106.

Hamm, Peter. "Die (wieder)einleuchtende Welt." *Die Arbeit am Glück.* Ed. Gerhard Melzer and Jale Tückel. Königstein: Athenäum, 1985. 102–10.

Hammer, Stephanie Barbé. "The Dance of Dishonesty: Satire of the Irredeemable in *Le Neveu de Rameau.*" *French Forum* 10.1 (1985): 5–19.

Harari, Josue. *Scenarios of the Imaginary: Theorizing the French Enlightenment.* Ithaca, NY: Cornell UP, 1987.

Harvey, A. D. "The Nightmare of *Caleb Williams.*" *Essays in Criticism* 26.3 (1976): 236–49.

Hatfield, Glenn W. *Henry Fielding and the Language of Irony.* London: Cambridge UP, 1968.

Havens, Raymond D. "The Sentimentalism of *The London Merchant.*" *English Literary History* 12 (1945): 45–61.

Hazard, Paul. *Études Critiques sur* Manon Lescaut. Chicago: U of Chicago P, 1929.

Hopkins, Robert. "Language and Comic Play in Fielding's *Jonathan Wild.*" *Criticism* 8 (1966): 213–28.

Hughes, Dean Thomas. *Romance and Psychological Realism in William Godwin's Novels.* New York: Arno, 1980.

Hunt, Herbert J. *Balzac's* Comédie Humaine. London: Athlone, 1964.

Hunter, J. Paul. "Fielding and the Modern Reader: The Problem of Temporal Transition." *Henry Fielding in His Time and Ours.* Los Angeles: U of California P, 1987. 3–28.

Hyman, Stanley Edgar. "Afterword to *A Clockwork Orange.*" *A Clockwork Orange.* New York: Norton, 1963. 180–85.

Irigaray, Luce. "When the Goods Get Together." Marks and Courtivron, eds. 107–10.

Irwin, Michael. *Henry Fielding the Tentative Realist.* Oxford: Oxford UP, 1967.

Irwin, William R. *The Making of* Jonathan Wild. Hamden, CT: Archon, 1966.

Jaccard, Jean-Luc. *Manon Lescaut, le personnage-romancier.* Paris: A. G. Nizet, 1975.

208 Works Cited

Jacob, Margaret C. *The Radical Enlightenment: Pantheists, Freemasons and Republicans*. London: Allen, 1981.

Jameson, Fredric. *The Political Unconscious: Narrative as a Socially Symbolic Act*. Ithaca, NY: Cornell UP, 1981.

Jones, Grahame. "*Manon Lescaut*: An Exercise in Literary Persuasion." *Romanic Review* 69 (1978): 48–59.

Jonnes, Denis. "Pattern of Power: Family and State in Schiller's Early Drama." *Colloquia Germanica* 20.2–3 (1987): 138–62.

Josephs, Herbert. "*Manon Lescaut*: A Rhetoric of Intellectual Evasion." *Romanic Review* 59.3 (1968): 185–97.

Kelly, Gary. "The Romance of Real Life: Autobiography in Rousseau and William Godwin." *L'homme et la nature*. Ed. Roger L. Emerson et al. Ontario: U of Western Ontario P, 1982. 93–101.

Kernan, Alvin. *The Cankered Muse*. New Haven: Yale UP, 1959.

Kiely, Robert. *The Romantic Novel in England*. Cambridge: Harvard UP, 1972.

King, Rolf. "The Figure of Luther in Kleist's *Michael Kohlhaas*." *Germanic Review* 9 (1934): 18–25.

Klossowski, Pierre. "Sade ou le philosophe scélerat." *Tel Quel* 28 (Winter 1987): 3–22.

Koc, Richard. "Fathers and Sons: Ambivalence Doubled in Schiller's *Die Räuber*." *Germanic Review* 61 (1986): 91–102.

Koelb, Clayton. "Incorporating the Text: Kleist's *Michael Kohlhaas*." *PMLA* 105 (1990): 1098–1107.

Kors, Alan Charles, and Paul J. Korshin, eds. *Anticipations of the Enlightenment in England, France, and Germany*. Philadelphia: U of Pennsylvania P, 1987.

Kraft, Herbert. "Erläuterungen zu Dramen 1." *Schillers Dramen 2*. Ed. Kraft. Frankfurt a. Main: Insel, 1966. 501–25.

Kuhns, Richard. "The Strangeness of Justice: Reading *Michael Kohlhaas*." *New Literary History* 15.1 (1983): 73–91.

Kuzniar, Alice. "Desiring Eyes." *Modern Fiction Studies* 36.3 (1990): 355–67.

Laborde, Alice. *Sade Romancier*. Neuchatel, Switz.: Baronnière, 1967.

Leidner, Alan C. "'Fremde Menschen fielen einander schluchzend in die Arme': *Die Räuber* and the Communal Response." *Goethe Yearbook* 3 (1986): 57–71.

Levine, George R. *Henry Fielding and the Dry Mock*. The Hague: Mouton, 1967.

Lewis, Peter. "The Beggar's Rags to Rich's and Other Dramatic Transformations." *John Gay and the Scriblerians*. London: Vision, 1988. 122–46.

Lindsay, J. M. "Kohlhaas and K. Two Men in Search of Justice." *German Life and Letters* 13 (1959/60): 190–94.

Linn, Rolf. *Schillers junge Idealisten*. Berkeley: U of California P, 1973.

Lotringer, Sylvère. "Manon l'écho." *Romanic Review* 53.2 (1972): 92–110.

Lüsebrink, Hans-Jürgen. *Kriminalität und Literatur im Frankreich des 18. Jahrhunderts*. Munich: R. Oldenbourg Verlag, 1983.

Lützler, Paul Michael. "Heinrich von Kleist: Michael Kohlhaas (1810)." *Romane und Erzählungen der deutschen Romantik Neue Interpretationen*. Ed. Lützler. Stuttgart: Reclam, 1981. 213–39.

McKeon, Michael. *The Origins of the English Novel*. Baltimore: Johns Hopkins UP, 1987.

Maddox, James H. "On Defoe's *Roxana*." *English Literary History* 51.4 (1984): 669–91.

Mann, Michael. *Sturm und Drang Drama: Studien zu Schillers* Räubern. Bern: Francke, 1974.

Marks, Elaine, and Isabelle de Courtivron, eds. *New French Feminisms*. New York: Schocken, 1981.

Marson, Eric. "Justice and the Obsessed Character in *Michael Kohlhaas, Der Prozess*, and *L'Etranger*." *Seminar* 2.2 (1966): 21–33.

Mead, William. "Manon Lescaut, C'est moi?" *L'esprit créateur* 6.2 (Summer 1966): 85–96.

"Medieval Romance." *Princeton Encyclopedia of Poetics*. 1974 ed.

Meitinger, Serge. "L'Irréel de Jouissance dans *Le Journal du Voleur* de Genet." *Littérature* 62 (1986): 65–74.

Miller, D. A. *The Novel and the Police*. Berkeley: U of California P, 1980.

Miller, Jacqueline T. "The Imperfect Tale: Articulation, Rhetoric, and Self in *Caleb Williams*." *Criticism* 20 (1978): 366–82.

Miller, Nancy. *The Heroine's Text: Readings in the French and English Novel, 1722–1782*. New York: Columbia UP, 1980.

———. "'I's' in Drag: The Sex of Recollection." *The Eighteenth Century: Theory and Interpretation* 22.1 (1981): 47–57.

———. "Justine, or the Viscious Circle." *Studies in Eighteenth Century Culture* 5 (1976): 215–28.

Morris, David B. "The Marquis de Sade and the Discourses of Pain: Literature and Medicine at the Revolution." Rousseau, ed. 291–330.

Mortier, Roland. "La Transition du 18e au 19e Siècle." *Dix-Huitième Siècle* 14 (1982): 7–12.

Moss, Martha Niess. "Balzac's Villains: The Origins of Destructiveness in *La Comédie Humaine*. *Nineteenth Century French Studies* 6.1–2 (1977–78): 36–51.

Mylne, Vivienne. *Manon Lescaut*. Series in French Literature. London: Arnold, 1972.

Nokes, David. Introduction. *Jonathan Wild*. By Fielding. Ed. Nokes Middlesex, Eng.: Penguin, 1982. 7–24.

Novak, Maximillian E. "'Appearances of Truth': The Literature of

Crime as a Narrative System (1660–1841)." *Yearbook of English Studies* 3 (1981): 29–48.

———. *Realism, Myth, and History in Defoe's Fiction.* Lincoln: U of Nebraska P, 1983.

Nussbaum, Felicity, and Laura Brown. *The New 18th Century.* New York: Methuen, 1987.

Pagels, Elaine. *Adam, Eve and the Serpent.* New York: Random, 1988.

Paglia, Camille. *Sexual Personae: Art and Decadence from Nefertiti to Emily Dickinson.* New York: Vintage, 1991.

Passage, Charles. *Friedrich Schiller.* New York: Ungar, 1975.

———. "*Michael Kohlhaas*: Form Analysis." *Germanic Review* (1954): 181–97.

Paulhan, Jean. "The Marquis and His Accomplice." *The Complete Justine.* By Sade. Trans. Richard Seaver and Austryn Wainhouse. New York: Grove, 1965. 3–36.

Paulson, Ronald. "Mock-heroic Irony and the Comedy of Manners." *John Gay's* The Beggar's Opera. Modern Critical Interpretations. Ed. Harold Bloom. New York: Chelsea House, 1988. 61–63.

———. *Satire and the Novel in Eighteenth-Century England.* New Haven: Yale UP, 1967.

Paulson, William R. *Enlightenment, Romanticism, and the Blind in France.* Princeton: Princeton UP, 1987.

Porter, Roy, and Mikulas Teich, eds. *The Enlightenment in National Context.* Cambridge: Cambridge UP, 1981.

Praz, Mario. *The Romantic Agony.* Trans. Angus Davidson. London: Oxford UP, 1933.

Preston, John. "The Ironic Mode, A Comparison of *Jonathan Wild* and *The Beggar's Opera.*" *Essays in Criticism* 16 (1966): 268–80.

Price, Lawrence. "George Barnwell Abroad." *Comparative Literature* 11 (1950): 126–56.

Reichler, Claude. "Le Récit d'Initiation dans le Roman libertin." *Littérature* 47 (1982): 100–112.

———. "On the Notion of Intertextuality: The Example of the Libertine Novel." *Diogenes* 114 (Spring/Summer 1981): 205–15.

Renner, Rolf Günter. *Peter Handke.* Stuttgart: Metzler, 1985.

Rex, Walter E. *The Attraction of the Contrary: Essays on the Literature of the French Enlightenment.* Cambridge: Cambridge UP, 1987.

Rich, Adrienne. *Of Woman Born.* New York: Norton, 1986. Reprint with new introduction of original 1976 publication.

Ricoeur, Paul. *De l'interprétation: Essai sur Freud.* Paris: Éditions du Seuil, 1965.

———. *Hermeneutics and the Human Sciences.* Trans. John B. Thompson. Cambridge: Cambridge UP, 1981.

Rivero, Albert J. "The Restored Garden and the Devil as Christ: Defoe's

Inversion of Biblical Images of Salvation in *Roxana*." *Essays in Literature* 12.2 (Fall 1984): 285–91.

Rodman, George Bush. "Sentimentalism in Lillo's *The London Merchant*." *English Literary History* 12 (1945): 45–61.

Rosa, Guy. "Jean Valjean (I,2,6): Réalisme et irréalisme des *Misérables*." *Lire* Les Misérables. Ed. Anne Ubersfeld. Mayenne: José Corti, 1985. 205–38.

Rothstein, Eric. "Allusion and Analogy in the Romance of *Caleb Williams*." *University of Toronto Quarterly* 37 (1967/68): 18–30.

Rousseau, George S., ed. *The Languages of Psyche: Mind and Body in Enlightenment Thought*. Berkeley: U of California P, 1990.

Rousseau, George S., and Roy Porter. "Introduction: Toward a Natural History of Mind and Body." Rousseau, ed. 3–44.

———, eds. *Sexual Underworlds of the Enlightenment*. Manchester, Eng.: Manchester UP, 1987.

Rückert, Joachim. "'Der Welt in der Pflicht verfallen . . .' Kleist's *Kohlhaas* als moral- und rechtsphilosophische Stellungnahme." *Kleist Jahrbuch* (1988/89): 375– 403.

Ruml, Treadwell. "*Jonathan Wild* and the Epistemological Gulf Between Virtue and Vice." *Studies in the Novel* 21.2 (1989): 117–27.

Sartre, Jean Paul. *Saint Genet: Actor and Martyr*. Trans. Bernard Frechtman. New York: Braziller, 1963.

Scheiber, Andrew J. "Falkland's Story: *Caleb Williams'* Other Voice." *Studies in the Novel* 17.3 (1985): 255–65.

Schlunk, Jürgen. "Vertrauen als Ursache." *Jahrbuch der Schillergesellschaft* 25. Jahrgang (1983): 185–201.

Sedgwick, Eve Kosofsky. *Between Men: English Literature and Male Homosocial Desire*. New York: Columbia UP, 1985.

Segal, Naomi. *The Unintended Reader*. Cambridge: Cambridge UP, 1986.

Shea, Bernard. "Machiavelli and Fielding's *Jonathan Wild*." *PMLA* 72 (1957): 55–73.

Sheringham, Michael. "Narration and Experience in Genet's *Journal du Voleur*." *Studies in French Fiction in Honour of Vivienne Mylne*. Ed. Robert Gibson. London: Grant, 1988. 289–306.

Showalter, Elaine. *Evolution of the French Novel*. Princeton: Princeton UP, 1972.

Simms, Karl N. "Caleb Williams' Godwin: Things as They Are Written." *Studies in Romanticism* 26.3 (1987): 343–63.

Singerman, Alan J. "A *fille de plaisir* and Her *greluchon*: Society and Perspective of Manon Lescaut." *L'esprit créateur* (1972): 118–28.

Smith, Ken Edward. "William Godwin: Social Critique in *Caleb Williams*. Studies on Voltaire and the Eighteenth Century* 263 (1989): 337–41.

Stallybrass, Peter, and Allon White. *The Politics and Poetics of Transgres-*

212   Works Cited

sion. London: Methuen, 1986.

Starr, G. A. *Defoe and Spiritual Autobiography*. Princeton: Princeton UP, 1965.

Steinhagen, Harald. "Der junge Schiller zwischen Marquis de Sade und Kant." *Deutsche Vierteljahrschrift für Literatur* 56. Jahrgang, Heft 1 (1982): 135–57.

Storch, Rudolph F. "Metaphors of Private Guilt and Social Rebellion in Godwin's *Caleb Williams*." *English Literary History* 34 (1967): 188–207.

Thalheim, Hans Günther. "Zeitalterkritik und Zukunftserwartung: Zur Grundkonzeption in Schillers früher Dramatik." *Wiener Goethe-Verein* 92/93 (1988/89): 101–16.

Thompson, James. "Surveillance in William Godwin's *Caleb Williams*." *Gothic Fictions: Prohibitions/Transgression*. Ed. Kenneth W. Graham. New York: AMS, 1989. 173–98.

Trainor, Stephen. "Tears Abounding: *The London Merchant* as Puritan Tragedy." *Studies in English Literature, 1500–1900* 18 (1978): 509–21.

Tyler, Carole-Anne. "Boys Will Be Girls: The Politics of Gay Drag." *Inside/out*. Ed. Diana Fuss. New York: Routledge, 1991. 32–70.

Tysdahl, B. J. *William Godwin as Novelist*. London: Athlone, 1981.

Uphaus, Richard. "The Fear of Fiction." *Man, God, and Nature in the Enlightenment*. Ed. Donald C. Mell et al. East Lansing, MI: Colleagues P, 1988. 183–90.

Vajda, Gyorgy M., ed. *Le Tournant du Siècle des Lumières 1760–1820*. Budapest: Akademiai Kiado, 1982.

Van den Abbeele, Georges. "Sade, Foucault, and the Scene of Enlightenment Lucidity." *Stanford French Review* 11.1 (1987): 7–16.

"Verbrechen." *Deutsches Wörterbuch von Jakob Grimm und Wilhelm Grimm*. Ed. Deutsche Akademie der Wissenschaften zu Berlin. Leipzig: Verlag von S. Hirzel, 1956.

Warren, Leland E. "*Caleb Williams* and the 'Fall' into Writing." *Mosaic* 20.1 (1987): 57–69.

Wehrs, Donald. "Rhetoric, History, Rebellion: *Caleb Williams* and the Subversion of Eighteenth-Century Fiction." *Studies in English Literature 1500–1900* 28 (1988): 497–511.

Weiskel, Thomas. *The Romantic Sublime: Studies in the Structure and Psychology of Transcendence*. Baltimore: Johns Hopkins UP, 1976.

Wendt, Allan. "The Moral Allegory of *Jonathan Wild*." *Journal of English Literary History* 24 (1957): 306–20.

Wexelblatt, Robert. "Thomas Hobbes and Michael Kohlhaas." *Southern Humanities Quarterly* 18 (1984): 109–28.

Wiese, Benno von. "Der Dichter der *Räuber*." *Friedrich Schiller*. Stuttgart: Metzler, 1959. 136–70.

———. *Novelle*. Tübingen: Metzler, 1963.

Winandy, Rita. "Prévost and Morality of Sentiment." *L'esprit créateur* 12.2 (Summer 1972): 94–95.

Winnack, Paul. "Some English Influences on Prévost." *Studies on Voltaire and the Eighteenth Century* 182 (1979): 285–302.

Witt, Mary Ann Frese. "Mothers and Stories: Female Presence/Power in Genet." *French Forum* 14.2 (1989): 173–86.

Wright, Andrew. *Fielding: Mask and Feast*. Berkeley: U of California P, 1965.

Index

Stephanie Barbé Hammer is an associate professor of comparative literature at the University of California, Riverside, where she teaches courses in literary theory and Enlightenment/romanticism as well as in German and French literature. Her work has appeared in *The Comparatist, French Forum, Essays in Theatre,* and other journals. She is the author of *Satirizing the Satirist: Critical Dynamics in Swift, Diderot, and Jean Paul.*